THE AA GUIDE TO
Cornwall

About the author

Laura Dixon has been entranced with the idea of Cornwall since reading stories of smugglers as a child. With an English degree from Oxford and a post-graduate Certificate in Journalism behind her, she left the corporate world to become a full-time travel writer in 2001 and has never looked back.

She has regularly contributed to national newspapers, style magazines and leading websites about travel and lifestyle issues, and currently works as the Communications Director of Kid & Coe, where her role is to help make family travel around the world easier. She can think of nowhere better to take kids than Cornwall.

Laura loves to surf, swim and play along Cornwall's coast. Hiking isn't her strong point but local culture, shopping and water-based activities are. Her favourite places are Mawgan Porth, The Lizard Peninsula and St Ives.

Published by AA Publishing (a trading name of AA Media Limited, whose registered office is Fanum House, Basing View, Basingstoke, Hampshire RG21 4EA; registered number 06112600)

© AA Media Limited 2016
First published 2014
Second edition 2016. Reprinted 2017
Third edition 2018

Maps contain data from openstreetmap.org
© OpenStreetMap contributors
Ordnance Survey data © Crown copyright and database right 2018.

A CIP catalogue record for this book is available from the British Library.

ISBN: 978-0-7495-7940-1
SS: 978-0-7495-7630-1

A05591

Cartography provided by the Mapping Services Department of AA Publishing.
Printed and bound in Italy by Printer Trento Srl.

THE AA GUIDE TO

Cornwall

CONTENTS

USING THIS GUIDE

Introduction – has plenty of fascinating background reading, including articles on the landscape and local mythology.

Top attractions – pick out the very best places to visit in the area. You'll spot these later in the A–Z by the flashes of yellow.

Before you go – tells you the things to read, watch, know and pack to get the most from your trip.

Campsites – recommends a number of caravan sites and campsites, which carry the AA's Pennant rating, with the very best receiving the coveted gold Pennant award. Visit theAA.com/self-catering-and-campsites, theAA.com/hotels and theAA.com/bed-and-breakfasts for more places to stay.

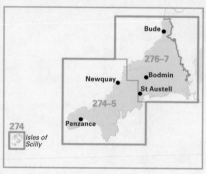

A–Z of Cornwall – lists all the best of the region, with recommended attractions, activities and places to eat or drink. Places Nearby lists more to see and do.

Eat and drink – contains restaurants with an AA Rosette rating, which acknowledges the very best in cooking. Pubs have been selected for their great atmosphere and good food. Visit theAA.com/restaurants and theAA.com/pubs for more suggestions.

Index – gives you the option to search by theme, grouping the same type of place together, or alphabetically.

Atlas – will help you find your way around, as every main location has a map reference, as will the town plans throughout the book.

INTRODUCTION

The stereotypical image of Cornwall is captivating enough: craggy cliffs, smugglers' coves and surfers hanging ten offshore. But peek behind the nautical bunting, past the rows of ceramic campervan-shaped moneyboxes and the sunburned tourists on the beach and you'll discover the real Cornwall – a compelling land of myth, legend, dramatic scenery and rich culture.

This county has independence, as well as tin, in its veins; a land once held to be a nation apart from England that still retains the right to veto any English laws it chooses. Its people are quirky and interesting: you'll find men who fish by day, sing in fishermen's choirs by night and host gig-racing championships at the weekend; former fashion designers turned boutique hoteliers and guesthouse owners dying to spill the local secrets; and gardeners who travel the world in search of exotic seeds to plant in the fruitful Cornish soil. There's an enormous pride in being Cornish and you can't disagree with that impulse – this is a place where giants have walked, King Arthur ruled and smugglers made

fortunes overnight. Cornwall has a mythical edge that is quite unlike anywhere else.

You don't need to be told why people visit Cornwall. From bucket-and-spade resorts to wild, windswept beaches, ocean swells heralding a great day of surf and fantastic clifftop walking paths with views of leaping dolphins, the sea's the thing. You're never far from it and you can reach either the north or south coasts, sometimes both, in under an hour from most places in the county. The unique environment inland – a patchwork of green fields, ancient woodlands, misty moors and headlands dotted with Iron Age remains – is a haven for wildlife and walkers. With Sites of Special Scientific Interest (SSSIs), Areas of Outstanding Natural Beauty (AONBs) and World Heritage Sites, the appeal is undeniable. And the unique climate, owing to Cornwall occupying the southernmost and westernmost parts of the UK, means that you can see astonishing floral displays, whales and sharks in the sea, and fascinating migratory birds that are rarely seen anywhere else in the country.

There's also something that you can't pin down about the county. It's in the air, in the sea and in the light, something free-spirited and distinct from the rest of the mainland UK. Stand by Tate St Ives and look at the sea: that turquoise-blue is unique to Cornwall and deserves its own Pantone colour reference.

Before you fall in love with Cornwall, as you almost certainly will, heed some words of warning. It's a treacherous place to desire, with a head-spinning number of places to stay and ruinously expensive homes to buy, not to mention a dearth of jobs. Travelling here by car every year will make your blood pressure rise, especially if you're stuck behind a tractor on a long, slow, sunken road. Make a mental note to look into other, more eco-sound options. Camping, though friendlier on the pocket, can be a depressing experience in a leaky tent on the top of a windy hill. Fish and chips, pasties, clotted cream and ice creams will add inches to your waistline that a gentle daily swim in the sea can't take off. And you'll never be a local, unless you can count your family back ten generations in the same village.

Those foolhardy enough to throw off these words of caution will already be contemplating how they can move down here, run a craft business, cream tea cafe or B&B, and spend their days eating fresh local produce, surfing, walking the dog on a blustery hilltop and sheltering from the rain in an ancient wood-beamed pub, dodging the odd ghost of a smuggler or two. It's hard not to.

Cornwall is an addictive place and, whether you come for a week or a weekend, you'll be back, for sure. Getting here's the easy bit; persuading yourself to holiday in any other part of the UK in the future is the struggle.

◄ St Ives (previous page) ▶ Porthcurno Beach from cliffs

TOP ATTRACTIONS

▲ Get lost in the gardens

Cornwall's climate means that the gardens here support plants and trees you're unlikely to see elsewhere in the UK. The lush country estates of Cornwall revel in it: not just at the Lost Gardens of Heligan (see page 168), but in more than 50 properties around the county, from Trebah (see page 102) to Tresco's Abbey Garden (see page 254).

▼ Visit Eden

Tim Smit's mega tourist attraction near St Austell (see page 89) is a monument to what Cornwall has achieved: a china clay quarry turned eco-centre with rainforests and jungles inside unique biomes. It's the county's top rainy day spot for families and always has something interesting and educational on show.

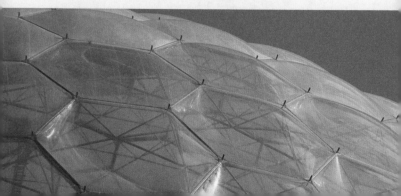

◄ Reach Land's End

The most southwesterly point of mainland Britain hosts a shopping complex and plenty of family attractions (see page 120), as well as the famous Land's End signpost and beautiful clifftop scenery. Something for everyone.

▶ Go underground at Geevor

A regular winner of Cornwall Tourism Awards, dramatically situated Geevor Tin Mine (see page 197) has a museum, visitor centre, underground tour and even mineral panning, so you can learn all about Cornwall's mining heritage – whilst keeping out of the rain.

◄ Book seats at the Minack

This incomparable open-air theatre near Land's End (see page 215) was originally made for *The Tempest*, with the wild, raging waters of the Atlantic as a backdrop. Created in the 1930s, it's just as good today, with a summer programme of classics, proms and children's shows. Even in poor weather it's a great adventure.

◂ Check out the National Maritime Museum

Half museum, half interactive experience, the National Maritime Museum Cornwall (see page 96) is right on the waterfront. Watch the tides turn from the safety of an underwater viewing gallery, or learn to sail a model boat in artificial winds.

▸ Be the king of the castle at St Michael's Mount

Walk across the causeway at low tide, beside rocks strewn with bladderwrack, to reach this unique island crowned with a castle and surrounded by sub-tropical gardens (see page 159). The modern-day home of the St Aubyn family is a real one-off, and is the former home of the mythical giant Cormoran.

◂ Visit the other Tate

Artists are drawn to St Ives for the quality of the light; less artistic visitors can appreciate the fruit of their labours at the fourth Tate (the others are in London and Liverpool). Tate St Ives (see page 237), hosts ever-changing exhibitions of contemporary art, frequently including the work of leading local artists of the 'St Ives School'.

▲ **Explore King Arthur's Tintagel**

Perched on a cliff edge with Merlin's cave down below, legend combines with landscape at the ruins of Tintagel Castle (see page 261). Visit on a wet, moody day for added drama.

HISTORY OF CORNWALL

People were already visiting Cornwall as far back as the Palaeolithic period, around 400,000–200,000 BC. Archaeologists have found flint axes and blades that show that these ancient people travelled through the southwest, but, so far as we know, none settled in Cornwall. By 10,000 BC, however, hunter-gatherers had started to settle around Cornwall's coastline, and from the New Stone Age or Neolithic period (4000–2400 BC), they farmed the lands, enclosing small fields and building settlements.

Tin mining brought great prosperity to the county in later centuries but it was a great boon in these early days too. In the early Bronze Age period, metalworking in bronze began, using the natural resources of tin and copper. Many of the stone circles, menhirs and barrows standing today commemorate this period: Cornwall has the second largest number of prehistoric remains in the UK, after Wiltshire.

Early settlers, labelled 'Celts', are thought to have colonised Britain during the early Iron Age of 600–400 BC. In Cornwall,

◀ Iron Age Village, Chysauster

weapons and farming tools were made from iron, settlements developed and trading centres were established on hilltops and headlands, such as Trevelgue Head near Newquay.

Ancient Greeks and Romans knew the southwest tip of Britain as Belerion or Bolerium, and the resident tribal group was the Cornovii. It is possible that they gave their name to the Cornish word for the area, *Kernow* or *Curnow*, which later mixed with the Anglo-Saxon word *Wealas* for Welshman or foreigner to make *Curnow-wealas*: Cornwall.

Roman times: Tin trading with Gaul
Cornwall was far enough west to escape most of the Roman dominance of Britain and was a place of refuge for many Celts. Romans did make it to the peninsula but there are only a few Roman sites in the county: Tregear, near Nanstallon, Restormel Castle and a fort near St Andrew's Church in Calstock. Likewise, only a few Roman road milestones have been found – and it looks likely that in Roman times the sea was more important than roads, forming trading routes between other parts of the British Isles and Gaul.

The Chysauster, Scilly Isles and Carn Euny archaeological sites date from this period, showing uniquely Cornish-style stone courtyard houses. Under Roman influence, rural life was largely unchanged in the county. Cornwall notably traded in tin at this time with other places, including Ireland, Wales and Brittany, which grew to influence its development, language and culture.

Post-Roman times: The Arthurian period
From around AD 500, Celtic kings ruled Cornwall, and lovers of legend say that the real King Arthur ruled in Tintagel during this period. The Saxons began to advance through the west, destroying Roman civilisation and bringing Christianity to England. In 710, Ina, the King of the West Saxons, attempted to destroy the kingdom of Dumnonia, as Cornwall was known. There were battles for the next 50 years until the Vikings visited the Wessex coasts in 807 and formed an alliance with the Cornish against the Saxons.

Over the next few hundred years, Cornwall was contested by the Saxons, Vikings and resident Cornish tribes. King Athelstan, grandson of King Alfred, fixed the boundary of Wessex and Cornwall as the east bank of the Tamar River.

Medieval times: Church building and an independent nation
In the later Medieval period, Cornwall showed great signs of development. After the Norman Conquest, the Earl of Cornwall

built a castle at Launceston. The Domesday Book recorded markets and fairs in various points in the northern part of the county, reflecting the rural and trading development of the area which continued for the next 100 or so years, with more and more markets granted legal status.

Like Wales, Cornwall was still held to be a nation apart from the rest of England. Cornish was the most widely spoken tongue. Men worked in the mines, in the fields and on the sea. Churches were built and rebuilt, according to the wishes of the Bishop of Exeter, and in 1284, the King of England's claim to jurisdiction over Cornwall was rebuffed. In 1338, Edward the Black Prince was created the first Duke of Cornwall and, in 1346, Cornish archers, who had longbows and a reputation for sharp shooting, distinguished themselves at the Battle of Crécy, where 4,000 French knights were killed, among many others.

The Black Death then swept through Cornwall, killing half the populations of Truro and Bodmin. During the next 100 years, almost every Cornish church was altered or enlarged.

Tudor and Stuart times: Sea forts and the English tongue
This period was distinguished by a gradual erosion of Cornwall's status as an independent nation as the English language became widely introduced.

This greater interaction and enslavement to the king began with Henry VII demanding taxation from the Cornish to pay for his war against the Scots – previously they had been exempt. Despite a spirited uprising, the Cornish failed and their leaders were

▼ Lanyon Quoit

executed. In 1508, Henry VII issued the Charter of Pardon to the county allowing the Cornish Stannary Parliament to veto English legislation – a law that still exists today albeit without legal force.

Later in that century, Henry VIII built fortifications along the south coast of Cornwall, including Pendennis Castle in Falmouth and its twin, St Mawes Castle, across the estuary from it.

The introduction of the *Book of Common Prayer* in English into Cornwall in 1549 heralded the final decline of the Cornish tongue and the county's independent status. The Cornish rebelled against it, preferring Latin over English as a language that was more widely understood in church, but were put down. Some 150 years later, only 5,000 people were still able to speak Cornish, most of whom lived at the furthest reaches of the county.

While Elizabeth I ruled, Cornwall came under repeated attacks from the Spanish, who attempted to burn Penryn and landed in Mount's Bay, attacking Mousehole, Newlyn, Penzance and Paul.

Small tin mines were worked at St Agnes, later to become a large source of wealth and jobs during Queen Victoria's reign.

17th–19th centuries: Tin mining and a tsunami

Through the 17th century, country estates were built in Cornwall and the county played a role in the English Civil War as a Royalist enclave in the largely Parliamentarian southwest. Cornwall's deepest copper and tin mines were built as the industrial revolution hit Cornwall, and china clay was quarried in locations including around St Austell – the future site of the Eden Project.

▼ Restormel Castle

▲ Wheal Coates Tin Mine, St Agnes

In 1755, an earthquake in Lisbon triggered a tsunami that reached Cornwall, causing great loss of life and property. In 1777, Dolly Pentreath, who was said at the time to be the last speaker of Cornish, died. In fact, Cornish was still spoken in part until the 19th century, but this shows how dramatically the language was overtaken by English. English was the compulsory language for teaching in schools in the 18th century.

Mining and china clay quarrying continued to build a prosperous Cornwall through the 18th and 19th centuries, and canals, horse-drawn rail links and railways were mooted and developed as ways to transport raw materials. In the 1860s, Great Wheal Vor near Helston was probably the richest tin mine in the world. Copper ore was also mined in much of Cornwall at this time.

From the 1830s onwards, the great Cornish migration began as Cornish mining skills were highly sought abroad, especially in the silver mines of Mexico and the iron mines of Canada. The migration continued following the decline of the mines in Cornwall as emigrants sought a better life elsewhere. It is said that the Cornish diaspora exported rugby union around the world and helped to develop the game in Australia, New Zealand and South Africa.

The flag of St Piran – a white cross on a black background, also known today as the Cornish flag – was first mentioned as such in 1838.

In legal arguments running through the mid-19th century, there was much debate about whether Cornwall was part of England and under the rule of the Crown, or independent and semi-autonomous. The Crown was defeated: Cornwall still had a degree of independence.

▲ The Eden Project

20th and 21st centuries: Tourism and a revival of the language

Some mines continued until the early 1990s in Cornwall, but most dwindled and closed in the early part of the 20th century. China clay is still excavated and exported today, but Cornwall's industrial glory days were drawing to a close and the mines gave up their last.

In the 1950s, attempts were made to support greater self-government of the county by the political party Mebyon Kernow, to no success; Cornish pride has however been fostered by the party's use of the flag of St Piran, which can be seen in many places today.

The 1990s saw Cornwall divided: an increasing population plus decreasing job prospects meant that the county had high levels of poverty, with three times more people unemployed than in 1961. At the same time, tourism was growing, bringing wealth to some, along with wealthy second homeowners from the rest of the UK. The division still exists.

The Eden Project opened in 2000 in a 160-year-old disused china clay quarry near St Austell, celebrating environmental sustainability as well as bringing a major and welcome boost to Cornish tourism.

In 2001, inhabitants of Cornwall were allowed to record their ethnicity as Cornish on the national census and Cornish culture was growing. Cornish is spoken in a number of places and is encouraged in select schools today. The people of Cornwall are proud of their heritage, and are intent on seeing their unique culture and customs going from strength to strength.

BACK TO NATURE

The story of Cornwall as told by its landscape starts
400 million years ago. Erosion, weathering and humans
have shaped this mass of rocks, with granite at their
heart, to create a county surrounded on three sides by
the sea and with views, nature and habitats seen
nowhere else in the country.

From the coastal villages and sandy beaches to windswept moors,
green fields and grazing pastures, estuary valleys and dramatic
cliffs, Cornwall's landscape is diverse and beautiful. Sustainable
tourism is essential to preserve the unique characteristics of
the Cornish landscape. That means obeying local bylaws, the
Countryside Code and common sense; it also means going out of
your way to enjoy the scenery and wildlife as much as you can, and
contributing to the conservation economy where possible.

There are 12 AONBs in Cornwall, 167 SSSIs and many
local nature reserves. If you're interested in wildlife, geography
and the landscape, the Cornwall Wildlife Trust runs events
and guided walks and has downloadable walks on its website,
cornwallwildlifetrust.org.uk. The places described below are a few
of the most notable areas.

▲ Golitha Falls; Cheesewring

Bodmin Moor

Bodmin Moor is the ancient heart of Cornwall. What makes it so special is its wild quality – the fens, bogs, wetlands and moor here are remote and unsettled in most parts, and some of the moor has never been tamed or enclosed. It includes valuable wildlife habitats and the remains of Neolithic tors, Bronze Age roundhouses, barrows and standing stones, plus Brown Willy, the highest point in Cornwall. There are stacks of eroded rocks on the tors, such as Cheesewring, one of the iconic views of the Cornish moorland, and rivers flow from the moor to the north and south coasts.

The Lizard Peninsula

Geologists are rightly fascinated by The Lizard, the most southerly tip of England, which is formed in part from a unique rock, serpentine, found nowhere else in the rest of Cornwall or the UK. This rock is a part of the Earth's mantle normally found tens of miles underground, but here it was thrust up to the surface as the continents shifted many millions of years ago. The Lizard's churches typically have fonts, lecterns and bible stands made from shaped and polished serpentine. The complex geology, together with the mild, maritime climate has made it possible for a distinct and varied flora to develop.

Hartland Peninsula

This part of north coast Cornwall, an AONB which is shared across the border with Devon, has remarkable creased and distorted cliffs with ridges of folded rock strata visible on the beach at low tide in corduroy-like lines. The views are dramatic. Away from the sea, the peninsula gives way to dairy farms, green fields and small hamlets.

St Agnes

For an example of Cornwall's mining heritage, visit St Agnes on the north coast. Known for its sandy surf beach, you don't have to look far along the headland to see engine houses, chimneys and shafts, along with rocky, bare patches of ground stained reddish brown by mineral waste. There are mining tracks across the fields and heathland, and small former mining villages all around the area.

Wildlife

With all these distinctive habitats comes a unique array of bird, mammal and sea life. It wouldn't be silly season in the UK press without a story suggesting that there are great white sharks cruising the sea around Cornwall waiting to pick off surfers – the truth is that there are sharks in the sea but none of them want to eat you.

▼ Basking shark

Cornwall's largest creature, excepting occasional visits from migratory minke whales, is the basking shark, which can often be seen from Land's End. While you're there, look out for dolphins too: Risso's dolphins and bottlenose dolphins are the most commonly seen, not just here, but from many beaches and cliffs in the county. Grey seals are also residents; Mutton Cove near Godrevy is a good place to see them, as well as nesting seabirds in the cliffs.

Inland, Cornwall's woods provide a fantastic habitat for native bird species. Tehidy Woods, one of the largest woodland areas in Cornwall, is a good stop for birders, where you might see robins, blue tits, jays, nuthatches and green woodpeckers.

Migrant waders, gulls and terns are seen in the Hayle Estuary, and Stithians Reservoir hosts unusual diving birds such as pochard and goldeneye, and there are buzzards and sparrowhawks in the surrounding farmland. The red-billed, red-legged Cornish Chough is Cornwall's 'national symbol' and many see it as the 'spirit of King Arthur'. The species died out during the 20th century but has now been re-introduced. Though a still vulnerable and small population, choughs can be spotted on the cliffs of West Cornwall.

Several animal centres focus on local wildlife, including the Cornish Birds of Prey Centre at St Columb Major and the Cornish Seal Sanctuary in Gweek.

▼ Dozmary Pool, Bodmin Moor

LORE OF THE LAND

The ancient lore of Cornwall is as wild as its scenery,
reflecting a history of Celts driven west by invaders.
They brought with them tales of giants, gods and fairies.
Among the fiercest of Cornwall's giants was Bolster,
so tall that he could plant one foot on Carn Brae,
near Camborne, and the other at St Agnes, six miles
away. St Agnes is named for the saint who, as a young
lass, destroyed Bolster – who was already married –
when he fell in love with her. Tasked by the beautiful
Agnes to prove his love by filling a hole in the cliff at
Chapel Porth with his own blood, he failed in his mission
because the hole is bottomless, leading directly to the
ocean, and he bled to death in the attempt.

Cornish little folk, still invoked today as tourist traps for the unwary
with money to spend, come in many guises. The Piskies, who live
on the moorlands and can come into homes to help around the
house, are thought to be the souls of the dead. Also indoors are the
ever-helpful Brownies. Underground, Knockers inhabit the old tin
mines and, by tradition, miners always left food out to placate them

and insure against fatalities. In old ruins and barrows, treasure is guarded by the Spriggans who, because they are purported to swell themselves to huge sizes, are believed to be giants' ghosts.

The king of legend

Arthur gets star billing in Cornwall's folklore. Atop the windswept crags of north Cornwall stands Tintagel Castle, believed to be the hero's birthplace. It was here in an ancient fortress that Uther Pendragon, assisted by the magician Merlin, disguised himself as Gorlois, the Duke of Cornwall, the husband of the beautiful Igerna. Igerna was indeed seduced and gave birth to the future king.

The home of Merlin, the young Arthur's teacher and guide, was the massive cave hollowed out by the waves below the fortress. According to the most popular version – there are several, and not just in Cornwall – the infant Arthur was found here by Merlin, plucked from the mighty waves and carried to safety. In the cave's echoing vaults, the wizard's ghost is still believed to wander, holding aloft Arthur's magical sword Excalibur to light his way.

Across the county, episodes from the Arthurian legends can be found at every turn. Arthur is reputed to have held court in the city of Celliwig, believed to be the modern Castle Killibury or Kelly Rounds, near Wadebridge, an ancient hill fort so high that it was said that from here Arthur's protectors could 'shoot an arrow through the legs of a wren in Ireland'. The still and brooding Dozmary Pool, just south of Bolventor – said to be bottomless – is allegedly where Excalibur was returned to the Lady of the Lake by Sir Bedivere after Arthur had been defeated by Mordred, his evil nephew, and was dying of his wounds. The Cornish Chough (see page 25), the embodiment of the spirit of King Arthur, has a characteristic harsh and dominant 'chawk' cry; its red bill and legs symbolise the king's bloody end.

Tragic lovers

The doomed lovers Tristan and Iseult (Isolde) featured in Cornish lore long before Wagner publicised them in an opera. Their demise is commemorated by the starkly simple Tristan Stone near Fowey. Tristan, nephew of King Mark of Cornwall, reached Ireland's shores having been wounded by a poisoned spear. There he was nursed to health by the beautiful Iseult before returning to Cornwall.

In time, Tristan was in Ireland once again, at the request of King Mark, on a mission to return with Iseult, who was destined to be the king's bride. But on the journey back, the pair accidentally drank the love potion intended for the wedding night. They fled into the Cornish countryside but eventually the royal marriage went ahead. On the way to their wedding, however, Mark and Iseult met a leper – actually Tristan in disguise – who carried her across a ford. At the ceremony she was then able to swear that apart from Mark and the leper no other man had ever touched her. On his deathbed Tristan sent a ship to fetch his love so that she could heal him, instructing a messenger to hoist white sails if she was on board when the ship returned. But only black sails were flown and Tristan died of his grief. A cross at Castle Dore near Fowey, Mark's fort, marks Tristan's last resting place.

Healing powers

All over Cornwall, rocks and stones that dot the landscape are believed to have magical or healing powers. Near Madron, 2.5 miles from Penzance, is Men-an-Tol, an alignment that includes the enigmatic circular 'holed stone'. At dawn, sick children were passed naked through the hole towards the sun to effect cures; for rickets the child needed to pass through nine times. Adults with rheumatism would also crawl through nine times while facing the sun, presuming their joints were not too stiff to make the moves. To ensure their fertility, women who had recently taken up with a new partner would also pass through the holes. And long before *Mastermind*, it was traditional to place a pair of brass nails across each other within the hole in the belief that the stone would then answer any question put to it.

Out on the moor

Even on the windiest night on Bodmin Moor – and there are many – the desperate cries of a dark spirit can be heard ringing out. This is the speaking soul of Jan Tregeagle, a man doomed to wander the moor as recompense for the sin of murdering his wife and children. He is said to have returned from the grave to bear witness in court in a case of fraud. As a reward his soul was saved but cruel spells were cast on him, such as requiring him to empty Dozmary Pool using a limpet shell with holes in it. But on a wild and windy night Tregeagle escaped from the power that bound him onto the moor, where his screams persist.

More mysterious yet is the Beast of Bodmin, possibly an escaped big cat. While it has not yet been identified, stories of the creature persist; perhaps it's more than just a shaggy cat story...

Woman power

Cornwall is witch country. At Trewa, in the rugged landscape near Zennor, was a rock where all the witches of the west were believed to meet on Midsummer's Eve to light fires. To touch the rock nine times at midnight – at any time of year – was a sure way of dispelling misfortune. Among the most notorious of these witches was Madgy Figgy, leader of a gang of witches who were notorious wreckers. From her 'seat of storms' on the cliffs of Gwennap Head near Porthgwarra, the hag whipped up the seas and led sailors to their doom. When the bodies were washed ashore they were stripped of their valuables and the jewels presented to local girls.

She may not have been a witch, but Sarah Polgrain of Mount's Bay also had powers from beyond the grave. Sarah was the lover of Yorkshire Jack and was hanged for the murder of her husband. On the scaffold Sarah and Jack exchanged wedding vows, and after her death sightings of her ghost – bearing telltale black bruises on her neck – were widely reported. Jack went off to sea but he was swept from the ship's deck in a terrifying storm. The last sight to reach his eyes was Sarah and the Devil screaming at him.

Mysteries of the sea

It's not just the land that's awash with myth and legend: phantom ships sail off the Cornish coast. Typical is the story of the vessel that was once seen approaching land between Penzance and Land's End. The night was clear, with a gentle breeze, but the ship appeared to be heading for the rocks. However, instead of crashing to its doom, it mounted the land from the waves and 'sailed' on to the village of Porthcurno, where it vanished for good.

And of course mermaids, or 'merry maids', swim in Cornish waters. Zennor (see page 271) has one famous mermaid legend, while at Doom Bar, Padstow, the sand that blocks the entrance to the estuary of the River Camel is said to have been put there as a curse by a mermaid: she used to guide ships safely into the harbour but a man with a gun took a pot shot at her while she was bathing. The sand bar, which can be dangerous to vessels, was her dying curse; something to remember if you overhear someone going into a pub saying, 'I'm dying for a Doom Bar...'

SMUGGLING IN CORNWALL

In the 18th and 19th centuries, Cornwall's coastline was awash with smugglers and wreckers evading the king's men and their excise duty, and hiding rum, tea and lace in caves and tunnels along the coast while the locals turned their eyes to the wall so they could say they had seen nothing.

At a time when high taxes were sought to finance wars, fishermen and packet ship crews needed to smuggle to survive. Miners too at this time experienced ruinous conditions: some were laid off in summer due to a lack of water to complete their tasks, leaving them penniless for months. Smuggling was a way of life for many people and was not so much romantic as desperate and steeped in poverty.

Cornish smuggling was also buoyed by a lack of prevention. Customs officers were not as plentiful in the county as elsewhere and, with so many coves and inlets to cover, they were stretched to their limit and were often easy to bribe. With sympathies to their fellow men, Cornish juries were said to rarely convict any smugglers in the dock.

'Harvesting from the sea', or wrecking, was a key Cornish activity but there's no hard evidence that local people lured ships onto the rocks, killed survivors and stole from them, as many fictional accounts would have it. The reality may be that such isolated incidents did take place but there is certainly much evidence of shipwreck victims being saved by locals, who would then, however, exercise a long-established 'right' of coastal communities to recover as much of the wrecked cargo as they could before customs officers arrived.

Smuggling and wrecking brought enormous wealth to some parts of Cornwall. Variously bringing in brandy, rum, gin, tea and spices from France and the Channel Islands, and selling it on upcountry, gangs of smugglers saw gold coins beyond their wildest dreams. They had inventive ways to evade the customs officers, from filling hearses with contraband to tying bladders full of spirits under the full skirts of local women and hiding goods under carts filled with seaweed. Stories of tunnels from the beaches to local houses and churches are the most evocative of this time, but while stories and documents mention pubs, churches and country houses with these passages, few actually survive today.

If you want to explore Cornwall's smuggling history, start on the south coast. Its gently shelving sandy beaches were more popular than those of the north shore, which were more exposed with heavy waves. Looe has a particularly strong smuggling history, with caves used to store goods and Looe Island as a strategic outpost. A farmer is said to

▲ Jamaica Inn

have ridden his white horse along Looe beach to alert those on the island to customs raids. Ye Olde Jolly Sailor Inn in Looe itself is a well-known smugglers' pub.

Pretty Polperro and the nearby Talland Bay have a strong smuggling history too: lace, brandy and tea were brought in here. The ghost of a smuggler, Battling Billy, shot while desperately trying to escape from the excise men with goods in the back of a horse-drawn hearse, can apparently still be seen around the neighbourhood.

Further west in Mount's Bay, at Prussia Cove near St Michael's Mount, the notorious Carter family ran their smuggling activity as a highly efficient business in the 18th century. John Carter styled himself 'the King of Prussia' after a childhood game that he played. Such was his fame that Prussia became the accepted name of the cove.

More risky locations on the north coast included Sennen, St Ives and Hayle, where alleged smugglers' caves have been found. An 18th-century mayor of St Ives, John Knill, was also Collector of Customs in spite of being allegedly involved in the smuggling trade. Knill built a memorial to himself, Knill's Steeple, a stone pyramid, on a prominent hill above the town. It is said that the steeple had a useful secondary use as a navigation aid to smugglers' vessels. There are caves in the cliff at Porthtowan where goods were stored, and Pepper Cove is so named because pepper and spices were regularly brought in to this perfect smugglers' cove, where ships were hidden from view by the high cliffs.

If you want to find out more about smuggling in Cornwall, there is a museum about it at Jamaica Inn on Bodmin Moor (see page 66). The inn dates from the 1760s and is the famed location for Daphne du Maurier's novel about a group of murderous wreckers. The inn itself was a staging post between the coast and Devon, and smugglers and traders regularly passed through it with their goods. As Rudyard Kipling's *Smuggler's Song* goes, 'Watch the wall my darling while the Gentlemen go by.'

CATCHING WAVES

It's hard to describe how exhilarating and addictive surfing can be unless you've tried it – after spilling off your board into cold water time and time again, gaining the balance to stand, and finally carving through bigger and bigger waves, you can feel as if you're in harmony with the water and landscape around you, and get a huge adrenaline rush at the same time.

It's enough to make serious fans travel for five hours each way at weekends to keep up the habit, or ditch jobs in the city and move to Cornwall just so they can surf every morning before work. All this, and it's good for you, too. Cornwall's status as the UK's top surf destination began in the 1960s, when surfing reached the UK and early pioneers realised that the waves of the North Atlantic combined with the beach breaks of Cornwall were ripe for the picking. Newquay was then, and is now, the surf capital of the county, with Fistral Beach one of the best beach breaks in

Cornwall. It hosts the annual Boardmasters festival, an international music festival which encompasses the surfing contest that has been running for more than 30 years. A huge surf industry has grown around it, including the O'Neill and Quiksilver surf schools, countless surf shops, and hotels and B&Bs geared up for surfing. Altogether, the sport brings £64 million to the county every year and provides 1,600 jobs.

Beyond the beach, surf lifestyle is a big deal, and certainly where the money is made. Huge VW transporters, hoodies and surf-style beach bars prop up the look: it's all about being carefree, trying hard to look as if you're not trying too hard and being cool. You don't need to surf to look the part.

If you are keen to get in on the action, there are many ways to do it. Just about every beach you visit will have a VW van advertising surf lessons; the more established hubs of Watergate Bay, Harlyn and Newquay are obvious spots. The north coast is considered better than the south coast, which is too sheltered for big waves aside from a few select beaches. Summer is a time to be avoided if you're a keen surfer: while there may be surf schools open for business everywhere, the beaches are crowded, weather patterns mean that swell is small, and it's likely to be a fairly frustrating experience. The spring and autumn are better, while winter brings an occasional monster wave, the Cribbar, in the sea off Newquay. It's not uncommon to see serious surfers in the sea at Christmas and on New Year's Day.

◀ Porthmeor Beach, St Ives ▼ Surfboards

The best advice for beginners is to start small. Shy away from the crowded beaches of Newquay and Watergate Bay – however famous they are, it's not fun to be hit by other people's surfboards in the sea, and there will be a lot of other learners there. Try Gwithian, Hayle, Polzeath, Perranporth or Towan Head for starters, all safe beaches for beginners.

Having lessons is essential – the last thing you want is to annoy local surfers by stealing their waves, or to find yourself in a rip current. Lifeguards aren't on every beach, especially out of season. Surf camps where you spend a week having lessons – one lesson is rarely enough – and staying in accommodation with other surfers tend to be clustered around Newquay; other surf schools are located at Harlyn Bay near Padstow, Godrevy Towans near Hayle, Perranporth, St Ives and Sennen. There are also various women-only surf camps.

One thing you'll learn very early on is that surfing is dependent on the weather, and not just the local weather either. Surfers check forecasts and learn to read weather patterns all across the globe to

determine what the wave patterns on their shores will be. Learning about wave patterns, geography, wind directions and coastal directions is just the start of becoming a full-blown surfer: you need a degree in oceanography to get your head round some of the finer details, or you could also use a shortcut and check magicseaweed.com for local surf forecasts.

The other unpublicised side to surfing is that it's not all about the surfers' arcane world of point breaks, aggressive short boards, fist pumping and shouting 'Gnarly' after you've been 'barrelled'. Surfing has a competitive edge, but at its best it's a soul-soothing sport, where you can be cruising along on a wave, looking out at the Cornish cliffs or hanging out in the line-up watching dolphins on the horizon as you wait for a set to come in. It's an uncommercial experience – despite all the labels flung around, once you're zipping along a wave, it doesn't matter what brand your board is, what car you drive or what type of wetsuit you're wearing – and you will need a wetsuit most of the year even when it's hot and sunny.

A MINI CORNISH PRIMER

Kernewek, the Cornish language, is a powerful entity in modern Cornwall. It effectively died out as a language of common use during the 19th century, and its subsequent revival is a token of how hard the Cornish people fought to maintain their independence and their unique culture.

Cornish was the main language of Cornwall until Tudor times, when law dictated that church services should be conducted in English. Its unique language, up to this point, meant that Cornwall was held to be a nation apart from the rest of the country; as soon as English became widespread in the county, it was rapidly accepted as part of England. Kernewek is now spoken fluently by a substantial number of people and is taught in some schools. It is one of the fastest-growing languages in the world.

In 2009, Cornwall Council adopted a policy encouraging its departments to use Cornish, including installing bilingual street

Some common components of Cornish words:

Bod	a home or dwelling, as in Bodmin
Bos	a homestead, house, as in Boscastle
Chy	a house, as in Chy-an-Mor
Pen	the end of something, for example a headland, as in Penryn, Penzance, Pentire
Perran	named after St Piran, the patron saint of Cornwall, as in Perranporth, Perranzabuloe, Perranuthnoe
Pol	a pool or inlet, as in Polbathic, Polzeath, Polruan
Porth	a port or landing place, as in Porthtowan, Perranporth
Ros	a moor, heath or promontory, as in Roseland, Roskear
Tre	a house, settlement or farmstead, as in Trerice, Trebarwith, Trelissick
Wheal	a mine or shaft, as in Wheal Kitty, East Wheal Rose

signs, although this has not been widely implemented. Existing street names and the names of countless farms and villages, although Anglicised, give some taste of the richness of Kernewek.

The components of Cornish largely reflect the landscape and history of Cornwall, with ports and mines named alongside villages, headlands and pools. Religion also plays a large role in place names. In Cornwall, this means that you'll find plenty of towns named after early Christian saints – St Erth, St Austell, St Agnes – which refer to church parishes. There are also references to Irish saints in place names – some less obvious than others – for example St Senan, as in Sennen, and St Senara, which has become Zennor. Padstow doesn't mean 'the seat of Rick Stein' but reflects St Petroc, the local saint, in combination with the Anglo-Saxon word for place, stow. Over time, Petrocstow has become Padstow; St Petroc's, one of Mr Stein's restaurants, is named after the saint.

Demelza, now used as a girl's name, is in Cornish Dyn Malsa, or Maelda's fort in translation. Puffin Island in the Scillies has clearly had some bright-beaked visitors in the past; Chacewater near Redruth means 'stream in the hunting grounds', suggesting more a vision of medieval pageantry and hunting in ancient forests than the small village in a valley that exists today. The village of Rock needs no explanation, while Calenick, meaning 'holly bushes' in Cornish, gives a clear indication of what was there in the past.

Some places sound more interesting in translation and hint at Cornwall's tapestry of myths and legends. Praa Sands, Poll an Wragh in Cornish, means 'witch cove' in translation. The village is the site of Pengersick Castle, said to be one of the most haunted buildings in the UK. Hessenford – Rys an Gwraghes in Cornish – means 'hag's ford' and, perhaps by coincidence, the Copley Arms in Hessenford is haunted by two ghosts, Matthew and The Lady.

Indian Queens has a lovely story behind it – and it's not what you think. Records show that there was a coach house on that spot called the Indian Queen, with an inscription on the porch telling the story of a Portuguese princess who landed in Falmouth and slept a night there on her way to London. Her dark appearance made locals think she was an Indian. Locals would like to link the story or visitor to Pocahontas, but no historian has yet found the proof.

While all these place names bring together items of topological and cultural information about Cornwall's places, there's no doubt that the things that jump out to a non-Cornish speaker are the funny ones. The name of the tor Brown Willy, far from meaning anything rude, actually means 'hill of swallows', from the Cornish Bronn Wennili. Mousehole, pronounced 'mouzel', is named after the tiny harbour entrance, while Lostwithiel has nothing to do with getting lost. The Cornish name, Lostwydhyel, means 'tail of a wooded area'.

LOCAL SPECIALITIES

Local specialities in Cornwall tends to mean food – as it's home to several Michelin-starred and TV chefs who do wonders with the produce grown here. While you might find a number of these delights elsewhere in the country, nothing beats eating this traditional food in its homeland.

FOOD AND DRINK

Cider
It's not a real West Country holiday if you don't get some cider inside yer. Healey's is the main producer, but you'll do well to knock on the door of any farm advertising its own version of Old Rosie. Watch out – things can get very fuzzy very quickly.

Clotted cream
Dairy farmers in the southwest specialise in this delicacy, made by heating full-cream cow's milk until the clots of cream rise to the top. Rodda's, based in Redruth, is the best-known brand name; don't tell your cardiologist, but the minimum fat content is 55 per cent.

Cornish fairings
These round ginger biscuits have been sold in Cornwall since before the 1800s and were given as a treat to children or by men to their sweethearts. These days, they're a good gift to take home to your work colleagues or housesitter.

Cornish pasty
The daddy of Cornish food is a semicircle of pastry with a crimped edge, filled with meat, vegetables and seasoning. All manner of varieties, including vegetarian pasties, are now available in most local bakeries.

Cornish yarg
This is a creamy, crumbly semi-hard cheese made from Friesian cow's milk, and is often sold round or heart-shaped and wrapped in nettle leaves. It's very pretty to look at.

Cream tea
A traditional Cornish cream tea consists of two halves of a scone spread with strawberry jam and topped with clotted

cream, served with a pot of tea. The best are served fresh with a sea view. Dodge any outlet trying to serve you a scone in a plastic wrapper – freshly baked scones are the only way to do it.

Hevva cake

Hevva, or 'Heavy' cake, is a type of fruit cake baked in a slab with a criss-cross pattern on the top. The name relates to the word the fishermen would shout when they saw shoals of pilchards in the sea; the pattern resembles a fishing net.

Ice cream

With all that lovely grass to munch, it's no wonder that Cornwall's cows produce such fantastic dairy products. Ice cream is a real treat here – Roskilly's is one of the bigger producers, but local independents such as Moomaid of Zennor are also well worth seeking out.

Real ale

Real ale is brewed down in these parts, with Sharp's, Skinner's and St Austell breweries being the producers of note. Cornish Knocker,

Heligan Honey and Doom Bar are some of the more intriguing names to look out for.

Stargazey pie

This classic Cornish dish is a pie containing pilchards. It is thought that the name comes from the fact that the fish heads protrude from the pastry, looking up at the sky. Cooked this way, the fish oil drains back into the pie and keeps it moist.

Wine

As the warmest county in the UK, Cornwall has a few vineyards. British wine once had something of a poor reputation but is now competing well, and Cornish wines – in particular Camel Valley wines – stand up to scrutiny. However, the wine does tend to cost more than imports.

A few other notable things have Cornish origins:

ART

Dame Barbara Hepworth

The godmother of Modernist sculpture, Dame Barbara Hepworth is best known for her powerful abstract sculptures and for being the doyenne of the St Ives modernist movement. The Barbara Hepworth museum in St Ives includes her home and former workshop.

Ben Nicholson

Barbara Hepworth's husband, Ben Nicholson, painted abstract still lives and landscapes in St Ives and is closely associated with the town. Some of his work can be seen at Tate St Ives.

Serpentine gifts

The distinctive mottled stone of The Lizard was once cut and shaped into everything from small ornaments to entire shop fronts. Today you can find small workshops and gift shops at Lizard Village and Lizard Point and at the nearby Church Cove.

MADE IN CORNWALL
Finisterre

This Cornwall-based surf label sells wetsuits, beanies, hoodies and just about everything you need for the lifestyle as a cold-water surfer down in Cornwall.

Seasalt

One of the modern classics to come out of Cornwall, Seasalt is a fashion label with dresses inspired by the Lost Gardens of Heligan, sporty deck shoes and a good range of quality rainwear.

NOT FROM CORNWALL
Cornishware

This distinctive blue and white-banded pottery has been made since the 1920s and the original egg cups, jars and crockery are highly prized by collectors. It was actually made in Derbyshire, not Cornwall; the name came about as an employee thought that the blue bands looked like the Cornish sky, and the white the white-capped waves.

▼ St Ives

BEFORE YOU GO

THINGS TO READ

Get in the mood for a Cornish holiday with these dramatic tales featuring windswept cliffs, stormy moors and long-lost family estates.

Rebecca –
Daphne du Maurier
'Last night I dreamt I went to Manderley again...' This gothic novel set in a rambling West Country estate has never been out of print and is du Maurier's best-known work. She lived and wrote in Kilmarth, near Par, and is Cornwall's foremost literary figure. *The House on the Strand*, *Jamaica Inn* and *Frenchman's Creek* also feature Cornwall.

The Poldark series –
Winston Graham
Following the Poldark family in Cornwall during the last half of the 18th century, these 12 novels are full of suspense, family feuds, tin miners and smugglers, bringing this period of Cornwall's history alive. It is now a hugely popular TV series (see page 45).

The Camomile Lawn –
Mary Wesley
The lawn in question belongs to a house on the Cornish cliffs where an extended family gathers to have an annual holiday in 1939, prior to the outbreak of war.

The Forgotten Garden –
Kate Morton
A four-year-old girl is found alone on a ship to Australia on the eve of World War I... and as the story unfolds, an inheritance, an estate and a forgotten garden in Cornwall become a key part of the story.

John Betjeman
Poet Laureate John Betjeman had a lifetime love of Cornwall and was buried at St Enodoc Church, Trebetherick, north Cornwall. Many of his poems are about Cornwall and his nostalgic love for its coast and countryside.

Thomas Hardy
Hardy was working as an architect near Boscastle in north Cornwall when he met his

first wife, Emma. Several of his poems about her, their meeting and their marriage have Cornwall as a backdrop.

The Lost Gardens of Heligan – Tim Smit

If you even have a passing interest in gardens and heritage, this will pique your interest. Until World War I, the gardens of the Heligan Estate were among the finest in Cornwall. When Tim Smit discovered them decades later, they were wild and overgrown. This is the story of his reinvention of the gardens.

The Levelling Sea – Philip Marsden

This highly rated historical story follows the town of Falmouth from the 16th to the 19th century as it grows from a single house to a significant Atlantic coast village. Marsden's 2014 book *Rising Ground: A Search for the Spirit of Place*, is a powerful and evocative reflection on the Cornish landscape.

THINGS TO WATCH

Get inspired and prepared for a trip to the far southwest with these TV shows and films.

Coast

This long-running BBC series has chased up and down every patch of sand and every cliff top around the UK, and remains a great point of reference for interesting stories about biology, history, marine life and living by the sea. The sections on Cornwall are particularly colourful and dramatic.

Doc Martin

Martin Clunes stars in this long-running ITV series about a grumpy urban surgeon with a fear of blood who moves to Cornwall to become a GP. It's a gentle comedy with love stories, strange maladies and peculiar

▼ Fistral Beach

people, and is filmed at Port Isaac. The eighth series aired on British TV in 2017. A ninth and, reportedly, final series will be shown in 2018.

Poldark

The remake of *Poldark* has become an ongoing BBC triumph, with Irish actor Aidan Turner starring as heartthrob Ross Poldark. The series taps into old-fashioned romanticism about Cornwall and, with the spectacular Cornish coast as the main co-star, is believed to boost tourism. A fourth series is due in 2018. Efforts at the Cornish dialect by the actors have led to YouTube comic spots becoming almost as popular as the real thing in Cornwall.

Saving Grace

This 2000 film is set in Port Isaac and follows the story of recently widowed Grace Trevethyn – Brenda Blethyn – as she discovers her husband's secret debt problem and turns to gardening, specifically the hydroponic cultivation of marijuana, to make ends meet. It features Martin Clunes as the local doctor, another Martin, in his pre-*Doc Martin* days.

The Witches

The Headland Hotel in Newquay is the site of the big witches' conference in this 1990 adaptation of Roald Dahl's children's book. These days, the transformations seem a bit dated – it's all pre-CGI – but it's fun nevertheless.

Wycliffe

Jack Shepherd played Detective Superintendent Wycliffe in the TV adaptation of the novels by W J Burley. It's worth a mention because Cornwall is as big a character as any of the others, and because the lifestyles portrayed reflect real life – well, real life but with more murders. One episode is about the Beast

▼ Port Isaac

▲ Coastal path towards Millook, Widemouth Bay

of Bodmin. The series ran from 1994–8 and you can buy them as a DVD box set.

THINGS TO KNOW

You'll find facts and figures, peculiar myths and legends dotted through this guide – Cornwall is full of wonderful places and incredible, unbelievable stories. Here's a taster of what's to come.

The Beast of Bodmin

More than 60 people claim to have seen the Beast of Bodmin, a large, black, cat-like creature that preys on local wildlife. Nobody knows for sure that there's a big cat living on the moor; one theory is that a panther escaped from a private zoo and it or its descendants are roaming the moor today.

Authentic pasties

The Cornish pasty really does taste better in Cornwall. For now, pre-Brexit, it enjoys EU Protected Geographical Indication status, so only pasties actually made in Cornwall can be called Cornish pasties. The authentic pasty recipe contains beef, potato, onion and swede and is said to date from as early as the 1300s.

Mutiny on the Bounty

Before we even mention pirates, Cornwall's best-known seafarer is probably William Bligh, the captain of the *Bounty*. He came from St Tudy near Bodmin, but is best remembered for the mutiny on his ship, bound for Tahiti, which led to many of the mutineers colonising Pitcairn Island.

Celebrity visitors

Cornwall seems to attract the rich and famous. David Cameron is a regular holiday visitor, Richard and Judy live near Polperro and Madonna has allegedly bought a mansion near Falmouth.

Beware the Spriggans

Cornwall has its fair share of fantastical creatures. Most mischievous of all are the Spriggans, fairy delinquents who take offence easily and respond mercilessly. Blame the traffic jams and disappearing tent pegs on them.

Local pride

Cornish people are rightly proud of their unique heritage and landscape. They display their own flag, the white cross on a black background, of St Piran or Perran, and St Piran's Day, 5 March, is celebrated as the national day of Cornwall.

Speaking Cornish

The Cornish language, which nearly died out in recent times, has been revived and is now taught in some nurseries, and primary and secondary schools in the county.

Let's talk statistics

Cornwall has the longest coastline of any county in Great Britain, running to nearly 435 miles. The Lizard is the southernmost promontory in Great Britain, and Land's End is one of the UK's most westerly points. The Isles of Scilly are the kingdom's farthest outcrop to the south. And the largest biome in the Eden Project is taller than the Tower of London.

How to eat a cream tea in Cornwall

In Cornwall, a cream tea consists of two halves of a scone slathered with strawberry jam and topped with clotted cream, while over the border in Devon you put the cream on first and then add the jam.

Waving, not drowning

The county's biggest wave is the Cribbar, also called the Widow Maker, a wave off the Towan Headland in Newquay that can top 32 feet.

THINGS TO PACK

Don't set off for Cornwall without these essentials:

Swimming kit

A towel and a swimming costume or trunks are the absolute first things you should put into your bag.

Warm clothes for the winter

You'll need a thick jumper, waterproofs, jeans and a few layers to stay warm in the sometimes biting winter wind. Add gloves and a woolly hat.

Warm clothes for the summer

You'll still need a warm jumper, waterproofs, jeans and a few layers to stay warm in the very occasionally biting wind. Add a sunhat and suncream.

Forgiving clothes

Pack these because it's easy to eat an ice cream, a pasty and two scones with cream every day of your stay in Cornwall, and loose, forgiving clothes will help to hide your weight gain.

Comfy shoes

Cornwall is not the place for high heels or power dressing unless you're staying at the Scarlet in Newquay, and probably not even then. If you're taking coastal walks, visiting pretty cobbled villages or larking about on the beach, you'll want to be wearing something comfortable.

A cameraphone

The best use for your phone in Cornwall is as a camera – mobile reception is patchy and being cut off from the world helps you to appreciate how lovely it is. Plus there are great things to photograph, from the sweeping views to your loved ones falling off a surfboard or having sand kicked in their faces by the kids.

Fishing gear

Bring a rod, a net and a bucket and try fishing for your supper. Crabbing is a popular pastime off Cornwall's piers and the whole family can explore rock pools so long as disturbance of tiny sea creatures is kept to a minimum.

A wetsuit

Even in the height of summer, most of the people in the sea will be wearing wetsuits, whether they're surfing, bodyboarding or swimming.

A dog

What better excuse do you need to get out and explore Cornwall's rural lanes and coastal routes? Dogs are welcome in most of the county's pubs and in select places to stay, but be aware that there are dog bans on some beaches.

Cash

Useful to have if you're staying somewhere a fair drive from a cash point. Most businesses in Cornwall will take a card, of course, but honesty food stalls by the side of the road, selling eggs and local produce, just have a box for coins.

National Trust and/or English Heritage membership

If you've got it, bring it with you: the National Trust and English Heritage look after a number of properties and places around Cornwall, including Tintagel Castle and Bedruthan Steps, and membership gives you free entry and free parking in plenty of beautiful spots.

Patience

Needed for the A30 and the summer traffic.

▶ Whipsiddery, Newquay

FESTIVALS & EVENTS

Most of the county's key events take place in the summertime; dates given are for 2018. For more information, see the 'What's on' page of visitcornwall.com.

▶ MAY

Padstow May Day
Padstow, 1 May,
May Day is celebrated all over Cornwall with parades and fairs. It's a particularly popular celebration in Padstow, when residents and visitors gather for a day of merriment.

World Pilot Gig Championships
St Mary's, Scilly Isles,
4–6 May
Crews compete to be the world champions in a colourful, energetic and friendly event, racing from St Mary's Quay to St Agnes or Nut Rock and back.

St Ives Food and Drink Festival
St Ives, 12–13 May
Porthminster Beach plays host to the region's finest food and drink producers and chefs for this two-day festival centred on the highly regarded Porthminster Beach Cafe with demonsrations, competitions and live music.

St Ives Literature Festival
St Ives, 12–19 May
This popular literary festival includes book launches, readings, writing workshops, live music and comedy.

▶ JUNE

The Royal Cornwall Show
Wadebridge, 7–9 June
A glimpse into Cornish rural life, this county show includes flower arranging, show jumping, a hunt relay and livestock judging.

The Electric Beach Festival
Newquay, mid-June
This hip-hop music beach party has moved from Watergate Bay to Fistral Beach in Newquay. Acts change every year, but recent headliners include Soul II Soul and De La Soul.

Falmouth International Sea Shanty Festival
Falmouth, 22–24 June
Get into the groove of Falmouth's seafaring past with maritime music, close harmony singers and a few bottles of rum. The festival supports the town and also the vital work of the RNLI.

▶ JULY

Penzance Literary Festival
Penzance, 4–7 July
The 'friendliest Lit Fest in the West' has national and international authors, book launches, creative writing

workshops and a colourful
LittleFest for youngsters.

Rock Oyster Festival
Dinham House, Wadebridge,
6–7 July
The Camel Estuary's fabled
oysters are celebrated in a festival
of music, food and art.

Port Eliot Festival
St Germans, 26–29 July
A glamorous, offbeat literary and
music festival in Port Eliot house
with speakers, wild swimming,
silent discos and creativity.

**St Endellion Summer
Music Festival**
Port Isaac, 31 July–10 August
This internationally famous music
festival includes classical music
concerts, Broadway show tunes
and brass band music. There is
also an Easter music festival,
running 12–20 April.

▶ **AUGUST**

Newquay Boardmasters
Newquay, 8–12 August
The UK's biggest surf festival has
a pro-surf competition as well as
live summer music from some of
the best names around, including
Bastille and Faithless in 2015.

**Fowey Royal Regatta and
Carnival Week**
Fowey, 19–26 August
This premier sailing event also
draws families for its carnival,
stalls and entertainment. The Red
Arrows do a fly past and locals
parade in fancy dress.

Newlyn Fish Festival
Newlyn, 27 August
This festival raises money for
the Royal National Mission to
Deep Sea Fishermen and
celebrates the town's most
famous produce with plenty of
food and drink.

▶ **SEPTEMBER**

Cornish Pasty Festival
Redruth, early September
This celebration of the Cornish
pasty revels in the history of the
former mining town of Redruth.
The three-day event is free and
the streets of Redruth are lined
with pasty stalls.

Newquay Fish Festival
Newquay, early September
Newquay isn't exactly famed for
its harbour, but in this local food
festival it's the centrepiece. The
local chefs show how to make a
fish dish to be proud of.

**World Bellyboard
Championships**
St Agnes, 1–2 September
A fun celebration of surfing using
old-style wooden boards. Expect
to see plenty of vintage gear, a
competition for the best
swimming hat, and fancy dress.
No wetsuits allowed.

Polo on the Beach
Watergate Bay, Newquay,
early September
This Veuve Clicquot-sponsored
annual event includes horse
displays, kite surfing, fantastic
food and Champagne alongside
polo games and tuition.

St Ives September Festival
St Ives, 8–22 September
This 14-day programme of events,
talks, concerts, theatre and much
more takes place in Cornwall's
most creative town.

▶ **DECEMBER**

Montol Festival
Penzance, mid-December
This historic six-day festival
celebrates the Midwinter
solstice and Cornish traditions
of the past. It culminates in
beacons being lit around the
town on 21 December.

CAMPSITES

For more information on these and other campsites, visit theAA.com/self-catering-and-campsites.

Carnon Downs Caravan & Camping Park ▶▶▶▶▶

carnon-downs-caravanpark.co.uk
Carnon Downs, Truro, TR3 6JJ
01872 862283 | Open all year
This is a beautifully mature park set in meadowland and woodland close to the village of Carnon Downs. An extensive landscaping programme has been carried out to give more spacious pitch sizes, and there is an exciting children's playground with modern equipment, plus a football pitch. Great for families.

Carvynick Country Club ▶▶▶▶

carvynick.co.uk
Summercourt, TR8 5AF
01872 510716 | Open all year
Set within the gardens of an attractive country estate, this campsite has self-catering holiday cottages and provides full facility pitches on hardstandings. The onsite amenities include an indoor leisure area with swimming pool, sauna and hot tub, fitness suite, badminton court and a bar and restaurant, plus the popular Signature Spa.

Padstow Touring Park ▶▶▶▶▶

padstowtouringpark.co.uk
Padstow, PL28 8LE | 01841 532061
Open all year
This popular park is set in open countryside above the quaint and fashionable fishing town of Padstow. The park is divided into paddocks by bushes and hedges that helps to create a peaceful and relaxing atmosphere.

Polmanter Touring Park ▶▶▶▶▶

polmanter.com
Halsetown, St Ives, TR26 3LX
01736 795640 | Open Spring BH to early Sep
A well-developed touring park on high ground, Polmanter has been tastefully landscaped, and includes a field with pitches for motorhomes. The fishing port and beaches of St Ives are just a mile and a half away, and there is a bus service in high season.

Porthtowan Tourist Park
▶▶▶▶▶

porthtowantouristpark.co.uk
Mile Hill, Porthtowan, TR4 8TY
01209 890256 | Open Apr–Oct
This neat, level grassy site is on high ground above Porthtowan, with plenty of shelter provided by mature trees and shrubs. It is almost midway between the small seaside resorts of Portreath and Porthtowan, with their beaches and surfing.

St Ives Bay Holiday Park
▶▶▶▶▶

stivesbay.co.uk
73 Loggans Road, Upton Towans, Hayle, TR27 5BH | 0800 317713
Open Easter–Oct
An extremely well-maintained holiday park with a relaxed atmosphere situated adjacent to a three mile beach. The park is specially geared for families and couples, and has a large indoor swimming pool and two pubs with entertainment. There are camping pods for hire.

St Mabyn Holiday Park ▶▶▶▶
stmabynholidaypark.co.uk
Longstone Rd, St Mabyn, Wadebridge, PL30 3BY | 01208 841677 | Open mid-Mar to Oct
St Mabyn is a family-run site close to the picturesque market town of Wadebridge and within easy reach of Bodmin; it's centrally located for exploring both the north and south coasts of Cornwall. The park is in a country setting and provides plenty of onsite activities including a heated swimming pool, and children's play areas.

Seaview International Holiday Park ▶▶▶▶▶
seaviewinternational.com
Boswinger, Mevagissey, PL26 6LL
01726 843425 | Open Mar–Sep
Seaview International is an attractive holiday park set in a beautiful, landscaped environment overlooking Veryan Bay. The beach is just half a mile away. There is also an 'off the lead' dog walk, and a 'ring and ride' bus service to Truro, St Austell and Plymouth.

Trethem Mill Touring Park
▶▶▶▶▶

trethem.com
St Just-in-Roseland, TR2 5JF
01872 580504 | Open Apr to mid-Oct
Trethem Mill is a quality park in all areas, with plenty of amenities. It's in a lovely rural setting, with spacious pitches separated by young trees and shrubs. The very keen family who own the site are continually looking for ways to enhance its facilities.

Wooda Farm Holiday Park
▶▶▶▶▶

wooda.co.uk
Poughill, Bude, EX23 9HJ | 01288 352069 | Open Apr–Oct
Wooda Farm is an attractive park overlooking Bude Bay, with lovely sea views. A variety of activities are provided by way of the large sports hall and hard tennis court, and there's a super children's playground. You can also try your hand at clay pigeon shooting or coarse fishing.

A–Z of Cornwall

▲ Bedruthan Steps

▶ **Bedruthan Steps** MAP REF 275 E2

nationaltrust.org.uk

Bedruthan, St Eval, PL27 7UW | Open all year for cliff walks;
cliff staircase closed Nov to mid-Feb

Cornwall has more than its fair share of ancient myths and
legends, but it turns out that the tale of the giant Bedruthan
who used the weathered rock stacks here – Queen Bess,
Samaritan Island and Diggory's Island among them – as a
shortcut across the sandy beach, isn't one of them. This
dramatic north coast beach, much loved by photographers, is a
National Trust site, along with the mine of Carnewas on the
clifftop overlooking it, and was a popular holiday spot for the
Victorians, along with Newquay down the coast. An enterprising
storyteller seems to have created the tale of a giant for tourism
purposes around this time – there are no older references to it.
But myth-busting aside, it's a gorgeous beach to visit, and the
clifftop path is perfect on a blustery day. Watch out if you're on
the beach – there are dangerous currents and nearby Mawgan
Porth (see page 164) is a better and safer bet for swimming.

EAT AND DRINK
Carnewas Cafe
nationaltrust.org.uk
Bedruthan, St Eval, PL27 7UW
01637 860701
Carnewas mine didn't yield up a vast fortune for its owners but it did leave behind some interesting buildings, repurposed today as the National Trust cafe and shop at Bedruthan Steps. The cafe serves cream teas and is a good stop after a blustery coastal walk. There's also a children's quiz and trail, walk leaflets and an information panel. Dogs are welcome.

▶ **Bodmin** MAP REF 276 C5

Bodmin might look like any other middle-sized town in mid-Cornwall, but its history shows it punching above its weight, often quite literally. It was always an important place for the Cornish to gather to defend their heritage, being the site of both the Cornish rebellion of 1497 and the Cornish uprising of 1549 when the Cornish people fought against the compulsory introduction of the *Book of Common Prayer* in English. During the mining boom of the 18th and 19th centuries, it was an important trading town and many of the impressive buildings of the town date to this period. Buildings that reflect Bodmin's one-time status as the former administrative centre of Cornwall include the neoclassical court building in Mount Folly and the old cattle market in Fore Street with its frieze of bulls' and rams' heads.

The church of St Petroc, in the centre of Bodmin, is the largest church in Cornwall. It has a plain face but, if you're looking for the heart of Cornish history and culture, it's here rather than in the surf beaches and tea rooms.

Bodmin has some unique ways of presenting its history – all of which make entertaining rainy day activities. You can participate in a trial in the old courthouse, where a Victorian-era murder case is played out for visitors. Then meet ghosts and hear chilling stories at Bodmin Jail, dating from 1779, as featured on TV's *Most Haunted*. There's also a light infantry museum, the town museum, which tells tales of life in Bodmin through to the post-war period, and a steam railway, which takes you out 6.5 miles beyond the town in a cloud of steam to the River Camel or the River Fowey.

Activity lovers may well find time to hire bikes and cycle to the coast on the largely level Camel Trail. It's a 22-mile cycle from Bodmin to Wadebridge then along the coast to Padstow. Bodmin is a down-to-earth working town but there's plenty for visitors to do and there is good access from here to the north and south coasts and to most major attractions.

VISIT THE MUSEUMS AND GALLERIES

Bodmin Jail

bodminjail.org
Berrycoombe Road, PL31 2NR
01208 76292 | Open all year
daily 9.30–6

This spook-filled jail held
murderers, cow stealers and
petty criminals from its opening
in 1779 and is now a popular
tourist attraction with a wine
bar, a restaurant and scary
nighttime ghost walks. The
ghost of a priest has been
seen in the chapel and many
visitors say they have been
followed around during
their visit. The jail features
regularly in *Poldark*.

Bodmin Museum

museumsincornwall.org.uk
Mount Folly Square, PL31 2DB
01208 77067 | Open Easter–Sep
Mon–Fri 10.30–4.30, Sat 10.30–
2.30, Oct Mon–Sat 10.30–2.30

On the site of the town's former
Franciscan friary, this museum
holds exhibits about life in
Bodmin, including materials on
trade and transport, rocks and
minerals, mining and
blacksmiths. The story of
Bodmin through World War II
is shown, and there's also a
quiz for children.

Cornwall's Regimental Museum

cornwalls-regimentalmuseum.org
The Keep, Lostwithiel Road,
PL31 1EG | 01208 72810
Open Mon–Fri 10–5

Atten–shun. This military
museum, in a former Victorian
barracks building, offers an
insight into military life and
the history of the Cornish
Regiment. Expect to see stirring
displays of uniforms, weapons,
medals and more. There's also
an extensive reference library
and the largest single section of
the Berlin Wall in the UK.

Shire Hall

bodminlive.com
Mount Folly, PL31 2DQ
01208 76616 | Court is in session
hourly Mar–May Mon–Fri 11–3,
Jun–Sep Mon–Sat 11–4, Oct–Feb
Mon–Fri 11–1

In 1844, the body of local girl
Charlotte Dymond was found on
Rough Tor on Bodmin Moor.
This 45-minute courtroom
experience takes visitors
through the trial of Matthew
Weeks, accused of her murder.
Will he be put to death, sent
to Australia, sentenced to
hard labour, or walk out a
free man?

GET OUTDOORS

Cardinham Woods

forestry.gov.uk/cardinham
Bodmin | 01208 72577
Open all year

This Forestry Commission-
managed woodlands area has
four different marked trails.
There is a 7-mile Bodmin Beast
blue-graded trail and two
red-graded trails for mountain
bikers, along with lovely
scenery, and a river with a
stone bridge. Some routes are
wheelchair- and pushchair-
friendly. There's also a cafe with
a play area for young children.

TAKE A TRAIN RIDE
Bodmin & Wenford Railway
bodminrailway.co.uk
Bodmin General Station,
PL31 1AQ | 01208 73555
Open 20 May–5 Oct daily
The Bodmin & Wenford Railway runs steam trains along a delightful 6.5-mile rural line, from Bodmin to Bodmin Parkway Station on the main Paddington to Penzance line. The views are lovely and there are tea rooms at or near the final destination stations in both directions. Check the website for precise train times and routes.

EXPLORE BY BIKE
Bodmin Bikes
bodminbikes.co.uk
Hamley Court, Dennison Road,
PL31 2LL | 01208 73192
Open Mon–Sat 9–5
What a choice: the Camel Trail, leading from Bodmin to Wadebridge and Padstow, or the peaceful network of narrow lanes that link the villages of Helland, Helland Bridge, Blisland, St Breward, St Tudy and St Mabyn in a circular tour. Brave the steep hills and reward yourself with a pub lunch or cream tea.

EAT AND DRINK
The Borough Arms
theboroughalms.com
Dunmere, PL31 2RD | 01208 73118
The Camel Trail skims past this updated Victorian railway pub outside Bodmin, and walkers come in to indulge in a range of West Country real ales and ever-reliable pub grub, including ploughman's, steaks, piri-piri chicken and freshly battered fish and chips. Families are well catered for, with a children's play area to burn off extra energy.

Woods Cafe
woodscafecornwall.co.uk
Cardinham Woods,
PL30 4AL | 01208 78111
Whether you're keen to ramble in the woods or just want somewhere pretty to stop for a while, this cafe in a woodsman's cottage is worth a visit and is rated as one of Cornwall's best places for a cream tea. They don't just serve the standard jam-and-clotted-cream treats, though – they also serve savoury cheese scones with cream cheese and onion relish.

▶ PLACES NEARBY
Close to Bodmin you'll find Cornwall's top winery the Camel Valley vineyard, and the Georgian house and estate Pencarrow (see page 83), known for its gardens, along with Lanhydrock, a stunning Victorian house and estate.

Camel Valley Vineyard
camelvalley.com
Nanstallon, PL30 5LG
01208 77959 | Guided tours
Easter–Sep Mon–Fri 10–5
Cornwall's most successful vineyard, Camel Valley has won plenty of awards for its still and sparkling fine wines from grapes grown in this boutique vineyard, including double

international gold medals in 2012. Stop by for a drink and a tour in the summer, or visit the wine bar/shop out of season.

Lanhydrock

nationaltrust.org.uk

Bodmin, PL30 5AD | 01208 265950

Gardens open all year daily 10–6; house open Mar–early Nov 11–5.30; closed Mon outside peak season

This magnificent Victorian estate and house, 2.5 miles north of Lostwithiel and reached from Bodmin on the A30, offers a glimpse of above-stairs elegance and below-stairs endeavours, along with a 1,000-acre garden. On first sight, the house gives every impression of being wholly Tudor, but in fact all that remains of the original house, built between 1630 and 1642 for wealthy Truro merchant Sir Richard Robartes, are the gatehouse, entrance porch and north wing. The east wing was removed and the rest fell victim to a terrible fire in 1881, but the house was rebuilt to match the surviving part.

The interiors are certainly very grand, notably the Long Gallery, and there are lavish furnishings throughout the house. Of all the 50 rooms that are open, visitors tend to find the below-stairs sections the most interesting, including the kitchen, larders, bakehouse, dairy, cellars and servants' quarters. In August and September there are Up and Under tours (free) exploring some of the history and workings of the Victorian-era house, and all year you can try out being a servant. The costumed volunteer team demonstrate how to lay a table setting properly and fold a napkin and invite you to join in. A lot of effort has been put

▼ Lanhydrock

into creating an experience rather than a static museum to visit.

Lanhydrock is surrounded by beautiful grounds, with a glorious bluebell wood in late spring and camellias, rhododendrons and magnolias in the higher garden. There is also a modern sculpture trail in the higher garden. Adjoining the house are formal gardens with clipped yews and bronze urns, and there's an adventure playground for children. Family events, particularly in the summer months, include trails and craft activities. Check the website for up-to-date details on events.

The house also holds gardening workshops and has a plant centre for those inspired by its estate, along with a secondhand bookshop. There is a restaurant in the old servants' hall and a cafe in the former stables serving Cornish ice cream and cream teas.

Pinsla Garden

pinslagarden.net
Pinsla Lodge, Glynn, Bodmin, PL30 4AY | 01208 821339
Open 23 Feb–Oct daily 9–5

On a far smaller scale than Pencarrow or Lanhydrock, which are the draw for many, the 2-acre Pinsla Garden and Nursery is bursting with colour and beautiful plants, all set around a fairytale cottage in the woods, where the owners live. It's beautifully thought out, unconventional, wild and romantic, all at the same

10 rainy day ideas

▶ Visit the Eden Project near St Austell
page 89

▶ Visit the National Maritime Museum in Falmouth
page 96

▶ Have some fishy fun at the Blue Reef Aquarium, Newquay
page 180

▶ Go coasteering or surfing – so what, you're wet anyway.

▶ Go swimming – either in the sea or in one of Cornwall's great indoor pools. Try Penzance (page 198), Falmouth (page 93) or Bude (page 70)

▶ Browse art and eat ice cream at Roskilly's Farm on the Lizard Peninsula
page 150

▶ Spend a morning at Tate St Ives
page 237

▶ Visit one of Cornwall's historic houses, such as Port Eliot (page 116) or Prideaux Place (page 190)

▶ Meet rescued seals at the Cornish Seal Sanctuary in Gweek
page 134

▶ Hunker down in a local pub until the rain stops

time. Dogs are welcome – and might make it on to the 'Dog blog' part of Pinsla's website – and it's a flat, easy walk around the garden with the option of a cream tea or homemade cake at the end.

▶ Bodmin Moor MAP REF 277 D4

Dominated by granite tors, peppered with Bronze Age relics
and coloured by myths and legends going back to the time
of King Arthur, Bodmin Moor is an essential part of the
Cornish experience. It feels larger than its boundaries, just
10 miles by 10 miles, perhaps because of its barren landscape
and its height – Brown Willy, the highest point in Cornwall at
1,377 feet, is on its western side along with the rocky crest of
neighbouring Rough Tor. Gaping holes in the ground left by the
mining and quarrying industries, such as Cheesewring Quarry
and Phoenix United Mine, add to the drama.

But let's start with the stories. The Beast of Bodmin is
the moor's most talked about inhabitant, a big, black, puma-
like cat that has been spotted more than 60 times since 1983
and investigated by multiple agencies, but to no avail. Nobody
has actually verified that there is a big cat living on the moor.
Like many similar sightings across the West Country, the
suggestion is that it is the descendant of a panther or similar
big cat escaped from a private zoo in the 1970s. Catch it on
camera if you can.

Going back to King Arthur, who reputedly lived at Tintagel
Castle on the north coast, the story goes that on his deathbed
he ordered his sword Excalibur to be cast into a lake. Locals
say that Dozmary Pool, on the south side of the moor, is
the home of Excalibur and the Lady of the Lake. It's also the
site of the myth or legend of Jan Tregeagle, a disgruntled

▼ Rough Tor

▲ Twelve Men's Moor

spirit condemned by the Devil to complete Sisyphean tasks, such as baling out Dozmary Pool with a holed shell. The Tregeagles were a powerful local family between the 16th and 18th centuries, and were notorious for their brutality and dishonesty.

More recent history swirls around Rough Tor: Charlotte Dymond, a local lass, was found murdered here in 1844. There is a monument to her at the foot of the tor and her ghost has apparently been seen in the area, a figure in a gown and a silver bonnet.

Unverifiable tales aside, the moor is great walking territory, with plenty to see. The remarkable layered granite formation known as the Cheesewring – named because it looks like the part of a cider press used to squeeze the 'cheese' or juice from apples – is a defining image of the moor. The Hurlers and the Pipers, a collection of early Bronze Age stone circles near Minions village, inspired a song by West Country folk singer Seth Lakeman. According to tradition, a group of hurlers – men playing Cornish hurling – were turned to stone for playing on a Sunday; likewise, a group of pipers played on the Sabbath and suffered the same fate. Rillaton Barrow and Trethevy Quoit, an entrance grave from the Neolithic period, stand nearby.

Craddock Moor to the west is also peppered with burial mounds from the Bronze Age, hut circles of the Iron Age and medieval field systems. There's quite some history here in the landscape. North of Minions is Twelve Men's Moor and the rocky ridges of Kilmar Tor and Bearah Tor.

Walking up the two most significant peaks is fairly straightforward. Brown Willy can be reached from a starting point in Camelford, while Rough Tor is reached via various paths across the open moorland and via Camelford too. Both offer views of the ancient landscape at its best, showing off the Bronze Age remains, wind-sculpted rocks, barren heath and mining history. Bodmin Moor is one of Cornwall's 12 AONBs and provides habitats for many unique species, including 23 species of butterfly, golden plovers, otters, bats, cows, sheep and wild ponies. It is the last world site of Cornish path moss. For this reason, dogs are not allowed off the lead.

What to do when visiting Bodmin Moor? Bring your walking boots and a picnic and explore, whatever the weather. Along with the obvious landscape-related sights, Jamaica Inn is an evocative and famed place, a pub on the through route for smugglers taking contraband upcountry and the setting for Daphne du Maurier's novel of the same name about murderous wreckers. Today it contains a museum of smuggling. To find out more about the human history of the moor, and the landscape, the Minions Heritage Centre is a good bet. The small villages dotted around the moorland also hold some interesting sights.

▼ The Cheesewring

EXPLORE THE MOOR
Brown Willy and Rough Tor
Approach from Camelford on the A39. Head southeast on a minor road to Poldue Downs; there is car parking at the end of the road

Cornwall's highest point can be reached in a couple of hours along a clear path. Rough Tor, pronounced 'Row tor', is the first peak, with a scramble of rocks at the top, rough Neolithic stone walls and the foundations of a medieval chapel; Brown Willy is less dramatic but has great views.

Cheesewring
Stowe's Hill, 4 miles north of Liskeard. A 4-mile walk, taking in the Hurlers as well, starts at the Hurlers car park in Minions

The weathered formation of layered granite gave its name to the quarry next to it. Granite from the quarry was used to build Devonport Dockyard, Birkenhead Docks and part of Copenhagen Harbour, and was included in the materials used in the Thames Embankment and Westminster and Tower Bridges. The quarry has long been a popular rock climbing venue.

Daniel Gumb's Cave
Southwest edge of Cheesewring Quarry; access via Hurlers car park in Minions as before

Back in the 18th century, stonecutter Daniel Gumb lived in a cave here with his family to avoid paying tax. Known as the 'mountain philosopher', he carved one of Euclid's theorems in the roof of his cave, still visible today. The cave has been partly reconstructed, as much of it was destroyed when the quarry was extended in the 1870s.

Dozmary Pool
On the A30, 1.3 miles south of Bolventor

This small lake is the only natural freshwater inland lake in the southwest peninsula. The pool is closely associated with Arthurian legend although its authentic history is illustrated by the large number of mesolithic and neolithic flint arrowheads and scrapers that have been found in the vicinity.

Golitha Falls
St Neot, Lanreath. Approximately 5 miles southeast of Colliford Lake. Car park

These cascades in the River Fowey as it drains from Bodmin Moor towards the south coast make for a beautiful walk in the ancient oak and beech woods. Otters and kingfishers have been seen in the stepped waterfalls. Good for a dog walk; some of the woodland is pushchair- and wheelchair-accessible.

VISIT THE MUSEUMS AND GALLERIES
Jamaica Inn
jamaicainn.co.uk
Jamaica Inn, Bolventor, PL15 7TS
01566 86250 | Museum open all year daily 8am–9pm

This 18th-century inn stands high on Bodmin Moor and was made famous by Daphne du Maurier. It boasts beamed ceilings, roaring fires and a children's play area, but is a tourist attraction in its own right rather than a gourmet destination. The small Smugglers Museum on the site explores the connection, with artefacts and period costumes. Best if you've read the book first or have a particular interest in smuggling in the local area around Bodmin and Bolventor.

Minions Heritage Centre
cornish-mining.org.uk
Close to the car park in Minions
Open daily all year
This heritage centre in the Houseman's Shaft engine house of South Phoenix Mine has displays on the history of the landscape from the Stone Age, through 18th- and 19th-century mining up until today. It's a great introduction to the moor and the archaeology, ecology and mining heritage of the Caradon Hill area.

GET OUTDOORS
Colliford Lake Park
swlakestrust.org.uk
Bolventor | 01566 771930
Open all year
Cornwall's second largest lake is easily accessed via the A30 and has an 8.5-mile perimeter walk and picnic areas. Watersports are not allowed on the lake: it's a peaceful spot for a walk and has an important nature reserve for overwintering wildfowl. Permits for fly-fishing for brown trout can be arranged through Jamaica Inn.

SEE A LOCAL CHURCH
Cathedral of the Moors
Altarnun, around 4.5 miles west of Launceston; there's a car park just off the A30 within walking distance of the village
This small village on the edge of Bodmin Moor boasts the remarkable church of St Nonna, known as the 'Cathedral of the Moors' because it is the largest on Bodmin Moor. With its decorated Norman font and some beautiful carved bench ends inside, it is the literal and figurative high point of the village. It's a tranquil spot and features in Daphne du Maurier's *Jamaica Inn*.

EAT AND DRINK
The Rising Sun Inn
therisingsuninn.co.uk
Altarnun, PL15 7SN
01566 86636
It's still fine to arrive by horse at this inviting 16th-century moorland inn – there's a hitching post in the car park. Lunch and dinner dishes include Fowey River mussels with fries, and Cornish ham with free-range eggs, washed down with local Cornish Orchards cider or Skinner's Betty Stogs ale.

▶ PLACES NEARBY
Close to Bodmin Moor there's an interesting church

at Laneast with medieval touches and a memorial to the man who discovered Neptune; and a family-friendly water park.

St Sidwell and St Gulvat's Church

Off the A935, Laneast, PL15 8PN

Set at the head of a wooded valley, Laneast's church has an almost complete and very well-preserved set of medieval benches and bench ends, a well-preserved rood screen, and a prayer desk from the beginning of the 16th century. In the church is a memorial to astronomer John Couch Adams, who discovered the planet Neptune in 1846.

Siblyback Water Park

swlakestrust.org.uk
Siblyback Water Park, near Liskeard, PL14 6ER
Ranger tel: 01579 346522
Open daily all year; wakeboarding May–Sep only

This water park on the edge of Bodmin Moor offers plenty of watersports, from family rowing-boat hire to sailing, windsurfing and canoeing, alongside the more gentle pursuit of rainbow trout fishing – permits are available from the centre on site. For a real adrenaline boost, try wakeboarding: being pulled along behind a speedboat on a surfboard. Novices can simply enjoy the ride while the experienced can use the take-off ramps to launch

10 mythical beings of Cornwall

▶ **The Beast of Bodmin**
page 62

▶ **The giant Bedruthan**
page 56

▶ **The giant Cormoran of St Michael's Mount**
page 159

▶ **The Hooper of Sennen Cove**
page 256

▶ **Joan the Wad**
Queen of the Piskies, associated with the elements fire and water and sometimes said to be married to Jack-o'-lantern

▶ **The Bucca**
A hobgoblin dwelling in coal mines and coastal villages

▶ **The Owlman of Mawnan**
A mysterious winged creature first spotted in 1976 and reported to be as big as a man

▶ **The Spriggans of West Penwith**
page 47

▶ **The Cornish Knocker**
page 26

▶ **Morveren, the mermaid of Zennor**
page 271

themselves into jumps. There's also a cycle centre with child seats and trailers as well as adult and child bikes, and Segways available to hire for an unusual way to get around the lake's edge. There are miles of walks, a small campsite and a cafe overlooking the water.

▶ **Boscastle** MAP REF 276 C3

The dramatic natural harbour of Boscastle makes it one of a
foursome of must-see north coast villages together with
Crackington Haven (see page 85), Port Isaac (see page 211)
and Tintagel (see page 257). It provides the dramatic scenery
that inspired Thomas Hardy while he was working as an
architect on the nearby St Juliot's church tower; he also met
his first wife, Emma, here. Today, the sea surges in and out of
the National Trust-owned harbour in an often dramatic way
between the slate and shale cliffs. The village made the
national news when extreme flooding in 2004 destroyed several
buildings, including the visitor centre, sending at least 50 cars
into the harbour and leaving 155 people clinging to trees and
rooftops. Most were rescued by helicopter.

Much engineering and renovation work has been carried out
to make sure that such a devastating flood cannot happen
again, and the National Trust and local businesses have done a
lot to restore the vitality of the village and make it a lovely place
to visit. In the 19th century, Boscastle was an important
commercial port, with up to 200 ships a year importing a variety
of goods and exporting mainly china clay and slate. The
opening of railway links in 1890 as alternative transport
heralded a decline in the shipping trade.

Walks along the coast are exhilarating. To the right, you'll
reach Pentargon Waterfall, while to the left the blowhole in
Penhally Point, the headland on the northern side of the
harbour entrance, erupts water an hour before and after low
tide. It is also known as the Devil's Bellows. To the south of
Boscastle you can see 'the Stitches' on Forrabury Common, a
pattern of medieval land tenure where long, narrow strips of
land were cultivated and farmed, now preserved by the
National Trust.

**VISIT THE MUSEUMS
AND GALLERIES**
**Boscastle Pottery
and Mochaware**
Boscastle, PL35 0HE
01840 250291
This unique little pottery
specialises in the Victorian art
of Mochaware, selling hand-
thrown pots, cups and teapots
with the characteristic cloud,
tree and fern patterns on a
painted background. Visitors to
the shop can meet the potter
and watch him at work.

Museum of Witchcraft
museumofwitchcraft.com
The Harbour, PL35 0HD
01840 250111 | Open Apr–Oct
Mon–Sat 10.30–6, Sun 11.30–6
This popular museum, which
opened in the 1960s, has the
world's largest collection of
witchcraft-related bits and
bobs, from sickles used to

gather medicinal herbs to mysterious stones carved with maze patterns, and information on wise women, curses, charms and sacred sites. Local legends a tell of witches changing into cats, hares and owls. It's fascinating, but perhaps not for sensitive children.

Pilchard Palace
nationaltrust.org.uk
The Harbour | 01840 250353
The National Trust visitor centre, shop and cafe are all in a light and airy renovated pilchard-packing building, where pilchards were previously salted, pressed and packed for export. You can get details of circular walks and children's trails, and enjoy great cream teas. There's WiFi access and dogs are welcome.

SADDLE UP
Tredole Trekking
Trevalga, PL35 0ED
01840 250495
Horse and pony trekking along the north Cornwall coast for all abilities and a wide variety of interests, from those seeking riding holidays to others wanting to hitch up a pony to ride them to a local pub. Sunset rides are particularly beautiful.

EAT AND DRINK
The Cobweb Inn
cobwebinn.com
The Bridge, PL35 0HE
01840 250278
Once a warehouse where customs agents guarded taxable imported goods, it's now a pub with a whitewashed restaurant serving pasties, seafood, steaks and more. Rumour has it that the beamed, flag-floored back room drew illicit drinkers; today Cornwall-brewed ales and farm ciders can be ordered without any need for subterfuge.

Harbour Light Tea Garden
The Harbour, Boscastle
PL35 0AG | 01840 250728
In a pretty whitewashed cottage with a characteristic undulating North Cornwall slate roof, and right by the Museum of Witchcraft, this popular cafe does light lunches, sandwiches, cream teas and cakes. Wash it all down with Cornwall's own Tregothnan tea.

Helsett Farm Cornish Ice Cream
helsettfarm.com
Helsett Farm, Lesnewth,
PL35 0HP | 01840 261207
A happy herd of Ayrshire cows produces thick organic milk to create this much-loved ice cream, sold in Waitrose, Harrods and Selfridges, which comes in delightful flavours such as Charlie's Chocolate. Drop into the farm – which has cottages to rent – or look out this brand in local shops.

The Wellington Hotel ◉◉
wellingtonhotelboscastle.com
The Harbour, PL35 0AQ
01840 250202
A coaching inn since the 16th century, The Wellington was renamed after the Battle of

Waterloo in 1815. The views over the harbour have hardly changed. The restaurant has plenty of charm, with its chandeliers and linen-clad tables, and there's a traditional bar with real ales. Cornish-sourced meat, fish and shellfish feature strongly and cream teas are available all day.

▶ Bossiney MAP REF 276 C3

Bossiney, a short distance from busy Tintagel, is a quiet relief from too much Arthurian legend. Much of the coast at Bossiney is in the care of the National Trust. The beach below the cliffs at Bossiney Haven is reached by a steep path where donkeys once carried seaweed up from the beach to be used as fertiliser on neighbouring fields.

A short distance to the east lies Rocky Valley, where the river cuts through a final rock barrier into the sea. At the heart of the valley are the ruins of an old woollen mill. Within the ruins are small maze carvings on natural rock, most likely to be Victorian. Rocky Valley's river can be followed inland through the wooded St Nectan's Glen to St Nectan's Kieve, where a 60-foot waterfall plunges down a dark, mist-shrouded ravine. A fee is payable to view the falls and there is a tea garden above. The site can be reached by public footpath, which starts behind the Rocky Valley Centre at Trethevy on the B3263, a mile northeast of Bossiney.

▶ Bryher
see **Isles of Scilly**, page 248

▶ Bude MAP REF 277 D2

Bude is considered to be one of the best and most popular beach destinations in the county. With two beaches in the town itself plus several more along the coast nearby, plenty of holiday accommodation and a bustling, friendly centre, it's a great place to be based.

Summerleaze Beach is the more attractive of the two, with its long stretch of sand where the River Neet runs into the sea and an open-air sea pool nestling against the cliffs; refreshed twice daily by the tide, it's a safe place to swim even when the sea is choppy. Campaigns are often under way to save it – it's a unique place, half artificial and half formed by rocks. Local children swap wild tales about the day a shark was caught in it; that has almost certainly never happened. The other main Bude beach is called Crooklets, and has more appeal for surfers than families. Nearby are Widemouth Bay, a long, sandy stretch for both surfers and families; Northcott Mouth, good for rock pooling; National Trust-owned Sandymouth, which has a cafe and a waterfall; plus Duckpool, Millook Haven, the Strangles and Crackington Haven.

Bude town centre has two main shopping streets, the Strand and Belle Vue. The former fishing port was a hub for commerce through the 19th century but tourism is its mainstay. You'll find souvenir shops, surf and activity shops, supermarkets, clothes shops and toy shops as you stroll through.

There are pleasant walks around the cliff top on level, close-cropped grassland, and also inland along the Bude Canal. In the 19th century this canal transported sand to inland farms, where it enriched the soil. It extended almost as far as Launceston, 18 miles away.

The Hartland Point area, just across the border with Devon, is a wild and spectacular section of coast. Just within Cornwall is Morwenstow (see page 170), once the home of the fascinating Victorial eccentric Robert Stephen Hawker, vicar of Morwenstow, who devoted much time to recovering the bodies of drowned sailors. He is said to have once dressed up as a mermaid and to have perched on a tidal rock at Bude – until a fisherman appeared with a gun.

VISIT THE MUSEUM
Castle Heritage Centre
thecastlebude.org.uk
Lower Wharf, EX23 8LG
01288 357300 | Open Easter–Oct Sun–Fri 10–4, Nov–Easter Mon–Fri 9–5
This local history centre covers the natural history and geology of the north Cornish coast, the area's industrial history and the famous wreck of the *Bencoolen* on Summerleaze Beach. Local character Reverend Robert Hawker, vicar of Morwenstow, is also depicted recounting his horror of watching shipwrecks from storm-lashed cliffs.

HIT THE BEACH
Both Crooklets and Summerleaze Beach have lifeguards from May to September, beach cafes, surf tuition and car parks. Crooklets is famed for having one of Britain's first Surf Life Saving Clubs, while Summerleaze has candy-coloured beach huts for hire and a tidal pool for safe swimming, much used by triathletes and children. There is a clifftop path between the two beaches.

TAKE A BOAT TRIP
Bude Rowing Boats
budeboathire.co.uk
Lower Wharf, Bude Canal, EX23 8LE | 07968 688782
Rowing boats, pedalos and canoes are available for hire on Bude Canal. Bude Marshes, beside the canal, are a

designated Local Nature Reserve, and are home to otters, swans, bats, herons, kingfishers and grass snakes. The canal runs from Petherwicks Mill to Helebridge, and canal boats often pass through too.

GO COASTEERING
Outdoor Adventure
outdooradventure.co.uk
Atlantic Court, Widemouth Bay,
EX23 0DF | 01288 362900
Coasteering trips and surfing lessons are provided by Outdoor Adventure, an activity centre based at Widemouth Bay. Coaches take you out to explore Cornwall from the sea, jumping off cliffs, riding waves and climbing barnacle-covered ledges. It's all a big adrenaline rush. Residential courses are on offer alongside one-off sessions, and the team caters for families and stag and hen parties – separately, of course.

EXPLORE BY BIKE
Bude Bike Hire
budebikehire.co.uk
Pethericks Mill, EX23 8TF
01288 353748 | Open Mon–Sat
9.30–5.30
Circular routes from Bude link to Widemouth Bay in the south, Northcott Mouth beach in the north and across inland to Marhamchurch and Stratton. Bude Bikes has suggested downloadable cycling routes for all the family, and offers tagalongs, bike seats and electric bikes. Book ahead during school holidays.

GO FISHING
Bude Canal
EX23 8LE
Coarse fishing in Bude's canal is an option for a relaxing day. The 2-mile stretch has carp, roach, rudd, dace, perch, tench and more. To fish, an Environment Agency rod licence from any post office, plus a day permit from the Crescent Post

▼ Bude

Office – next to the canal – are required. Additional fishing options include Hele Barton Fishery, Lower Lynstone Lakes and the Tamar Lakes (see page 170).

SADDLE UP
Broomhill Manor Stables
broomhillmanor.co.uk
Poughill, EX23 9HA
07886 434740 | Open daily all year
Individual tuition, group rides and hacks along the north Cornish countryside and beaches, for all ages and experiences. There are plenty of country lanes and bridleways in the area to explore; this stables also has its own sand school and can run family lessons and taster sessions. Call for further details.

GO SURFING
Big Blue Surf School
bigbluesurfschool.co.uk
12 Summerleaze Crescent,
EX23 8HH | 01288 331764
Lessons Apr–Oct
Bude's beaches are for more than just picnics. Join the surfers with lessons or a week-long course with Big Blue Surf. They also offer surf hire, as do several shops in the centre of Bude, and vans in season at both beaches. This surf school has BSA accreditation and a low pupil-to-teacher ratio.

WALK THE WILDFLOWER COAST
The sand and pebble beach at Northcott Mouth lies about a mile north of Bude and can be reached by road or on foot along the clifftop coast path from Bude's Crooklets Beach through the wildflower haven of the National Trust's Maer Down. From spring onwards, the short, grassy clifftops are speckled with typical coastal flowers such as pink thrift, kidney vetch and sea campion, among many more. It's a level, exhilarating walk and there's a tearoom at Northcott Mouth (see page 74).

PLAY A ROUND
Bude and North Cornwall Golf Club,
budegolf.co.uk
Burn View, EX23 8DA
01288 352006 | Open daily all year
The traditional links course at Bude and North Cornwall Golf Club, dating from 1891, is in the centre of Bude with magnificent views of the sea. It's known as a challenging course with super greens and excellent drainage, making the course playable throughout the year off regular tees and greens.

EAT AND DRINK
Bay View Inn
bayviewinn.co.uk
Marine Drive, Widemouth Bay,
EX23 0AW | 01288 361273
Dating back around 100 years, this welcoming, family-run pub has fabulous views of the rolling Atlantic from its restaurant and the large raised decking area outside. The menu includes a signature

dish of fish pie, and plenty of variety for meat eaters and vegetarians.

Life's a Beach

lifesabeach.info
Summerleaze Beach,
EX23 8HN | 01288 355222

The best place to eat out in Bude is this stylish cafe with a view of the beach, which serves beachgoers during the day, cafe-style, and a more sophisticated clientele from 7pm, with some of the best seafood in the town. It also has an ice cream parlour and a beach shop.

Margaret's Rustic Tea Room

Northcott Mouth, EX23 9EG
01288 355241

In a field in Northcott Mouth, this tea room is one of Cornwall's finest and is a sight for sore walkers' eyes – or should that be feet? Margaret serves up tempting teatime treats, including a classic cream tea, in her open-air lounge with a bridge and stream running through it, just as her mother did since the 1940s.

▶ PLACES NEARBY

There are a number of places to visit from Bude itself, including the remains of a moated manor house, the pretty town of Stratton, neighbouring villages with interesting churches and Widemouth Bay, where you can learn to surf or relax with the family.

Penhallam Manor

english-heritage.org.uk
Week St Mary, south of
Widemouth Bay | 0370 333 1181
Check website for opening times

Not another Cornish country estate, but a low, grass-covered and complete ground plan of a 13th-century moated manor house surrounded by woods. Built by Andrew de Cardinham, it's a rare example of a moated manor house in the southwest – they are mainly found in central and eastern England. It's an interesting place to wander around if you're staying nearby – the full medieval ground plan has survived unaltered after the property was abandoned in the 14th century. Dogs on leads are welcome.

St Olaf's Church

Off Poughill Road, Poughill,
EX23 9ER

The 16th-century woodwork and wall paintings are the main reasons for visiting here. St Olaf's has two wall paintings of St Christopher, a medieval south door and roof bosses dating from the 1530s. Records show that in the 1520s the church had at least five guilds, including one to St Christopher and another to St Olaf, a Scandinavian saint.

St Winwaloe's Church

Off Vicarage Lane, Poundstock,
EX23 0AX

St Winwaloe's is set in a wooded hollow and has features

from many ages, including a Norman font, a 16th-century chest and an early 17th-century pulpit. Most notable are the wall paintings, including one with the message 'Don't work on Sundays' and another of the seven deadly sins. Parts of the rood screen survive, as does a symbol of St Luke in a panel of medieval stained glass.

Stratton

The nearby market town of Stratton, inland from Bude, is also a lovely place to visit, all narrow streets and ancient through-routes. The town is reached by turning off onto the Holsworthy road from the A39, just east of Bude. The Tree Inn, on Fore Street, was once the home of Antony Payne, aka the Cornish Giant, who grew to 7ft 4in. When he died in 1691, his coffin had to be lowered through the ceiling as it was too big for the stairs. Colebrook Farm near the town offers Pick Your Own gooseberries,

raspberries and strawberries in season. There is a car park at Howells Bridge on the eastern edge of Stratton. From the car park, walk up Spicer's Lane to the church and from there into the centre of the town.

Widemouth Bay

Marine Drive, Widemouth Bay, EX23 0DF

Pronounced 'Wid-muth', this wide surf beach 3 miles or so south of Bude is great for families and has a lifeguard during the summer season. At low tide there are rock pools, and you'll find plenty of surf schools touting for business in peak season – it's a great place to learn, especially because it's uncrowded and has beach and reef breaks. A seasonal ban on dogs applies to the northern part of the beach but they are welcome all year at the south part, called Black Rock locally. There's free parking at the north and south ends of the beach.

▶ Cadgwith
see **The Lizard**, page 131

▶ Calstock MAP REF 277 F5

Calstock lies on the Cornish side of the River Tamar looking over to Devon, and is known today for an eclectic mix of festivals, including those of the motorbike, rock music and art varieties. The village is dominated by an elegant rail viaduct built in 1906 from precisely manufactured rocks, a triumph of good design and successful engineering. The coming of the railway saw a decline in Calstock's centuries of river trade and industry, and today the village is a serene enclave to which river boats carry visitors from Plymouth. As well as its popular festivals, Calstock is well known for its attractive mix of pubs, restaurants, shops and art galleries. There are numerous woodland walks in the area and canoe trips are available from Cotehele Quay. In summer, a ferry runs from Calstock Quay to Cotehele House, a National Trust-run Tudor mansion with extensive gardens that attracts most of the area's visitors.

TAKE IN SOME HISTORY
Cotehele
nationaltrust.org.uk
St Dominick, PL12 6TA, between Tavistock and Callington. Turn off the A390 at St Ann's Chapel, signed 2.5 miles south of junction
01579 351346 | Garden open all year, 10–dusk; house open mid-Mar to Oct, limited opening Nov–Dec
One of Cornwall's great gardens and finest Tudor houses, Cotehele is tucked away in a huge estate in the Tamar Valley. Visitors have marvelled at the Great Hall with its armour and arched timber roof since the 18th century. The layout owes much to the medieval period, with three internal courtyards, a fine old kitchen, ancient furniture and tapestries on the walls. Later additions include a tower built in the 1620s and a splendid bedroom where Charles I was said to have spent a night in a four-poster bed.

Go into the garden and you'll be blown away. It's not so much a case of stepping back in time as stepping into another world, with enormous ferns and a garden tunnel leading from the formal East Garden into the wild Valley Garden, planted with azaleas and rhododendrons. There's also a tiny chapel in the wood, a thatched Victorian summerhouse, a medieval stew pond, used for storing live fish, and a dovecote.

Cotehele Quay – part of the wider Cotehele estate, which is 1,300 acres in total – has an onsite discovery centre in the former stone lime kiln buildings telling the story of the Tamar. You'll find the restored sailing barge, *Shamrock*, built in 1899

10 sub-tropical gardens

and used to carry cargo, including manure, coal and limestone, up and down the river. She's in the port every day and the hold is open for visits from 1 to 4 on Sundays. There are also fantastic walks around the estate from here, with river views, deep woods and glimpses of the riverside wildlife. You can download walking trails from the National Trust website.

MEET THE WILDLIFE
Tamar Otter and Wildlife Centre
North Petherwin, Launceston, PL15 8GW | 10.30–6
The ideal outing for all ages. Watch the British and Asian short-clawed otters playing and being fed, and stroll through the 21 acres of woods spotting a fascinating range of animals from fallow deer, muntjac deer, meerkats and wallabies. There are several owl species and birds of prey. The centre has an award-winning tea room.

TAKE A TRAIN RIDE
Tamar Valley Line
greatscenicrailways.com
Gunnislake–Plymouth, via Calstock
01752 584777 | Check website for timetable
Known as one of England's loveliest country branch lines, this particular stretch of the Cornwall–Devon border can be traversed on a main-line train over Brunel's Royal Albert Bridge and along the Bere Peninsula. Stop at local village stations for a cream tea. It

▲ Calstock Viaduct

takes approximately 40 minutes to reach Plymouth from Gunnislake and vice versa, through a largely hidden and lesser-visited part of the county.

CANOE THE TAMAR
Tamar Trails
tamartrails.co.uk
Cotehele Quay | 01822 833409
Open daily Feb–Nov
Sample everything from tree surfing to mountain biking, canoeing, archery and hiking in the beautiful Tamar Valley. The tree-top adventures are great fun for all the family and there are canoeing and cycling trips. The centre also houses an interpretation area with live webcams of local wildlife.

PLAY A ROUND
St Mellion International Resort
st-mellion.co.uk
St Mellion, PL12 6SD
01579 351351 | Open daily all year

Set in 450 acres of glorious Cornish countryside, St Mellion is heralded as the premier golf and country club in the southwest. The Kernow Course is perfect for golfers of all abilities, while the sculpted fairways and carpet greens of the Jack Nicklaus Course offer a challenge. The culinary focus is the An Boesti restaurant, which steers a course between traditional beef Wellington and more modern lamb with rhubarb fare.

EAT AND DRINK
The Rising Sun Inn
Gunnislake, PL18 9BX
01822 832201
The pretty terraced gardens here afford fabulous views over the Tamar Valley and the river. Draught beers include Dartmoor Brewery's Jail Ale and Legend, while the menu features old British favourites such as fish and chips and curry, but with the likes of duck breast and ribeye steak also on the menu. Great walks start from the pub.

▶ PLACES NEARBY
Not far from Calstock and Cotehele, you'll find more historical sights, plus a country park, a donkey sanctuary and the wonderful Port Eliot (see page 116).

Cotehele Mill
nationaltrust.org.uk
St Dominick, near Saltash,
PL12 6TA | 01579 351346
Open mid-Mar to Oct daily 11–5

More than just a 19th-century watermill, Cotehele Mill next to the Morden stream in the Tamar Valley is a working mill selling wholemeal flour. Outbuildings provide a historical insight into the wheelwright's, saddler's and blacksmith's workshops, and there is a traditional furniture maker, a potter and a hydro-electric scheme bringing everything bang up to date.

Dupath Well
english-heritage.org.uk
Callington | Open all year
In the medieval period, holy wells were held in high regard, and this pretty stone-built well-house standing over an ancient stream is a good example. It was believed to cure whooping cough when sufferers were immersed in the pool, and was built by the Augustinian canons of St Germans Priory around 1500. Entry is free.

Kit Hill Country Park
Callington | 01822 83503
The magnificent granite dome of Kit Hill rises to just over 1,000 feet above the town of Callington, about 4 miles northwest of Calstock. It stands in splendid isolation between the granite masses of Bodmin Moor to the west and Dartmoor to the east. For centuries Kit Hill was quarried for stone and mined for tin, copper, zinc, lead and even silver, but it is now a country park. The hill is topped by an 80-foot chimneystack built in 1858 as part of the

engine house of the Kithill Consols mine. There's a waymarked walking trail, as well as a heritage trail.

Saltash Heritage Museum

saltash-heritage.co.uk

17 Lower Fore Street, Saltash, PL12 6JQ | 01752 848466

Open Apr–Jun, Oct–Nov Wed 2–4, Sat 10–4, Jul–Sep Wed 2–4, Fri 10.30–12.30, 2–4, Sat 10–4

This small local museum celebrates the history and heritage of Saltash, covering everything from wartime life in the area to the impact of Isambard Kingdom Brunel in the southeast district of Cornwall. There is also a heritage trail around Saltash, including a stop at Mary Newman's cottage, a historic preserved site where Francis Drake's wife reputedly lived.

Tamar Valley Donkey Park

donkeypark.com

St Ann's Chapel, Gunnislake, PL18 9HW | 01822 834072

Open late Mar–Sep daily 10.30–5 (Jul–Aug 10–5), Oct Thu–Sun 10.30–4; at most other times weekends only 10.30–4

A great option for small children if it's raining, this donkey sanctuary includes a small petting zoo/farm with guinea pigs, goats, sheep, rabbits, pigs and, of course, donkeys, which you can take for a walk. There's also a large indoor play barn with a soft play area and cafe.

▶ Camborne MAP REF 274 C4

Camborne was once a cradle of Cornish industry, in tandem with adjoining Redruth (see page 220). This central swathe of Cornwall was once one of the richest tin-mining areas in the world and famed for its mines; the Camborne and Redruth Mining District with Wheal Peevor and Portreath Harbour are now designated as World Heritage Sites by UNESCO. Today the mining spirit lives on – although all its mines have fallen silent. Only South Crofty Mine, at Pool, between Camborne and Redruth, has shown any hope of reopening, although there is no current activity there. At Pool, the National Trust has restored two great steam engines used for pumping water and for bringing men and ore up and down deep mine shafts.

The town's most famous son, Richard Trevithick (1771–1833), was an early steam engine inventor who invented a steam threshing machine, an early road vehicle and the first railway engine. A special Trevithick Day is held in his honour in April, when the town remembers his achievements.

Beyond the industrial heritage, there are two key areas of countryside to visit: Tehidy Country Park, with leafy walks, streams and ornamental lakes; and Tuckingmill Valley Park, an award-winning park that has conservation at its heart.

GET INDUSTRIAL
East Pool Mine

nationaltrust.org.uk
cornish-mining.org.uk
Illogan Highway, Pool, near Redruth,
TR15 3ED | 01209 315027
Open mid-Mar to Oct Tue–Sat
10.30–5

This former Cornish mine and World Heritage Site has two great beam engines at its centre, preserved in towering engine houses that were originally powered by high-pressure steam boilers invented by local lad Richard Trevithick. The restored winding engine is in action every day, and there are family trails and plenty of displays about the industrial mining past in Cornwall.

GET OUTDOORS
Tehidy Country Park

TR14 0HA
01872 222000

This, the largest area of woodland in West Cornwall, is a great place to go bird watching or to simply wander through the woods. With more than 9 miles of paths and 250 acres of woods and lakes to discover, plus a picnic area and visitor centre/cafe for refreshment, you can roam freely. The woodlands were formerly owned by the Basset family, once one of the four most powerful families in Cornwall. As well as exploring the many paths and tracks that criss-cross the park, an

▼ An engine house near Camborne

extended walk leads out to the open coast of the North Cliffs past dramatic, wind-sculpted woods to make a contrasting circular route.

Tuckingmill Valley Park
tcv.org.uk
Just a mile east of Camborne, this country park has won awards for its conservation work and is a great place for families, with a bespoke skate park, walking trails, playgrounds, picnic areas and art installations. You can't miss the mining history, with mine stacks on the hill and the Red River that runs through it, so named for the colour it gained because of the minerals from the mines. Cornish wildlife is now flourishing here, including interesting and unusual species of dragonfly.

PLAY A ROUND
Tehidy Park Golf Club
tehidyparkgolfclub.co.uk
TR14 0HH | 01209 842208
Open daily all year
This well-maintained parkland course is a good bet for holiday golf and offers a challenge for golfers of all abilities.

▶ Camelford   MAP REF 276 C3

Legend has it that King Arthur died at the hands of Mordred, his nephew, near to Camelford at the small settlement of Slaughterbridge. There, at the Arthurian Centre, you can find 'Arthur's tomb', marked by an inscribed stone dating back 1,500 years. The local Arthurian connection begs the question: does the old market town of Camelford have a strong connection with Camelot? Could it actually *be* Camelot?

Sadly, no evidence has been found to suggest that the name of Camelford relates to Camelot rather than being an ancient Cornish place name, but the town is pretty close to some key Arthurian sights, including Tintagel Castle (see page 261) and the Slaughterbridge Arthurian Centre, so it's a rewarding place to visit if you are an Arthurian fan.

Camelford is 6 miles inland from the north coast and around 10 miles north of Bodmin. To its southeast lies the rocky ridge of Rough Tor and Bodmin Moor. Camelford is well placed for exploring the north coast of Cornwall. Port Isaac (see page 211) is a short drive away, as are many north coast surf beaches. Pleasant walks through the surrounding countryside can be started from the town's two free car parks, while both Rough Tor and Brown Willy can be reached from a car park 2 miles to the southeast (see Bodmin Moor, page 62), though the access road can be a little tricky to find.

Other things to see nearby include the Delabole Slate Quarry (see page 88), which runs guided tours.

VISIT THE MUSEUMS AND GALLERIES

Arthurian Centre

arthur-online.co.uk
Slaughterbridge,
PL32 9TT | 01840 213947
Open Easter–early Nov daily 10–5
Walk through the fields where King Arthur and Mordred supposedly had their final battle; look at the 6th-century stone by 'Arthur's tomb' and find out more about the legends of King Arthur at the Arthurian Centre. Archeological digs are sometimes going on in the 20 acres of property here. One such dig in 2005 uncovered a secret garden dating from the 18th century, now called Lady Falmouth's Secret Garden. If that's not enough for the children, there's brass rubbing, a play castle and more.

North Cornwall Museum and Gallery

bodminmoor.co.uk
The Clease, PL32 9PL
01840 212954 | Open Apr–Sep
Mon–Sat 10–5
This small private museum about life in Cornwall covers the last 100 years or so and concentrates on farming life. It includes a reconstructed moorland cottage with a section on tools, an exhibition on lace bonnets and a collection of Cornish and Devonshire pottery as well as a collection of early vacuum cleaners. The museum is noted for its painting and craft exhibitions throughout the season, and doubles as an information centre.

GO FISHING

Crowdy Reservoir

swlakestrust.org.uk
near Camelford | 01566 771930
Open for fishing 15 Mar–12 Oct
Within Bodmin Moor's SSSI, Crowdy Reservoir offers free trout fishing in its 115 acres for Environment Agency rod licence holders in season – buy online at environment-agency.gov.uk. The moorland lake attracts a lot of birders, and no other activities, beyond walking and fishing, are allowed in the area.

SADDLE UP

Lakefield Equestrian Centre

lakefieldequestriancentre.co.uk
Lower Pendavey Farm, PL32 9TX
01840 213279 | Open daily all year
This equestrian centre on a local farm caters for all abilities, from lessons in the school through to show jumping. Short rides around the farm are great for beginners; off-road hacks for the more experienced are also available. There's also a tea room, the Lakeside Teapot, which serves cream teas and cakes.

PLAY A ROUND

Bowood Park Hotel and Golf Course

bowood-park.co.uk
Lanteglos, PL32 9RF | 01840 213017
Open daily all year
This hotel and golf course in Lanteglos near Camelford are set in 230 acres of ancient deer park once owned by Edward the Black Prince. The rolling parkland course has 27 lakes and ponds and is a haven for

wildlife. Summer golf breaks in the three-star hotel are good value; there's also a fine dining restaurant on site.

▶ **PLACES NEARBY**
The Georgian estate of Pencarrow, south of Camelford, is known for its gardens.

Pencarrow
pencarrow.co.uk
Washaway, PL30 3AG
01208 841369 | House open Apr–Sep Sun–Thu 11–3; gardens

Mar–Oct daily 10–5.30; cafe, shop and plants Apr–early Oct Sun–Thu 11–5
Still a family home, this Georgian house has a superb collection of pictures, furniture and porcelain. The 50 acres of formal and woodland gardens include a Victorian rockery, a lake, more than 600 varieties of rhododendron and an acclaimed conifer collection. There is also a children's play area. There are special events throughout the year.

▶ **Cawsand**
see **Kingsand & Cawsand**, page 113

▶ **Charlestown**   MAP REF 276 C6
Georgian Charlestown, on the south coast of Cornwall just beyond St Austell, is a sight to behold. With square-rigged ships in its traditional harbour, it looks like something from *Treasure Island* or Cornwall's glorious past, when pirates roamed the high seas and the local sailors travelled the world. The harbour, its ships and its surroundings are used regularly in period films – scenes from the BBC's 2015 remake of *Poldark* were filmed there. You can wander down to two shingle and sand beaches and the rest of the harbour, where modern fishing boats bob about. It's a peaceful spot.

The port was created by a local entrepreneur, Charles Rashleigh, in the late 18th century and is named after him. Before that, it was known as West Polmear and was a modest fishing cove. Rashleigh's grandiose ambition extended to the broad, tree-lined avenue, called Charlestown Road, that leads to the port. Rashleigh commissioned John Smeaton, designer of the Eddystone Lighthouse, to design Charlestown's emblematic harbour. The Grade II listed harbour has been up for sale for some time; the public loos were sold in 2015 for £115,000. Overall, Charlestown is a rewarding place to visit, with cream tea cafes, a handful of pretty interiors shops, a pub overlooking the beach and a Shipwreck and Heritage Centre to visit with the children, where you can see items from a number of shipwrecks, including the *Titanic*.

10 top museums

▶ The National Maritime
Museum, Falmouth
page 96

▶ Tate St Ives
page 237

▶ Barbara Hepworth Museum,
St Ives
page 236

▶ Bodmin Jail
page 58

▶ Charlestown Shipwreck and
Heritage Centre
see below

▶ Cotehele
page 76

▶ Smuggler's Museum,
Jamaica Inn
page 66

▶ Royal Cornwall Museum
page 264

▶ Penlee House Museum
page 201

▶ Pendennis Castle
page 95

VISIT THE MUSEUM
Charlestown Shipwreck and Heritage Centre
shipwreckcharlestown.com
Quay Road, PL25 3NJ
01726 69897
Open Apr–Oct 10–5

This family-friendly museum is the largest private collection of shipwreck items on display in Europe and includes unique items from local shipwrecks as well as a large exhibit on the *Titanic*. There's an audio-visual theatre that tells you the history of Charlestown harbour. Children under 10 go free and there's a good selection of pocket-money treats in the museum shop. Outside, you can examine a lifeboat and a 1920s German diving suit.

HIT THE BEACH
Crinnis Beach and Carlyon Bay
As well as the two beaches in Charlestown, a short hop down the coast will take you to Carlyon Bay, a wide, white-sand beach. It's not all as pretty as it sounds, as development plans mean that some of it is marred by fences and steel; head to Crinnis Beach, as the westerly end of it is called, for the easiest access. There are no facilities here and dogs are not allowed, but even so it gets very popular in season.

PLAY A ROUND
Carlyon Bay Hotel Golf Course
carlyonbay.com
Beach Road, Carlyon Bay,
PL25 3RD | 01726 814250
Open daily all year

The Carlyon Bay Hotel course is a championship-length, clifftop parkland course, running east to west and back again – uphill and down. The fairways stay in excellent condition all year, as they have since the course was laid down in 1925. Enjoy the magnificent views from the course across St Austell Bay; particularly from the ninth green, where an approach shot remotely to the right will plummet over the cliff edge.

EAT AND DRINK

Charlies Coffee House
79 Charlestown Road, PL25 3NL
01726 67421
This family-friendly cafe in
Charlestown's former post
office serves enormous
sandwiches, delicious cakes,
and great coffees and teas.
Charlies Boathouse, up the
road, offers proper meals.

Harbourside Inn
harboursideinncharlestown.co.uk
Harbour Front, Charlestown Road,
PL25 3NJ | 01726 68051
This traditional late 19th-
century inn, with a lively
atmosphere, overlooks
Charlestown Harbour. It offers
good pub snacks and the
meals include such treats as
a spicy Seafood Jambalaya of
cod, smoked mackerel,
mussels, prawns and chorizo.
A speciality Bubble & Cheek
serves up pan-fried vegetables
and potatoes topped with
smoked bacon, pork cheek and
fried eggs.

Tall Ships Creamery
The Harbour,
PL25 3AJ | 01726 654444
Rated as one of the finest ice
cream shops in Cornwall,
this delightful place has
some interesting flavours and
a host of intriguing names
inspired by the town. Take your
pick from Chocolate Booty,
Peaches of Eight, Buccaneering
Banoffee, Swashbuckling
Strawberry or the inventive
Bacon, Pancakes and Maple
Syrup variety.

▶ PLACES NEARBY
Near to Charlestown, you'll find
a large sandy beach, and a hotel
and golf course. A short drive
and you'll find yourself in St
Austell (see page 229) and can
visit some lovely villages
nearby, including Mevagissey
(see page 165) and Fowey (see
page 104).

Carlyon Bay Hotel ◉
carlyonbay.com
Sea Road, Carlyon Bay,
PL25 3RD | 01726 812304
Surveying the rugged Cornish
coast from its clifftop perch
above St Austell, the creeper-
curtained Carlyon Bay Hotel is
an imposing presence. Inside,
the Bay View Restaurant is
smartly turned out and has
a menu that includes St Ives'
sourced fish and award-winning
Cornish cheeses.

▶ Coverack
see **The Lizard**, page 133

▶ Crackington Haven MAP REF 276 C2
Between Boscastle and Bude on the north coast, the pretty
cove of Crackington Haven has a small cafe and pub at its heart
and a large, sandy beach with rock pools at low tide.

Crackington Haven has given its name to a geological phenomenon, the Crackington Formation – fractured shale that has been shaped into incredibly twisted and contorted forms. On the sheared-off cliff faces of the area, you can see the great swirls and folds of this sedimentary rock that was metamorphosed by volcanic heat and contorted by the geological storms of millions of years ago. Even the name 'Crackington' derives from the Cornish word for sandstone, 'crak'.

There are some great walks on the dramatic cliffs nearby. The steep coast path leads north to Castle Point where there are the remnants of Iron Age embankments. A mile or so further on is Dizzard Point, where an old oak wood clings to the slopes.

South of Crackington Haven you'll find Strangles Beach, a secluded cove with Northern Door, a natural rock arch where the soft shale has been eroded by the waves. High Cliff, to the south, is the highest cliff in Cornwall at 731 feet.

HIT THE BEACH
Crackington Haven beach
The beach is the thing to do in Crackington Haven, a stretch of rock and shingle beach giving way to deep rock pools and sand when the tide goes out. There's a pay-and-display car park at the top of the beach and there are lifeguards on duty in early June and from July to September. Dogs are only permitted October–Easter. Bring a bucket for rock-pool finds and some money for ice creams from the nearby shop.

▼ Crackington Haven

WALK AROUND CRACKINGTON HAVEN

For clifftop walks, start at St Gennys church. You can see the drama of the coastline and geology from here without a need to plunge steeply down to the centre of the village.

The area above Strangles Beach is National Trust land and similarly dramatic. Park along the coast road south of Crackington to explore it. There is also a lovely walk from the National Trust farm at Trevigue, down through the wooded valley and into Crackington Haven.

Wherever you walk, watch your step. The whole area is affected by landslips and though the coast path is stable, don't stray from it.

EAT AND DRINK

Cabin Cafe
cabincafecrackington.co.uk
EX23 0JG
01840 230238
Whether you're looking for pasties, cream teas or ice creams, this cafe makes all its food on the premises and offers takeaway for the beach or dining in. It's also a farm shop, handy if you're self-catering nearby, and there's a beach shop and surf hire if you plan to spend your day on the beach.

▶ Crantock   MAP REF 275 D2

Just 2 miles south of the most popular beaches in Cornwall, at Newquay, Crantock stands beside the long, narrow estuary of the River Gannel. It's a good place to check out in the height of summer to remember why Cornwall is so special. Founded by Irish hermits in AD 460, Crantock has a strong religious history, with two holy wells, one in the centre and one on the road to the beach, and a church with 13th- and 14th-century features.

These days, the beach is the key pilgrimage site: a surf beach with lifeguards and a beach kiosk in season. It's backed by Rushy Green, an area of sand dunes. Lifeguard advice must be heeded as changes in the course of the River Gannel have affected the topography of the beach and there are strong and potentially dangerous currents in places.

To the west of Crantock is West Pentire, a headland bursting with wild flowers and plants that has been designated an SSSI. There's also a car park. From here you can take the zigzag track south to Porth Joke, also known as Polly Joke, an unspoilt sandy cove. There are some lovely coast path walks around the area.

HIT THE BEACH

The beach at Crantock is manned by lifeguards in the summer. It's a wide sandy beach with caves to explore. When the tide is out, to the left-hand side of the beach in one of the caves you can see a rock carved with a woman's face, a horse and a poem. Great care should be taken, however, with a close eye kept on the movement of the tide.

VISIT HOLYWELL BAY

This large sandy bay is great for families and popular with surfers. At low tide you can see the remains of a 70-year-old shipwreck. There are lifeguards on duty from May to September. Always heed their advice. There are cafes and toilets at the beach and pubs and shops in the adjacent village.

EAT AND DRINK

Cosy Nook Tea Gardens
Langurroc Road, TR8 5RB
01637 830324
Located in Crantock village, this pleasant cafe has a lovely walled courtyard filled with plants and sunlight. They serve breakfasts – try the eggs Benedict – light lunches of sandwiches and jacket potatoes, and cakes and cream teas. Dogs are welcome. An added attraction is the Wheelhouse Gallery with its selection of paintings, prints and photographs.

▶ Delabole   MAP REF 276 C3

Delabole's biggest claim to fame, once you've discounted the fact that it's en route to the tourist haven of Port Isaac, Doc Martin's town, is its slate. Back in medieval times, Delabole slate was being taken from this deep pit in the earth; at 500 feet it's the deepest quarry in England and is still being quarried. The village itself is named after the quarry and is also the birthplace of the Cornwall Air Ambulance. There's not much to see, beyond the quarry and its visitor centre; every July it holds a week of events as part of its annual carnival.

About a mile north of Delabole, along the B3314, you can see Britain's first commercial wind farm. The tall white towers and their whirling vanes generate electricity for 3,000 homes. Just south of Delabole is St Teath, a pretty village with an attractive church.

GET INDUSTRIAL

Delabole Slate Quarry
delaboleslate.co.uk
Pengelly, Delabole, PL33 9AZ
01840 212242 | Tours and presentations May–Aug Mon–Fri 2pm
If you're keen to know more about slate quarrying, this is the place to get a first-hand look at it. With walkabout tours around the quarry plus access to the showroom, the quarry invites visitors to find out more about its operation. Small group tours can be organised on an individual basis; otherwise visit the website for precise tour information.

▶ The Eden Project MAP REF 276 C6

edenproject.com
Bodelva, St Austell, PL24 2SG | 01726 811911 | Open daily 9–6; closed 6 days
in Jan; check website for details

Cornwall's blockbuster attraction near St Austell is a modern
marvel, an eco-tourism site that aims to educate and entertain
and, perhaps most importantly, is somewhere that you can take the
children for a whole day when you're camping and it's raining.
Everything about it is good – even the obligatory gift shop, which is
packed to the rafters with eco-friendly and ethical goodies. For
those of you who want a refresher, here's a little background to
how this Cornish super-garden was created.

How Eden was made

In the mid-1990s, Bodelva Quarry near St Austell was exhausted.
Worked for more than 160 years, its china clay had run out
and it seemed that it would stand ravaged and empty forever
as the quarrymen moved on to a more fruitful site. But not so.
Enter visionary businessman Tim Smit, architect Nicholas
Grimshaw and a whole host of top-level building and engineering
talent. After the success of the Lost Gardens of Heligan, Smit
recognised that people were interested in the environment and that
he could create something extraordinary, which he did by
developing a series of biomes: dome-shaped structures like large
glasshouses, housing plant life in unique hot-house environments.

▼ Biomes, Eden Project

The vision was not just that of a unique rainforest garden under cover in Cornwall, but of something much larger: a social foundation, education programmes, and a focus on biodiversity and climate change. It's so much more than an impressive display of plants and butterflies.

Eden opened in March 2001 and counted its millionth visitor just three months later. It's been a runaway success and continues to develop its programmes and diversity today. One of the greatest things about the attraction is that it never stands still. Perhaps because it has multiple aims and public engagement at its heart, you can guarantee that every time you visit you'll see something new: maybe some of the 100,000 plants that you missed the first time or maybe a whole area that you hadn't discovered before. Eden is huge and warrants at least a full day's attention.

The Rainforest Biome

This, the largest biome, includes the plants and products of West Africa, South East Asia, Amazonia, Malaysia and Oceania. It's a huge space, 164 feet high, with the capacity to accommodate trees from tropical rainforests, and contains, as they put it, the largest rainforest in captivity. There are teak, mahogany and rubber trees interspersed with bamboo, a banana plantation and a host of intriguing tropical plants, all fed by the moisture from a cascading waterfall. The temperature is kept between 18°C and 35°C. Glasses wearers will realise that immediately as their specs fog up. What's missing are the larger animals that populate a rainforest in the wild – lizards, insects and butterflies are fun to spot, but you don't need to worry about chancing on anything with big teeth and a threatening growl.

The Mediterranean Biome

The temperature is cooler and the environment is a notch less exotic in the Mediterranean Biome, which replicates the habitats of Southern Africa, the Mediterranean and California, with hundreds of vividly coloured flowers intermingled with olive groves and vines. In these environments, plants thrive on drought and poor, thin soils. Summers are hot, while winters are wet and cool. Tales are told through this area, as through the Rainforest Biome, to help you put the plants and environment in context, showing you which plants are used for food and medicine, construction and entertainment. The idea is that you start to see the way that plant life supports our lives, and to develop an understanding and appreciation of them, and their importance to the world and the way we live.

▶ The Mediterranean Biome

Beyond the biomes

The walk down into the quarry takes you past sculptures and Eden's stunning outdoor gardens, which cover 30 acres and include the best West Country plants alongside those of the Himalayas, Chile and Australasia. It's fun to run and play here; there are outdoor stages set up in summer with events; theatre companies and local choirs put on performances, and the Eden Sessions, a short season of gigs and comedy shows, take place in the summer months and demand advance booking. The music and comedy are as cutting edge and remarkable as the venue. Previous acts have included Tim Minchin, The Vaccines and Mumford and Sons.

Seasonal events take place through the year, including an ice-skating rink and winter attractions, Easter egg hunts and an autumn harvest festival. There's always a reason to go and new things to see and do.

If you're visiting as a family, there is a cafe at Eden, serving local and seasonal dishes of course, or you can bring a picnic. While the ticket prices are on the high side, there is an option to convert your ticket to an annual pass for no extra money – ask when you buy – and those arriving by public transport, on foot or by bike get a discount. Buying online in advance is cheaper too.

Beyond the visitor attraction, Eden is a social enterprise and charity and runs, among many things, the Big Lunch, an initiative seeking to get people talking to their neighbours and strengthening their communities by having lunch together in their street. It's another part of Eden's mission – not just to get people talking and thinking about biodiversity and the future of the planet, but also to help us realise that we're all connected and all have a role to play in the future.

▼ Biomes, Eden Project

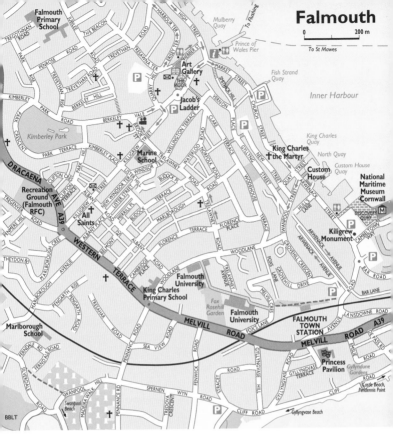

▶ Falmouth   MAP REF 275 E5

Cornwall's fifth-largest town has a distinctive atmosphere
entirely its own. Falmouth will never lose its seagoing
ambience. The Fal Estuary is one of the world's biggest natural
harbours, and this archetypal Cornish port has a timeless
maritime history. Because of the university's strong art and
design elements and the town's long association with the
previous Falmouth School of Art, there is a colourful, vibrant
pulse to life and a creative, youthful element that mixes well
with Falmouth's strong Cornish identity. While eyebrows would
certainly be raised in the more traditional villages of the
county, nobody bats an eyelid in Falmouth.

It's a town with diverse appeal as a result: if you like your
boats, the harbour, which is the third largest natural harbour
in the world, is the place to visit. It's been in use for hundreds
of years and, during the 17th century, gold and silver came in
and out of it on routes from the Americas, Indies and Spain.
Smuggling and privateering are key components of the town's
history, while today shipbuilding and yachting continue to
contribute to the town's economy. This isn't a town that exists

solely for tourists. Key sailing events take place in Falmouth each year, including Henri Lloyd Falmouth Week and the Pendennis Cup. For those in love with the sea and its daily rise and fall, Philip Marsden's excellent book *The Levelling Sea* recounts the tale of Falmouth from the very beginning. Take a stroll around Pendennis Head and you'll see yachts, fishing boats, and huge tankers and liners. The excellent National Maritime Museum is worth a visit for an in-depth look at boats; it's also great for children.

Pendennis Castle, built by Henry VIII at the same time as St Mawes Castle opposite (see page 244) to protect the Fal Estuary, can be visited and is looked after by English Heritage. You can explore inside to see barracks, cells and tunnels, and then enjoy a cream tea with a view of the sea on the terrace. There's a lovely walk around the headland to Gyllyngvase Beach, with a stretch taking you through rock pools at low tide.

Falmouth's beaches are great – as long as you're not a surfer. Being on the south coast and fairly sheltered, the town's beaches rarely get enough swell for surfing. Gyllyngvase Beach has one of the county's best beach cafes, and is sandy and safe for swimming.

Falmouth is one of the best shopping towns in Cornwall, with a broad mix of outlets serving both locals and visitors.

▼ Falmouth Bay

Down its narrow streets you'll find vintage stores, independent shops, design shops and some high street shops nestled amid the boat chandlers and watersports shops, pubs and pasty vendors. Strolling the back streets and side streets is a pleasant way to spend an afternoon.

Falmouth's layout can make it hard to navigate as the town follows the riverside and has plenty of winding, linking streets. Offshoots from them take you to the town quays, where you can watch buskers, eat snacks from food wagons and stalls, and watch the world go by. From the broad, open central area known as The Moor, the 111-step Jacob's Ladder leads up the side of a steep hill and is named after its creator, a builder and property owner called Jacob Hamblen who needed access to his business. You may also spot a number of characterful 'opes' in the town, narrow passageways between the town's buildings which were used to give easy access to the sea.

As the streets are narrow and parking in town is expensive and limited, the best way to access Falmouth, especially in summer, is by using the Park-and-Float service, parking at Ponsharden on the edge of Falmouth. A 10-minute ferry ride takes you into the centre of the town. It runs Mon–Fri only.

TAKE IN SOME HISTORY
Pendennis Castle
english-heritage.org.uk
Pendennis Headland,
TR11 4LP | 0370 333 1181
Open Apr–Sep daily 10–6, Oct 10–5,
Nov–Mar Sat–Sun 10–4, Feb half
term. Parts of castle may be closed
for private events
Together with St Mawes Castle, Pendennis forms the end of a chain of castles built by Henry VIII along the south coast as protection against attack from France. Journey through 450 years of history and discover the castle's wartime secrets, from Tudor guns to a World War I guardhouse and a World War II Experience. The cafe serves the usual pasties, snacks and treats, with ingredients sourced where possible from local suppliers.

VISIT THE MUSEUMS AND GALLERIES
Falmouth Art Gallery
falmouthartgallery.com
Municipal Buildings,
The Moor, TR11 2RT
01326 313863 | Open all year
Mon–Sat 10–5
This free town art gallery is dynamic and innovative – like the town's art-school residents. With engagement programmes and workshops for children and the community, the idea is to get people involved, not just hang some dusty old oil paintings on the walls. The permanent collection includes works by Man Ray, John William Waterhouse and Laura Knight, and is considered one of the most important in Cornwall. There's a good gift shop too.

▶ National Maritime Museum Cornwall MAP REF 275 E5

nmmc.co.uk

Discovery Quay, TR11 3QY | 01326 313388

Open all year daily 10–5

This award-winning museum offers something for everyone, from ever-changing exhibitions, hands-on family activities, talks, lectures, displays and events to crabbing and the opportunity to sail and see marine and bird life. Admire the views from the 95-foot tower or descend the depths in one of only three natural underwater viewing galleries in the world. The purchase of a full-price individual ticket gives you free entry to the museum for a year.

National Maritime Museum Cornwall
See highlight panel opposite

MEET THE LOCAL SEALIFE
AK Wildlife Cruises
akwildlifecruises.co.uk
01326 753389 | Open all year
Join an AK sea adventures cruise where you might see seals, porpoises, pods of dolphins and even minke whales and leatherback turtles. It's an exciting prospect. As well as sea safaris, they run wildlife and birding trips around the Fal Estuary. Consult the website for precise trip information – some sailings are four hours long, some are seven, and all depend on the weather and tides.

HIT THE BEACH
There are four beaches to choose from in Falmouth.

Gyllyngvase Beach
Ten minutes' walk from the town centre, Gyllyngvase Beach is a wide arc of golden sand with lifeguard cover from May to September and some great facilities, including a stand-up paddleboard hut, an ice cream hut and an award-winning beach cafe. It's a sheltered and safe beach for children. Parking is on the road beside a landscaped garden or in the large car park nearby. Near the beach are the early 20th century Gyllyngdune Gardens and Princess Pavilion, reached through a lovely old grotto.

Castle Beach
Castle Beach is the most northerly beach, by Pendennis Point and overlooked, of course, by the castle. It's rocky and is a good beach at low tide for rock pooling. Divers and snorkellers love to visit too. There's a small beach cafe and parking is at Pendennis Point. At high tide the beach is submerged, so check your tide times before you lay out your towels.

Maenporth Beach
Only 2 miles from the town centre, Maenporth beach is a sheltered sandy cove with lovely views and good rock pooling. It's family friendly – although there are no lifeguards – with a cafe and toilets. There is also a kayak hire company, Arvor Sea Kayaking, based here offering lessons, guided trips and simple day hire. The car park is behind the beach.

Swanpool Beach
Further out of town, Swanpool Beach backs on to Swanpool Lake Nature Reserve, an SSSI, and has a decent watersports centre offering dinghy sailing, kayaking and windsurfing. There's also a beach cafe. The lake itself has plenty of resident swans, hence the name, as well as an extremely rare plant-like creature called the trembling sea mat.

TAKE A BOAT TRIP
Prince of Wales Pier
falriver.co.uk
TR11 3DF | 01326 741194
Easter–Sep only
Enterprise boats run along the Fal River between Truro, Falmouth and St Mawes, and other river and sea cruises are available from Falmouth's Prince of Wales Pier and from other boarding points around the estuary. Evening cruises on the Fal are another option, along with sea-angling trips.

GO DIVING
Cornish Diving School
cornwalldivers.co.uk
Marine Crescent, TR11 4BN
01326 311265 | Open Tue–Sat 9–5.30
This top local dive centre offers small group and one-to-one tuition plus dive trips, diver training, boat charter and spear fishing. There is a lot of shallow wreck diving in the sea around Falmouth and trips also go as far as the Manacles, Hayle, Penzance and Rock. Contact them for lessons, hire or trips.

GO FISHING
Argal Reservoir, Penryn
swlakestrust.org.uk
Falmouth | 01209 860301
There are beautiful walks around this reservoir near Falmouth and plenty of picnic and barbecue areas. It's also a well-stocked course fishery with permits available from a self-service unit in the barn beside the lake.

PLAY A ROUND
Falmouth Golf Club
falmouthgolfclub.com
Swanpool Road, TR11 5BQ
01326 314296 | Open daily all year
Falmouth's par 72 golf course dates from 1894 and has great sea views over the Cornish cliffs. There's a modern clubhouse and the website provides a set of top tips for each hole, which makes for essential reading. Golf lessons are also available at the club.

EAT AND DRINK
de Wynn's
55 Church Street,
TR11 3DS | 01326 319259
For a traditional Cornish cream tea, de Wynn's is the place to go. This traditional tea shop located in a historic listed building with bow windows offers eight different types of tea plus sandwiches, scones and cakes. It's justifiably popular, with specialities including Granny Nunn's bread pudding. You may need to book in advance in the summer to avoid disappointment.

Fal Falafel
falfalafel.com
Adjacent to The Moor (Oct–May) and Prince of Wales Pier (Jun–Sep)
Delicious takeaway falafel in pitta bread, drenched in tasty sauces, from the town's premier food cart. It's a Cornish take on the Israeli delicacy and is better for you than fish and chips or a pasty. Herb teas and Turkish coffees are served.

Falmouth Hotel ◉

falmouthhotel.com
Castle Beach, TR11 4NZ
01326 312671

Nothing becomes a seaside town like a great white hotel, lording it over the waters from the headland. The eponymous Falmouth went up in the 1860s as the Great Western Railway reached Cornwall. The elegant dining room offers sweeping views over the bay and a menu that works its way round the seasonal calendar in both British and international modes. Dishes include West Country beef and pork, while seafood features such treats as pan-seared sea bream.

The Greenbank Hotel ◉◉

greenbank-hotel.co.uk
Harbourside, TR11 2SR
01326 312440

The house that grew up into the Greenbank Hotel has occupied this prime spot on the Fal estuary since 1640, and is famous for its outstanding views: full-length windows fold back to reveal a panorama that sweeps right across the harbour. The restaurant offers everything from fresh crab sandwiches and vodka-cured salmon starters to chicken gnocchi and chorizo, while the evening menu includes such treats as a seafood grill of monkfish, mackerel, king prawn and scallop. Meat eaters and vegetarians can enjoy equally delicious offerings.

Gylly Beach Cafe

gyllybeach.com
Cliff Road, TR11 4PA
01326 312884

This superb modern beach cafe has won awards for its locally sourced food and has to be one of the best beach cafes in Cornwall. Young, friendly staff, beach views and a veranda sheltered from the wind get a thumbs up, as does the menu including nachos, Cornish mackerel sandwiches and burgers. It's family friendly, but at the same time a fairly upmarket spot in the evening, with music and a slightly more sophisticated menu.

Rick Stein's Fish

rickstein.com
Discovery Quay,
TR11 3XA | 01841 532700

It's no surprise to find a Rick Stein outpost right at the entrance to Falmouth's superb Maritime Museum – alongside a raft of cafes, other eateries, and shops. But Stein's still exudes fish and chip class with grilled sea bream fillets, lobster, oysters and moules marinières on the menu as well as classic fish and chips. There are takeaways and special deals for families and senior citizens. Interiors are Stein classic, with oak tables and chairs as chunky as the chips, white-tiled walls, pebbled counter tops and slate floors merging traditional chippy style with classic deco-Stein.

The Royal Duchy Hotel @@
royalduchy.co.uk
Cliff Road, TR11 4NX
01326 313042

With palm trees framing splendid views across the bay towards Pendennis Castle from its alfresco terrace, the Royal Duchy certainly has that Riviera touch. Plush furnishings, crisp white linen-clad tables, chandeliers, a tinkling grand piano and gracious, unobtrusive service together create a sense of occasion. Contemporary cooking is the order of the day, based on simple combinations that reflect the seasons.

St Michael's Hotel and Spa @@
stmichaelshotel.co.uk
Gyllyngvase Beach, TR11 4NB
01326 312707

5 beach cafes

▶ Porthminster
Beach Cafe
page 240

▶ Godrevy Cafe,
near Gwithian
page 109

▶ Gylly Beach Cafe,
Gyllyngvase Beach,
Falmouth
page 99

▶ The Beach Hut,
Watergate Bay
page 183

▶ Kynance Beach Cafe,
Kynance Cove
page 143

St Michael's Hotel's award-winning Flying Fish Restaurant bags a fabulous vista and has a genuine local flavour to its contemporary menus, with lots of Cornish seafood on offer such as whole dressed crab, oysters, and baked turbot. Delicious meat and vegetarian dishes are also available.

▶ PLACES NEARBY

Falmouth is close to the Lizard Peninsula (see page 129) and some of Cornwall's most beautiful sub-tropical gardens, including Glendurgan and Trebah. Watersports enthusiasts have two nearby lakes to choose from as well.

Glendurgan
nationaltrust.org.uk
Mawnan Smith, Falmouth,
TR11 5JZ | 01326 252020
Open mid-Feb to early Nov Tue–Sat
10.30–5.30 (also Mon in Aug)

Glendurgan's sub-tropical gardens spread across three valleys and include giant rhubarb (*Gunnera manicata*) plants, a huge laurel maze dating from 1833 and the Giant's Stride, a pole that the estate-owning family's children have been swinging round for a hundred years. Developed in 1820 by Alfred Fox, the brother of Charles Fox who created nearby Trebah, the National Trust estate includes trees and shrubs from all over the world, including the Japanese loquat and tree ferns from New Zealand. There are garden tours on the first Thursday of the month, and it is only the gardens that are open to the public – the house is not.

Lizard lakes

Cornwall has few natural lakes of any size but there are reservoirs that make a pleasant change from the sea. The Argal and College lake reservoirs are only about 2 miles from Falmouth along the A394. The lakes are tree fringed and very peaceful, with much birdlife and pleasant paths skirting the shoreline. Coarse fishing is available all year and the fly-fishing season is Mar–Oct. Stithians Lake is within easy reach of Falmouth and Helston along the A394.

Miss Peapod's

misspeapod.co.uk
Kitchen Cafe, Jubilee Wharf, Penryn, TR10 8FG
01326 374424
An eco-eatery within Jubilee Wharf on Penryn's revitalised waterfront. The river views from the alfresco decking and the food are the stars, with excellent breakfasts, coffee and cakes and delicious lunches prepared from local produce, including organic meats from Rosuick Farm.

Penjerrick Garden

penjerrickgarden.co.uk
Budock, Falmouth, TR11 5ED
01872 870105 | Open Mar–Sep Sun, Wed, Fri 1.30–4.30
Far less commercial than some of the bigger Cornish gardens, you won't find a tea shop at Penjerrick but what you will find is a gardener's paradise with 15 acres of forest, jungle and huge tree ferns. The garden dates back 200 years to when it was created by Robert Were Fox, another green-fingered brother of the Fox family behind the gardens at Trebah and Glendurgan. Look out for waterfalls, dense valleys, ponds and a tranquil garden, best enjoyed in April and May.

Stithians Lake

swlakestrust.org.uk
near Redruth, TR16 6NW
01209 860301
Open mid-Apr to May Wed, Fri–Sun 10–4.30, Jun–Sep daily 10–4.30
The Outdoor + Active centre at Stithians Lake has options for watersports – sailing, windsurfing, kayaking and canoeing – as well as archery and climbing activities. Lessons and equipment hire are on offer and there are less strenuous activities such as a lakeside walk, a trim trail and a children's park. Birders will find bird hides and there's a cafe, a campsite and a fly-fishing area too. You'll find a car park on the east side of the lake near the dam and another at its north end, near the watersports centre. The nearby village of Stithians is a peaceful place, with its handsome church tower a major focus.

Trebah

See highlight panel overleaf

▶ **Trebah** MAP REF 275 D5

trebahgarden.co.uk

Mawnan Smith, near Falmouth, TR11 5JZ | 01326 252200

Open daily all year 10–4.30

One of Cornwall's most exceptional gardens, Trebah is known for its hydrangea valley, excellent children's facilities including an adventure playground, and miles of trails that lead to a private beach on the Helford River. It also has an award-winning cafe and, seasonally, a beach cafe and ice cream hut. The gardens themselves cover 25 acres in a steep ravine running from a fine 18th-century house down to the river.

Charles Fox, Trebah's original creator, came to Cornwall in 1826 and planted a screen of maritime pines to protect the ravine from fierce coastal winds. Behind this shelter he was able to plant seeds collected from all over the world, and the garden has developed to become one of the finest in the county. More recent additions include a water garden in the upper part of Trebah, created in the 1980s, where small pools are edged with primulas and water irises, and bamboos and ferns provide a colourful background.

In the lower part of the ravine, the Brazilian 'rhubarb' is probably the largest you'll ever see. Follow a dense network of paths to find the koi pond and waterfall, or amble along the camellia walk to a viewpoint overlooking the beach. As much of the garden dates to Victorian times, you can expect to see a lot of rhododendrons. Many are spring and early-summer flowering – and the Trebah Gem, planted in 1900, now reaches 42 feet in height. The garden has been created to have interest all year, with plants flowering through to Christmas.

Trebah is also famous for its tender trees and shrubs. A large Chilean laurel with bright green, aromatic leaves can be seen in the Chilean Combe, and the dogwood 'Bentham's Cornel', with its yellow bracts, does well. Magnolias, including *Magnolia x soulangiana*, and the pink tulip tree are also well represented, as are many varieties of eucalyptus, pieris and tree fern. Two extremely tall Chusan palm trees dominate the view down the ravine, and you can also see a pocket handkerchief tree and an exotic, though actually quite hardy, Chinese fir.

▶ **Fowey** MAP REF 276 C6

Fowey is one of the must-see maritime towns of south Cornwall. Pronounced 'Foy' – don't embarrass yourself by trying to call it 'Fow-ey' – this pretty town on the west side of the Fowey estuary attracts the boating fraternity with their yachts, foodies who love to eat the local seafood and Fowey River mussels in particular, and families and holidaymakers browsing interiors shops, supping tea in cafe gardens and playing on the beach at Readymoney Cove.

The town was a major port from medieval times thanks to its natural deep-water anchorage – hence so many well preserved medieval houses – and supplied more boats to the Siege of Calais in 1346 than London. The town's sailors were well known for their arrogance and contempt for the law. Unsurprisingly, as time went on, this town became a haven for smugglers and you can still imagine them rolling barrels of rum up the narrow, cobbled streets in the moonlight. China clay exporting is one of the legal ways in which people have earned money around here for hundreds of years, and unlike the smuggling it's still going on today.

One of the first things you'll notice is that, while Fowey is a waterfront town, it centres around a river rather than the sea, which gives it quite a different feel from other towns nearby. Pubs cluster down by the water with views of white-sailed yachts and the wide river beyond it from their terraces. The shopping is interesting too, with delis, craft shops, independent shops and plenty of nautical touches to bring home from the streets of the old town where medieval and Georgian buildings stand beside each other.

St Catherine's Castle, built by Henry VIII to protect the estuary from attack, stands at the edge of the harbour beside Readymoney Cove at the far end of the town and is its only bona fide sight. People don't visit Fowey to tick off attractions on their to-do list, though; it's a place to enjoy for its food and atmosphere. One great way to see it is from a river cruise departing from the Town Quay steps and taking you out to sea. Cruising the other way, up the estuary in a canoe, gives you access to an array of river wildlife, and maybe a kingfisher if you're lucky.

Daphne du Maurier was the town's most famous resident. She lived and wrote nearby, inspired in part by this beautiful area.

▶ Washing Rocks headland viewed from St Catherine's Castle

Access to Fowey

A word of warning: don't try to drive through Fowey. It's one of those towns where you might get stuck trying to turn a corner and will almost certainly not find anywhere to park. You'll certainly regret it. The main car park is at the entrance to the town. An alternative and relaxing way to visit is to take the ferry from Polruan. Park up and walk down to the slip; you can also take a bike. Ferries go about every 10–15 minutes and it saves a long drive round. In the summer, there's also a passenger ferry to Mevagissey and, if you have to bring the car, the Bodinnick to Fowey ferry is the one to look for. All are subject to weather conditions and have a reduced service in the winter months. Consult the website (ctomsandson.co.uk) to check timetables.

TAKE IN SOME HISTORY

St Catherine's Castle

english-heritage.org.uk

0370 333 1181

Open any reasonable time

All the way through Fowey (park at Readymoney Cove), this small 16th-century fort is one of a pair built by Henry VIII to defend Fowey Harbour. Entry is free and there are no facilities; climb to the top storey for views of the town and harbour.

VISIT THE MUSEUM

Fowey Museum

foweyharbourheritage.org.uk

Town Hall, Trafalgar Square, PL23 1AY | 01726 833513

Open Easter–Sep Mon–Fri 10.30–4.30

Housed in one of Fowey's oldest buildings, this small local museum shows something of the history and heritage of the little harbour town. Some displays are changed on a yearly basis; regular items on show include a cape worn by Garibaldi and some archaeological finds from the medieval period.

MEET THE SEALIFE

Fowey Aquarium

foweyaquarium.co.uk

Town Quay, Fowey, PL23 1AT

07815 840467 | Open Apr Fri–Mon, Wed 10–4, May daily 10–4, Jun–Jul 10–5, Aug 10–late, Sep 10–4.30, Oct Fri–Tue 10.30–4

This small local aquarium holds a collection of fish and sealife from the waters around Fowey. It looks a little worn from the outside, but inside you can get up close and personal with eels, flatfish and starfish and quiz the owner on the lot. It's very different from the big-budget aquarium in Newquay.

HIT THE BEACH

A walk through the town and up the hill takes you to a small, sandy cove, Readymoney Cove, just to the south. St Catherine's Castle overlooks the beach, which can be accessed by the Southwest Coast Path. There are no facilities; it's a safe place to swim but can be very busy in summer.

TAKE A TOUR AROUND THE TOWN

Guided Town Walk

Town Quay, PL23 1AT

01726 833616

Tours early Apr–Sep Tue 11–2

A stroll round Fowey reveals a fascinating mix of historic Cornish buildings, hidden corners and nautical quirks, as befits a town that was once one of the busiest ports in England. The Church of St Fimbarrus, also known as St Nicholas, sets a dominant tone with its richly decorated tower. Close to the church is Place, the seat of the Treffry family, a complex of high battlemented walls that reflect yet again Fowey's fractious history. Joining a town walk uncovers a host of other fascinating details. The walks starts at Town Quay; you can just turn up or book ahead by phone or in person at the tourist information centre.

TAKE A BOAT TRIP

Fowey Quay

foweycruise.co.uk

07776 141241 | Open Apr–Oct

Short harbour and longer river cruises take place from the town quay, running as far afield as Polperro and Charlestown, or closer to Lostwithiel, Lerryn and around the town's historic harbour. The crew aim to provide an interesting sightseeing tour and can answer questions.

EAT AND DRINK

Crumpets Tea Shop

1 Fore Street, Polruan-by-Fowey, PL23 1PQ | 01726 870806

Just a 5-minute boat trip across the estuary from Fowey, Crumpets is a traditional tea shop decked out in yellow and blue, with sea-related prints on the walls. Just the ticket for light lunches, home-baked cakes or a delicious cream tea served with homemade jam.

The Fowey Hotel ◉◉

thefoweyhotel.co.uk

The Esplanade, PL23 1HX

01726 832551

If you're ambling the town's narrow streets of crooked houses and shops and fancy a pitstop to dine on excellent local produce keep an eye out for this handsome Victorian hotel amid landscaped gardens. Its restaurant – Spinnakers – basks in the sweeping views across the water, while the kitchen delivers an upbeat repertoire of simple classic combinations and is renowned for its traditional puddings and for its fine selection of Cornish cheeses.

Lifebuoy Cafe

thelifebuoycafe.co.uk

8 Lostwithiel Street, PL23 1BD | 07715 075869

This fun, friendly and bright tea shop specialises in homemade cakes and serves its tea in deliberately mismatched patterned china cups. Bread comes fresh from the baker down the road, sausages from the local butcher and crabs are caught locally. Great for children too, the menu includes breakfast, sandwiches and afternoon tea.

The Ship Inn

Trafalgar Square, PL23 1AZ

01726 832230

One of Fowey's oldest buildings, the Ship was built in 1570 by John Rashleigh, who sailed to the Americas with Walter Raleigh. It serves great pub grub with plenty of local fish on the menu, including River Fowey mussels as a starter or main, and grilled sardines in garlic. There's St Austell ales to sup, real fires to sit by, and a tradition of genial hospitality adds the final touches.

▶ PLACES NEARBY

The area around Fowey is fantastic for walkers – particularly Gribbin Head, with its striped tower. You'll also find the pretty village of Golant worth a visit.

Golant

This pretty village is 1.5 miles north of Fowey and is reached from the B3269. The small church of St Sampson in the middle of the village remembers one of Cornwall's great Celtic saints. The village holds a carnival in mid-August each year and has a friendly riverfront pub, the Fisherman's Arms.

Gribbin Head

nationaltrust.org.uk
Gribbin Head | 01726 870146

This headland, commonly known as the Gribbin, lies to the west of Fowey and has an unusual 84-foot tower, the daymark, painted in barbershop red and white. It was put there to distinguish the Gribbin from St Anthony's Head at the entrance of Falmouth Bay – the two headlands look so similar from the sea that sailors regularly mistook them, to catastrophic effect: St Austell Bay is in no way as deep as Fowey's legendary harbour.

There's a circular walk from Fowey or Coombe around the headland. It's a rewarding path, with wildflowers and wild garlic in the woods in the spring and stunted elm trees running down to the shore, covered in lichen and blown into contorted shapes by the wind. Don't forget a camera – along with scenic views and wildlife, there are also Bronze Age barrows and some long-disused cliff gardens en route.

Inland from the Gribbin, Daphne du Maurier made Menabilly her home and found inspiration for a number of her novels there. In the eastern shelter of the Gribbin is Polridmouth Cove, with adjoining beaches and an ornamental lake.

The Gribbin can be reached on foot from a car park at Menabilly Barton, a mile inland. To the west, the small village of Polkerris faces into St Austell Bay; you can park halfway down the approach and walk to the beach.

▼ Fowey

▶ Gunwalloe
see **The Lizard**, page 133

▶ Gweek
see **The Lizard**, page 134

▶ Gwithian   MAP REF 275 C4

This coastal village 4 miles east of St Ives on the north coast is known for its sand dunes and has a church and a friendly pub. Gwithian Towans – 'towans' means sand dunes – are the site of a Bronze Age farm, though nothing can be seen there today apart from glorious dunes and native wildlife. In summer, you might see butterflies and skylarks amid myriad minibeasts. The local area was heavily mined for tin until the late 20th century, staining the river running through Gwithian red with iron ore. There are views across the nature reserve and beach to Godrevy Lighthouse and it's a great place to watch the sunset. Surfers love the beach, as do children, who can scramble across rocks and swim in natural pools. There is a local campaign ongoing to save the beaches here from sand extraction.

HIT THE BEACH

Gwithian's 3.5-mile-long sandy beach is popular with families and surfers and is backed with holiday chalets, a small tea room, a surf shop and the famous dunes. There is a lifeguard service here from Easter to September. Some of the rocks nearby and the beach bear witness to the iron-mining industry of the 20th century. At low tide there are caves and rock pools to explore; one of Cornwall's oldest churches is buried in the sand of the beach. You can park in the car park and walk through the dunes to the beach. Be aware that dogs are banned from the beach in the summer.

EAT AND DRINK

Godrevy Cafe
godrevycafe.co.uk
Godrevy Towans, Gwithian,
TR27 5ED | 01736 757999
Godrevy Cafe stands isolated within the dunes at Godrevy Beach near Gwithian. Beautifully designed, it has spacious terraces that make

5 local celebrities

▶ Dawn French

▶ Sir Ben Ainslie

▶ Rick Stein

▶ Tim Smit

▶ Richard and Judy
(OK, make that 6)

the most of the view, and an unusual attic dining space. It's open all day, for breakfast, coffee and cakes, a light lunch, or a sunset dinner from the evening menu.

The Red River Inn
1 Prosper Hill, TR27 5BW
01736 753223
The name of this 200-year-old pub recalls the colour of the village river when tin was mined locally. Close by runs the South West Coastal Path, and the beach is popular with surfers as well. Among its attractions are up to five ever-changing Cornish real ales, an Easter weekend beer and cider festival, and delicious food that ranges from crab sandwiches and haloumi salad to fresh sea bass, steaks and Middle Eastern, Mexican and Indonesian dishes. An in-house shop sells artisan bread, pastries and farm produce from April to October. Dogs are welcome.

▶ Hayle MAP REF 274 C4

The town of Hayle lies to the east of St Ives at the head of a tidal estuary that penetrates deep inland. The sheltered mudflats of the estuary attract migratory birds in spring and autumn and make the Hayle area a paradise for birdwatchers.

Hayle was once a powerhouse of Victorian industry in conjunction with Cornwall's tin and copper mining until a general industrial decline left the town with a degree of dereliction. Much has been done to preserve the integrity of Hayle's history, and the disused hinterland of the town's harbour area is slowly being developed and modernised. Hayle itself is a bustling, attractive place with a broad range of shops, traditional pubs, restaurants and art and craft galleries, together with a number of historic buildings.

There are various pleasant strolls around such features as the town's Copperhouse Pool and Millpond Gardens. Hayle's great glory, though, is the long sweep of golden sand that extends northwards from the mouth of the estuary and that offers everything for the holidaymaker, from sunbathing to surfing and windsurfing. The beach is best reached via the village of Phillack, which has a lovely old church.

MEET THE WILDLIFE
Paradise Park
paradisepark.org.uk
Trelissick Road,
TR27 4HB | 01736 751020
Open daily from 10am. Last entry summer 5pm, winter 3pm

Paradise Park is a mini-zoo with plenty of wildlife to meet, from red pandas to guinea pigs. The main event is the birds – they have more than 650 species to see, including parrots, flamingos, toucans

▲ Hayle Beach

and Cornish choughs. There's also a small petting zoo with donkeys and goats, and an indoor play barn for a rainy day.

HIT THE BEACH

Hayle Towans, along with Mexico and Upton Towans, provides plenty of sand for everyone. Backed by sand dunes, the beaches here are generally safe, good for surfing and have lifeguards in residence from Easter to September. There are mudflats by the River Hayle estuary, great for birding, and the sand dunes are full of wildlife, from wildflowers to rare butterflies and dragonflies. Hayle Canoe Club offers sea kayak and canoe lessons on the beach and, if you look out to sea, you'll spot the 19th-century octagonal form of Godrevy Lighthouse, which inspired Virginia Woolf's famous novel *To the Lighthouse*.

GO BIRDING

Hayle Estuary

Hayle's sheltered estuary is home to a vast number of birds and plays host to migratory species in the winter. Some very rare sightings are possible during autumn migrations when vagrant species from America may be pushed off their north-to-south migratory path and driven across the Atlantic to Cornwall.

The stretch between Copperhouse and Lelant Saltings is the best to begin with, accessed off the A30 on the Penzance and St Ives road by the Old Quay House Inn. There is a public hide at Ryan's Field: the Eric Grace Memorial Hide. Look out in particular for wintering wildfowl and migratory birds, golden and grey plover, widgeon, shelduck and curlew, and hovering kestrels and peregrine falcons. Water voles have burrows in the estuary bank and there is a select colony of European pond turtles here too. Grey seals sometimes make an appearance, as do basking sharks way offshore. There's plenty to look out for: bring binoculars if you can. Spring, autumn and winter are the best seasons.

EXPLORE BY BIKE
Hayle Cycles
haylecycles.com
36 Penpol Terrace,
TR27 4BQ | 01736 753825
Open Mon–Tue, Thu–Fri 9–5.30,
Sat 10–5

In the centre of Hayle, close to the Towans beaches, Hayle Cycles offers bike hire and servicing. There are some lovely routes along the coast and inland here, along quiet country lanes. You could tackle a route along the coast to St Ives (6 miles) and back, or over to Marazion and St Michael's Mount (5 miles).

GO SURFING
Shore Surf School
shoresurf.com
St Ives Bay Holiday Park,
TR27 5BH | 01736 755556

Various packages are on offer for those wanting to find their feet on the waves, from a 2.5-hour taster to a three- or five-day course. The surf school has a centre of excellence at the St Ives Bay Holiday Park and a surf school at Godrevy National Trust car park. You can hire wetsuits and boards too.

EAT AND DRINK
Mr B's Ice Cream
mrbsicecream.co.uk
24 Penpol Terrace, TR27 4EQ
01736 758580

With a quite frankly ridiculous 260 flavours to choose from, Mr B's has been roundly declared one of Cornwall's top gourmet ice cream destinations. Strange to think, then, that former cockney Mr B himself spent 10 years making just vanilla ice cream before developing this extraordinarily long list. Try caramel and fudge, lemon meringue pie or Turkish delight.

Rosewarne Manor ⊚⊚
rosewarnemanor.co.uk
20 Gwinear Road,
TR27 5JQ | 01209 610414

After a period when this grand 1920s' building had fallen into neglect, the current owners have resurrected Rosewarne as a venue with a keen eye to the weddings and functions market, and with good food to boot. The modern British repertoire is driven by seasonality and local sourcing, and the confident cooking delivers well-defined flavours. There is a lively bar menu and tasting menus, and the à la carte offers a good choice of locally sourced meat, poultry and fish dishes.

▶ PLACES NEARBY
Close to Hayle is the attractive Godolphin House, while the small village of Gwinear has an interesting church with historical details.

Godolphin House

nationaltrust.org.uk
Helston, TR13 9RE | 01736 763194
Estate open all year; garden open
mid-Jan to mid-Oct daily 10–5,
mid-Oct to mid-Jan 10–4; house
selected weekends only. Check
website for details

This historic house with a medieval garden was one of Cornwall's most fashionable houses back in the 17th century and is a still a knockout today. The garden is one of the most important historic gardens in Europe and has barely changed since the 16th century. Its Tudor raised walkways and walls are of particular note; some parts of the side garden date from 1300. Godolphin Hill, on the southwesterly side of the estate, gives good views to St Ives Bay in the north and St Michael's Mount in the south.

St Winnear's Church

Gwinear, Churchtown, TR27 5JZ

This church's battlemented granite tower dates from 1441. Inside you can see much of historical interest including a carved rood screen, a Norman granite-based font and some interesting bench ends. Close by is part of a Celtic cross with a figure of Christ on it that may date back to the 9th century.

▶ Helford

see **The Lizard**, page 135

▶ Helston

see **The Lizard**, page 138

▶ Isles of Scilly

see page 246

▶ Kingsand & Cawsand   MAP REF 277 F6

You don't have to drive miles into the depths of Cornwall to find a true Cornish experience – here, just 3 miles from Plymouth, the twin villages of Kingsand and Cawsand have narrow streets, pretty houses, gig boat races and cosy pubs. They are not the best known of Cornwall's villages, being tucked away on the Rame Peninsula, and are all the better for it, with several pubs and cafes and only one or two shops. Hidden from Plymouth by the high ground of Mount Edgecumbe, you'd never know the big city was so close.

   Start in Cawsand, and do use the car park. The streets here are narrow, and watching a tourist in a large vehicle attempt to manoeuvre around them is considered a sport by the locals.

Cawsand has a charming little square above its small, sandy beach, overlooked by a pub, and from here you can walk along Garrett Street to Kingsand, and past a grand clock tower built to commemorate the coronation of George V. Explore the narrow alleyways and flights of steps that sidle to and fro above the rocky shoreline.

Running south from Cawsand is a level walk that leads along part of a Victorian drive, built by the Earl of Edgcumbe. Wealthy landowners of the 18th and 19th centuries often built such driveways through their properties in order to show them off to their full advantage to arriving guests. The way leads through shady woods to Penlee Point, where there is a grotto built against the slope of the headland. From here you can enjoy views of the curve of Rame Head as it heads to the west. The villages have a strong smuggling and fishing past; sadly all the known smugglers' tunnels have been sealed up.

Kingsand has a wider and rockier beach, popular with children and dogs, as well as an ice cream cafe open in season, a beautiful art gallery and a pleasant pub. You can walk along the beach to Mount Edgcumbe, beside fishermen's boats.

Once upon a time, Kingsand and Cawsand were divided by the Devon–Cornwall border – and there's a sign to that effect on Garrett Street. For many generations those born in Kingsand were recorded as Devon-born, while those born in Cawsand were considered Cornish; today the merged villages are both considered Cornish.

▼ Cawsand

TAKE IN SOME HISTORY
Mount Edgcumbe Country Park and House
mountedgcumbe.gov.uk
Cremyll, Torpoint, PL10 1HZ
01752 822236 | Park open all year;
house and Earl's Garden open
Apr–Sep Sun–Thu 11–4.30
The original Tudor house at Mount Edgcumbe was destroyed by a bomb during World War II, a victim of the massive raids on Plymouth. It was rebuilt during the 1960s to replicate the original and has been handsomely restored. The landscaped park has many lovely features, including follies, mock temples and Gothic ruins, and exquisite formal gardens. The park's woodland has a network of paths and fallow deer roam among the trees. Nearby is the little river port of Cremyll, from where there is a passenger ferry to Plymouth.

VISIT THE GALLERY
Westcroft Art Gallery
westcroft-gallery.co.uk
Market Street, Kingsand,
PL10 1NE | 01752 822151
This fine, small art gallery attached to an exquisite B&B is worth looking out for its contemporary expressions of Cornwall by talented local artists, including watercolours, oils and pottery. It's a cut above the typical souvenir shop offering; the friendly owners can also arrange art tutorials and painting sessions around the coast with local artists.

HIT THE BEACH
Both Kingsand and Cawsand have safe beaches for families. Cawsand's sandy beach is overlooked by the Cawsand Bay Hotel and is the home of the local boat club. Kingsand's beach is longer and is sandy and shingly; it's better for rock pooling when the tide goes out. Both are dog friendly and there are several slopes and steps leading down to them.

EAT AND DRINK
Edgcumbe Arms
edgcumbearms.co.uk
Cremyll, PL10 1HX | 01752 822294
Close to the foot ferry from Plymouth, this inn next to Mount Edgcumbe Country Park has fabulous views from its bow window seats and waterside terrace. Real ales from St Austell and quality home-cooked food are served in characterful rooms, with American oak panelling and flagstone floors.

The Old Boatstore
cafetheoldboatstore.co.uk
The Cleave, Kingsand, PL10 1NF
01752 829011
A short step away from Kingsand beach, this cheerful, unfussy cafe with its views across Plymouth Sound serves good Cornish fare. Many of the ingredients are locally sourced. Breakfasts are generous and the rest of the day sees a choice including light lunches, pasties, cream teas and ice cream. The Old Boatstore is licensed and has free internet access.

▶ PLACES NEARBY

Along the headland from Kingsand and Cawsand, Whitsand Bay is overlooked by holiday chalets but remains a beautiful, wild, unspoilt beach, while the granite-faced 18th-century Antony House is 5 miles inland. The wonderful Port Eliot country house can be found at St Germans.

Antony House

nationaltrust.org.uk
Torpoint, PL11 2AQ
01752 812191 | Open Mon–Fri 12–5, some seasonal variation; check the website for full opening hours
Antony House, home of the Carew family for generations and now cared for by the National Trust, stands in more than 100 acres of woodland garden on the grassy banks of the Lynher River near Torpoint. The original Tudor house was pulled down in the early part of the 18th century and replaced by the finest Georgian house in Cornwall, perfectly proportioned with fine granite stonework facings of Pentewan stone and elegant colonnaded wings of red brick.

Port Eliot

porteliot.co.uk
St Germans, PL12 5ND
01503 230211 | Open 11 Mar–6 Jun, 10 Jun–15 Jul Sat–Thu 2–6
With vast lawns, woodland gardens, a maze and a rip-roaring summer festival, Port Eliot is a particularly special country house. As the historic seat of the Earl and Countess of St Germans, it's a grand and impressive place, with Rembrandts above the fireplaces and a magnificent collection of exquisite furniture as well as some very odd murals. The family still live there and on a tour you may meet their dogs. The landscaped gardens were laid out by Humphrey Repton and the house was remodelled by Sir John Soane in the 18th century. Its more recent claim to fame is as the setting for the Port Eliot Festival at the end of July, a bohemian mix of writers, speakers, wild swimming and creativity, where the likes of Dominic West, Tracy Chevalier and Ali Smith have spoken. At other times of the year it's a great dog-walking and picnicking spot, regularly holds unique fairs and events, and has a buzzing, arty tea room called the Long Gallery.

St Germans

The village of St Germans lies just north of the A374 approach to Rame Head and Kingsand and Cawsand. The village is remarkable for its preserved old buildings, not least the splendid Norman church of St Germanus, once a monastic priory and the medieval cathedral of Cornwall. The interior of the church is suitably sombre and atmospheric, but it is the external features that make the building so appealing, especially its superb west doorway, considered to be one of the finest Norman doorways in England. Other notable buildings include the Old Galleries, almshouses dating from 1583. Nearby is the Port Eliot estate (see above).

St German's traditional May Fair, complete with election of a 'mock mayor', appeared in records as long ago as the 13th century and was re-established in 2012.

Whitsand Bay

Whitsand Bay is a gorgeous curve of white sand – hence the name – and is popular with surfers. There's nothing here but sand and waves – no shops, no ice cream stalls, no surf hire – but that makes it all the more appealing. Access is limited to the beach – the cliffs are very steep so you have to tackle many steps – and there are some rip currents. A little further along the coast, Freathy Beach is a good place to swim, with a car park at the top and steep steps to the bottom of the cove.

Whitsand Bay Hotel and Golf Club

whitsandbayhotel.co.uk
Whitsand Bay, PL11 3BU
01503 230276 | Open daily all year

This testing seaside course is laid out on cliffs overlooking Whitsand Bay. It's pretty easy walking after first hole; the par 3 third hole is acknowledged as one of the most attractive in Cornwall. The hotel also has a spa, restaurant and bistro and is dog friendly.

▶ Kynance Cove
see The Lizard, page 143

▶ Lamorna MAP REF 274 B5

Lamorna, a small former fishing village turned artist colony 4 miles south of Penzance, is in the most sheltered of the narrow valleys that lead gently down to the south-facing shores of Mount's Bay. It's an arty community that drew the Newlyn School in the 19th and 20th centuries; these days it celebrates this heritage with an arts festival each autumn bringing together professional artists working in the area. Down at the cove, Colin Caffell's bronze sculpture 'Naiad' lends a little magic.

The road that leads down to Lamorna Valley is narrow and can become congested during Bank Holidays. It is quite a journey through shady woodland to reach an unexpected bay fringed by granite cliffs, but there is charm around every corner of Lamorna. On the way down to the cove is the Wink, a classic Cornish pub so named for the blind eye that locals turned to smugglers. The village has a granite quay and in

Victorian times the granite from the hillside quarries was highly prized. Some went to build lighthouses while more went to construct the Thames Embankment.

Note that Lamorna's car park is pay-and-display, even if you patronise the cafe; plenty of tourists have missed the notice and found themselves landed with big penalty fines.

HIT THE BEACH

Lamorna Cove does not have a lifeguard and is only a small curve of sand – read: busy in summer – but there is a car park right nearby, a cafe and, in season, motorboat and kayak hire. The small pebble cove is backed with boulders andis popular with swimmers and scuba divers. There is a car park above the cove. At the time of writing, the historic quay suffers from storm damage and should be avoided. There are outstanding cliff walks to either side of the cove.

EAT AND DRINK

Lamorna Wink Inn

lamornawink.co

Lamorna Cove | 01736 731566

Famous for its smugglers 'blind eye' name, The Wink, and its eponymous pub sign, this classic inn is located at the heart of the leafy Lamorna valley. It offers cheerful pub food covering all needs, and pleasant outside seating.

▶ PLACES NEARBY

You might like to visit Penlee House in Penzance (see page 201) if you're interested in local artists; walkers can walk the coastal path through the cove to the home of a well-loved writer. Just west of the valley there's a famous stone circle and a Bronze Age grave.

The Minack Chronicles

A lovely half-mile walk along the coastal footpath west from Lamorna Cove leads to the world of the late Derek Tangye. His *Minack Chronicles* detailed his life with his wife in their idyllic clifftop cottage. The deeply sentimental books with a cast of character cats and donkeys appealed to animal lovers. An 18-acre section of clifftop land is now a peaceful

◀ Lamorna Cove

nature reserve that is reached from the coast path through a gate.

The Merry Maidens
A mile west of Lamorna Valley in a field alongside the B3315 is a stone circle dating from the early Bronze Age – the famous Rosemodress, or Boleigh, Circle of 19 upright stones. It is popularly known as the Merry Maidens, from the legend of young girls turned to stone for dancing on a Sunday. In nearby fields are two tall standing stones, the Pipers, who suffered the same fate. They are all more likely to have been ceremonial sites of the local Bronze Age peoples. A short distance west of the Merry Maidens, and close to the road, is the Tregiffian entrance grave. Also from the Bronze Age, it comprises a kerbed cairn with a chamber roofed with slabs.

▶ Land's End MAP REF 274 A5

And so to Cornwall's most southwesterly point, the start of many a walk to John O'Groats and the location of 'that' signpost. Land's End draws tourists like bees to honey so go with that expectation. The 200-foot granite cliffs are majestic when nobody else is around and the best way to get a clear shot is to walk there, along the cliff path. The South West Coast Path runs from Sennen (see page 256), 1 mile to the north, and Porthgwarra (see page 216), 3 miles to the southeast.

Land's End is a wet weather attraction on a grand scale, with its mix of themed entertainment and commercial outlets, although the spectacular Atlantic scenery is the real deal. You'll find shops, exhibitions, cinemas and enough to keep you busy for a few hours. There is a good choice of cafes and restaurants and the Land's End Hotel is in a splendid position overlooking the Longships Lighthouse. There may be queues on the approach on public holidays and during peak holiday periods. The car park operates a flat fee for an all-day stay.

ENTERTAIN THE FAMILY
Land's End
See highlight panel overleaf

EAT AND DRINK
Apple Tree Cafe
theappletreecafe.co.uk
Trevescan, TR19 7AQ
01736 872753
This cheerful cafe is an escape from the Land's End crowds. It's in the little hamlet of Trevescan a short distance inland. Every diet is catered for including vegetarian, vegan and gluten-free, as well as meat-eaters. Key ingredients are locally sourced and the cafe offers breakfasts and delicious light lunches, as well as sandwiches, cream teas and a selection of tasty cakes all day.

▶ Land's End   MAP REF 274 A5

landsend-landmark.co.uk

TR19 7AA | 0871 720 0044 | Open all year daily 10–4, later in peak season

This complex includes the West Country Shopping Village, for all your souvenir needs, along with Arthur's Quest, a 4D family cinema experience '20,000 Leagues Under The Sea', an Air Sea Rescue motion theatre attraction, the End-to-End exhibition and Greeb Farm, a family farm park with a small petting zoo. All the attractions are pay as you go, and there are restaurants and cafes in the complex too.

▲ St Mary Magdalene Church

▶ Launceston MAP REF 277 E3

Launceston, on the A30 just over a mile west of the Tamar, is the largest town in the Cornwall/Devon borderlands and is dominated by its castle. Known as the gateway to Cornwall, it's a historic town with Georgian buildings, restaurants and museums that has suffered a little during the recession, with many shops closing down.

The key attractions are the town's 11th-century castle, which hosts the local Castle Rock music festival in July each year and is a good site for a picnic; the Lawrence House Museum, which showcases the town's history from the Bronze Age to World War II; and the dark granite and beautifully carved St Mary Magdalene Church.

To enjoy Launceston, park as soon as you can (there are car parks near the market and at Thomas Road and Tower Street) – Launceston's handsome South Gate forces traffic to pass through in single file while pedestrians pass comfortably three abreast beneath an adjacent arch.

At the centre of the town, the Square has some very fine Georgian buildings, including the White Hart Hotel, which has the added flourish of a Norman arch over its doorway. Launceston Castle is reached by going down Western Road from the Square. The Launceston Steam Railway is based at the bottom end of St Thomas Road and runs for 2 miles through the valley of the Kensey River.

TAKE IN SOME HISTORY

Launceston Castle

english-heritage.org.uk

Castle Lodge, PL15 7DR

01566 772365 | Open daily Apr–Sep 10–6, Oct 10–5

Built by Henry III's brother Richard in 1227, Launceston Castle is a shell keep, a circular wall with buildings inside it. Richard later added to the castle with another tower and a fighting platform, making this castle the dominant building for miles around. It's still fairly impressive today. Climb the battlements for impressive views, picnic on the grass around it or read up on its 1,000-year history in exhibitions inside. The castle has an impressive history not just as the fortress of the Earl of Cornwall but also as a prison in the 17th century, where George Fox, founder of the Quakers, was imprisoned for eight months in the North Gatehouse. Today the castle is the site of a summer music festival, Castle Rock, and the start of the Two Castles walking trail, linking it to Okehampton Castle (see opposite).

▼ Launceston Castle

VISIT THE MUSEUM
Lawrence House Museum
lawrencehousemuseum.org.uk
9 Castle Street,
PL15 8BA | 01566 773277
This Georgian townhouse
museum run by the National
Trust preserves the town's
history, focusing particularly
on its links with Australia.
There is also a display of
costumes dating from the
18th century to the 1960s, and
a toy room with historical
exhibits and toys that visiting
children may play with.

TAKE A TRAIN RIDE
**Launceston Steam
Railway**
launcestonsr.co.uk
St Thomas Road,
PL15 8DA | 01566 775665
Open Jul–Sep Sun–Fri 11–4.30;
check the website for other times
The Launceston Steam Railway
links the historic town of
Launceston with the hamlet of
New Mills in a 5-mile round trip
through the Kensey Valley.
Tickets are valid for unlimited
travel on the day of issue and
you can break your journey.
Launceston station houses
railway workshops, and a
transport museum, gift shop
and book shop.

GO WALKING
There are two long-distance
walking trails starting in
Launceston. The Tamar
Discovery Trail is a 30-mile
waymarked route from the
town to Plymouth, through
villages and woodlands.

The Two Castles Trail is a
24-mile route from Launceston
Castle to Okehampton Castle,
waymarked through northwest
Dartmoor. A visit to the
Tourist Information Centre
gives you access to leaflets
on the routes and Ordnance
Survey maps.

PLAY A ROUND
Launceston Golf Club
launcestongolfclub.co.uk
St Stephens, PL15 8HF
01566 773442 | Open daily
all year
The highly rated Launceston
Golf Club course has
magnificent views over the
historic town and moors and is
noted for superb greens and
lush fairways.

Trethorne Golf Club
trethornegolfclub.com
Kennards House,
PL15 8QE | 01566 86903
Open daily all year
A challenging and scenic
par 71 parkland layout, with
numerous water hazards
and tree-lined fairways with
greens built to USGA
specification, making them
playable all year.

▶ PLACES NEARBY
The villages around Launceston
have several beautiful
historic churches; families
and nature-lovers will enjoy
seeing otters in the wild at the
Tamar Otter and Wildlife
Centre, or enjoy some family
fun at the Hidden Valley
Discovery Park.

Hidden Valley Discovery Park

hiddenvalleydiscoverypark.co.uk
Tredidon, Launceston, PL15 8SJ
01566 86463 | Open late Apr–Sep
daily 10–5; check the website for
other times

This family mini theme park is
great fun, with a miniature
railway, Forbidden Mansion
crazy house with its mind-
bending perspectives, and the
Sherlock Holmes, Moriarty and
Indiana trails, three graded
adventure-themed detective
treasure hunt trails. Six new
themed gardens are being
created for 2016.

St Paternus' Church

Hellescott Road, North
Petherwin, PL15 8LR

This is a very large and
splendid church for a small
rural community. The village
was originally in Devon, though
it lies west of the Tamar and
has always been part of the
archdeaconry of Cornwall.
The architectural features of
the church include round
columns with scalloped
capitals dating from around
1200, and a clerestory dating
from the 14th century.

St Petrock and St Keri's Church

Egloskerry, PL15 8RU

This church has Norman
details – a simple font and an
unusual pillar piscina
– alongside a section of early
17th-century stained glass and
the alabaster tomb probably of
Edward Hastings, Lord of
Penheale, dating from 1510. It
is interesting because he is
shown in civilian clothes,
not the military attire that
was the norm.

St Winwallo's Church

Tremaine, PL15 8SA

Set on its own among trees,
Tremaine's little church is
peaceful and rugged. It has
Norman details that include
a tympanum and window,
both on the north side of the
church, and, inside, a Norman
font with a round bowl and
cable moulding. The wagon
roof and its bosses date from
the early 16th century. The
unusual steps cut into the
thickness of the north wall
led to the rood loft.

Tamar Otter and Wildlife Centre

tamarotters.co.uk
North Petherwin, near Launceston,
PL15 8GW | 01566 785646
Open Apr–Oct daily 10.30–6

Visitors to this wildlife centre
will see British and Asian
short-clawed otters in large
natural enclosures. They will
also be able to see fallow and
muntjac deer, and wallabies
roaming freely around the
grounds. There are also birds of
prey – including a tame kestrel
and buzzard – a pair of Scottish
wild cats, peacocks and a large
selection of waterfowl on two
lakes. A special treat for kids –
young and old – are the giant
rabbits and even meerkats.
Otters are fed at noon and 3pm,
accompanied by a talk.

► Lelant MAP REF 274 B4

The small, pretty village of Lelant is a mile west of Hayle and a little further than that up the coast from St Ives. With a sandy beach and sandy coves on the estuary, it's a pleasant spot – but beware fast-running tides on the estuary coves, which are not completely safe for swimming. Surrounded by countryside, dunes, and former tin mines and granite quarries, the village used to be a fishing port until the estuary silted up. Now it's best known as the start of St Michael's Way, a 13-mile pilgrimage route from Lelant church to St Michael's Mount, via the coast path to St Ives and an overland path. There's an information board on the route outside the church.

The village is a stop on the jaw-dropping St Ives Bay train line – if you get a chance to ditch the car and try it out, do. And Lelant Saltings is the place to leave your car for a park-and-ride service into St Ives in the summer months.

GO BACK IN TIME

Trencrom Hill

The rocky hill of Trencrom, the site of an Iron Age encampment and the highest hill in West Cornwall, stands above the Hayle Estuary and can be reached from Lelant or from the B3311 St Ives to Penzance road. Trencrom is in the care of the National Trust and there is a small car park on its southern side. The path to the summit is short and steep in places, but the views are outstanding. Just west of Trencrom is the little village of Nancledra, from where the green and peaceful Towednack Valley runs north to the sea through a gap in the coastal hills.

HIT THE BEACH

Carbis Bay beach is one of the finest in Cornwall, and can be reached by train from St Ives (see page 238).

WALK THE LINE

A trip on the branch line railway to St Ives is one of Britain's loveliest scenic outings. The line hugs the coast and the edge of the Hayle estuary for 4 miles. It is a wonderfully stress-free way of getting to St Ives and there is a park-and-ride facility at Lelant Salting halt.

A great outing for walkers is to catch the train from either St Erth station alongside the A30 Penzance road or from St Ives to one of three halts along the way – Lelant Saltings, Lelant Halt or Carbis Bay – and then to walk to St Ives, catching the train back. Visit the Woodland Trust's charming little nature reserve of Anne's Wood, opposite Lelant Halt, with its 2 acres of young woodland, and revel in the exhilarating views across the golden expanse of Porth Kidney Sands and the ever-widening view of St Ives.

SADDLE UP
Old Mill Stables Riding School
oldmillstables.com
Lelant Downs, Hayle, TR27 6LN
01736 753045
This riding school in nearby Hayle offers half-day rides and pony trekking on Lelant Downs. It's a scenic spot to ride along country lanes and farmland with views of the beach and sea.

PLAY A ROUND
West Cornwall Golf Club
westcornwallgolfclub.co.uk
TR26 3DZ | 01736 753401
Open daily all year
Established in 1889, this is a seaside links with sand hills and lovely turf adjacent to the Hayle Estuary and St Ives Bay. It's a real test of the player's skill, especially Calamity Corner starting at the fifth. The beautiful Lelant church lies at the eastern perimeter.

EAT AND DRINK
Scarlett Wines & Deli
scarlet-wines.co.uk
The Old Forge, TR27 6JG
01736 753696
They really know their wine and coffee at this attractive cafe-deli, located near to Lelant Saltings rail halt. Breakfast, lunch and coffee and cake are all on offer.

▶ Liskeard MAP REF 277 D5

With Bodmin Moor close by to the north and the lovely resort of Looe to the south, Liskeard makes for an ideal holiday base. The town has much to offer, with its many historic buildings reflecting its prosperity during the heyday of Cornish copper mining. This former market town has grand Victorian buildings and a number of high street shops. In recent times, in response to the Mary Portas High Street Review, it has made a lot of effort to develop its independent streak and embrace unusual ideas, holding regular festivals and events. Under the shadow of retail parks, the town team has been keen to develop the town's personality to attract shoppers.

As a coinage town in medieval times, Liskeard was always the seat of prosperity in this part of east Cornwall. When copper mining took off in the 19th century, the town grew ever wealthier. It's still important for its rail routes today, connecting with London and as the northern terminus of the branch railway connecting with Looe. There's a lovely train ride through the trees and along the estuary from Liskeard to Looe that's well worth the train fare, with sights of ancient woods, wading birds and sailing boats that you can't otherwise see unless you're on foot.

If Victorian market town architecture is your thing, the town has some key buildings to look out for: Webb's Hotel, which overlooks the Parade; the Guildhall and its Italianate tower on

Market Street; the Public Hall and Forester's Hall, both dating fron the 1890s; and the church of St Martin, which is the second largest church in Cornwall. There's also an ancient well, the Pipe Well, gated off on Well Lane, off Market Street.

Around Liskeard, reaching up to near Bodmin Moor (see page 62) and down to the area around Looe (see page 151), there are lots of attractions, walking routes and countryside sights.

VISIT THE MUSEUM
Liskeard Museum
visitliskeard.co.uk
Foresters Hall, Pike Street,
PL14 3JE | 01579 346087
Open Mon–Fri 11–4, Sat 11–1.30
This small town museum tells the tale of Liskeard, including its early days as a cattle-farming district, through to the 19th-century copper boom. Much of the museum is about mining, of course. The museum is housed in the former East Cornwall Savings Bank, and is free.

TAKE A TRAIN RIDE
Looe Valley Line
greatscenicrailways.co.uk
Liskeard Station, PL14 4DX
01752 584777 | Trains run daily;
Sun in peak season only
A trip on the Looe Valley Line from Liskeard to Looe is a stress-free way of going to the seaside and back, recapturing some of the excitement of those days when such a journey was a rare treat. The trains descend through the lovely East Looe Valley from Liskeard Station, with station halts on the way giving access along narrow lanes to pleasant villages such as St Keyne.

EXPLORE BY BIKE
Liskeard Cycles
liskeardcycles.co.uk
Pigmeadow Lane, PL14 6AF
01579 347696
The narrow tree-lined lanes around Liskeard are the perfect place for a cycle ride. This bike shop offers cycles for all the family. From Liskeard, there are routes to Tavistock, Bodmin Moor and even Land's End.

▶ PLACES NEARBY
The area surrounding Liskeard has a lot of activities, small museums, independent attractions and places to visit. Carnglaze Caverns in particular are a good spot on a rainy day, and host occasional concerts and events. See also Bodmin Moor (page 62).

Carnglaze Caverns
carnglaze.com
St Neot, Liskeard, PL14 6HQ
01579 320251 | Open Jan–Jul
daily 10–5, Aug 10–8,
Sep–Dec 10–5
Not just another Cornish mining heritage sight, the Carnglaze slate caverns and gardens are also a concert venue and have an intriguing history. Visitors can take a self-guided tour of the three largest caves, one of

which has a subterranean lake. Check the website for details on concerts and events in the Rum Store, the first of Carnglaze's caverns, which got the name because the Royal Navy used it to store its supply of rum during World War II. The acoustics are outstanding. There are also gentle walks to be had in the gardens around the caves, including an easy 25-minute loop around the woods with a view of St Neot's village. The woodland walk has a lot of bluebells in late spring and is open later on Tuesday evenings in season to view them.

King Doniert's Stone

english-heritage.org.uk
St Cleer | Free access

For serious fans of ancient Cornish history and heritage, these two carved pieces of Celtic cross commemorate Dumgarth, the British King of Dumnonia, who drowned around AD 875. They are the only surviving examples of a 9th-century stone cross in Cornwall. The stones are in a walled enclosure by the road, a mile northwest of St Cleer. Park in the adjacent layby.

Moyclare Cornish Garden

moyclare.co.uk
Lodge Hill, Liskeard PL14 4EH
01579 343114 | Open Apr–Aug
Sun–Tue 2–5

This lovely garden, near Liskeard railway station, reflects a labour of love by Moira and Louis Reid from Ireland, who transformed an open field in 1927 with a planting programme using plants and seeds from their County Clare home. The garden now displays variegated and evergreen plants and shrubs from all over the world. There is wheelchair access, but dogs are not allowed.

Trethevy Quoit

Tremar Coombe,
between St Cleer and Darite

Trevethy Quoit, or 'the Giant's House' as it's called locally, is an impressive 9-foot tall megalithic tomb of five standing stones crowned by a large, flat, sloping slab. Originally covered by a mound, this type of grave dates from 3700–3500 BC. For those seeking Cornwall's ancient history, this site is one of the highlights.

TM International School of Horsemanship

tminternational.co.uk
Henwood, Upton Cross,
PL14 5BP | 01579 362895

This riding centre offers lessons, hacking on the moors and activities for children, as well as residential riding holidays for those aged 12 and up. Book in advance, at least up to a day before you wish to ride.

Adrenalin Quarry

adrenalinquarry.co.uk
PL14 3PJ | 01579 308204 | Open
Mar–Sep Mon–Fri 10–5, Sat–Sun
10–6, Nov–Feb Sat–Sun 10–5

This is a 1,608-foot long and 164-foot high zipwire above a flooded quarry.

▶ The Lizard MAP REF 274 D5

Along with rocks that make geography teachers' hearts beat double time, dolphins cruising in the sea, seabirds calling and wildflowers bending in sea breezes, the Lizard is visited by most people because its point is the most southerly piece of land on the UK mainland. But there's much more to the peninsula than that. None of this area is overdeveloped – although the number of pasty shops and ice cream parlours around Lizard Village can feel a little much – and if you can avoid the coach parties heading to the point, it feels a world away from touristy Cornwall.

Surrounded by the sea on three sides, with fishing villages seemingly untouched by time at the foot of dramatically steep roads, and with some of Cornwall's very best beaches to boot, it is a dazzling place to visit. Helston is held as the 'gateway' to the Lizard – meaning that it's the largest town hereabouts and you have to drive through it to reach the countryside and southernmost point beyond it. Back in the seafaring days, the rocky coast around here was considered highly treacherous and many sailors lost their lives on the Manacles and other protruding rocks nearby. The large lighthouse overlooking the point acknowledges this today, and churches remember the lost sailors in stained-glass windows.

Regardless of whether or not you're keen to check off the furthest points of land on the UK mainland, this peninsula

▼ Coverack

is worth a visit for Kynance Cove alone. This sensational beach has a long clifftop route down to it and a welcoming cafe on the cliffs when you make it, and features on many postcards and images of Cornwall. Other coves and beaches around the Lizard are family friendly, sandy and worth a visit for sure.

The Southwest Coast Path winds all the way around the peninsula and it's hard not to walk at least a mile of it while you're there, looking out to sea and perhaps spotting dolphins or basking sharks along with rare wildflowers and seabirds. The geology of the area is quite incredible: the rocks found here are not found anywhere else in the UK and are the result of the earth's crust being pushed up many miles higher than it would normally sit. Just ask a geography teacher.

The Lizard Downs areas, including Goonhilly Downs and Predennack Nature Reserve, are rich in ancient artefacts dating from a time when early people found reasonable grazing on the poorly drained soil. The soil over serpentine rocks also supports a remarkable variety of rare plants. The Lizard's mild climate encourages these plants, but the main reason for the area's unique botanical nature is that the Lizard was joined to the European land mass thousands of years ago, when these plants spread and flourished on what are now the peninsula's coastal fringes. Look out for *Erica vagans*, a type of heather with dark green leaves and spikes of small pink or lilac flowers. It's only found in substantial quantities on the Lizard. Closer to the cliff tops, blue spring squill, pink thrift and creamy sea campion contribute to a mosaic of wild flowers in spring and summer.

▼ Beach from Halzephron cliffs, Gunwalloe

▲ Cadgwith

▶ Cadgwith MAP REF 275 D6

It feels a little as if time has stood still at Cadgwith, where a whitewashed pub stands beside thatched and slate-roofed cottages, waiting for the fishermen to come home with their catch. Aside from the odd blackboard advertising cream teas, it's as if the community here doesn't know that the rest of Cornwall has hi-tech aquariums, WiFi and a roaring surf-fashion industry. And in fact, fishing boats do still go out here to bring in the catch, with inkwell-shaped pots trapping lobster and crab, and nets for cod, pollock, monkfish and mackerel. Pilchards were the catch of the day here for decades, until the fishery declined in the early 20th century, and now the cellars where pilchards were once salted and pressed for oil have been converted for modern use.

The best way to visit is on foot. Park in the car park on the hill before you reach the village – the main street is very narrow and there's no parking. Cadgwith has a small, shingly beach called Cadgwith Cove, used mainly by fishing boats, with another beach, Little Cove, beyond it. There are some lovely cliff path walks from the village. A short walk south takes you to the spectacular Devil's Frying Pan, a huge gulf in the vegetated cliffs where a sea cave collapsed centuries ago leaving an arch of rock connecting both sides. On the cliff to the north of the cove, there is a small building that was built over 100 years ago and used as a coastguard watch house.

The Lizard area is especially noted for the variety and value of its plant life. Pink thrift, the powder-blue squill, cliff bluebells and kidney vetch grow in profusion here, but insignificant-looking plants may well be very rare and vulnerable. Visitors are asked not to pick even the most prolific wild flowers and to take care while walking.

HIT THE BEACH
Kennack Sands
Kennack Sands is everything that Cadgwith Cove isn't: a vast, wide, sandy beach with space to build sandcastles, fly kites, surf and grab a coffee or ice cream from one of the two beach cafes. The remains of boats that have run aground can be seen here at low tide. The beach is split in two, with a small hill, Carn Kennack, in the middle; the easterly beach is designated as a wildlife reserve.

▼ Devil's Frying Pan

GO FISHING
From Easter to mid-September the Cadgwith Cove Inn (see below) runs daily fishing trips with breakfast from Cadgwith's beach. The hour-long trips depart at 8am and travel along the coast to finish up with a full English breakfast at the pub. From Easter to mid-October, longer fishing trips leave from Porthleven Harbour for some serious sea angling. Book via the Cadgwith Cove Inn and reserve in advance.

EAT AND DRINK
Cadgwith Cove Inn
cadgwithcoveinn.com
TR12 7JX | 01326 290513
Relics in this 300-year-old pub's atmospheric, simply furnished bars attest to a rich seafaring history; the cove itself is just across the old pilchard cellar from its sunny front patio. Meals include fish and chips, crab salad, and vegetarian trio. Tuesdays are folk-music nights, and the Cadgwith Singers pitch up every Friday.

▶ PLACES NEARBY
A couple of miles north of Cadgwith, beyond Ruan Minor, you'll find a wide, sandy, family-friendly beach that is popular with surfers.

▶ Coverack MAP REF 275 D6

Towards the southeast tip of the Lizard Peninsula, Coverack is another of the area's characterful fishing villages, defined by steeply sloping roads down to the sea and encompassed by a dramatically undulating part of the Southwest Coast Path. Pilchard fishing was Coverack's main industry from the medieval period until the early 20th century and it still feels like a busy fishing town today. Despite modern developments around the area, the village retains its authentic atmosphere.

The sand and pebble beach is fun to visit; offshore you can see the Manacles, a group of dangerous rocks that have sunk many a ship. Today it's a popular dive site. And if you should wonder why a Cornish fishing village has a Paris Hotel, it is named after a ship that was stranded off the coast of Coverack in 1899, rather than the glamorous French city.

GO WINDSURFING

Coverack Windsurfing Centre
coverack.co.uk
Cliff Cottage, Sunny Corner,
TR12 6SY | 01326 280939
Open Apr–Oct
This local RYA-recognised windsurfing centre makes use of Coverack's protected sandy bay and offers windsurfing lessons at all levels plus surf kayak hire. Residential courses are on offer for a weekend or longer, and all courses are small with groups having a maximum size of 12.

▶ Gunwalloe MAP REF 274 C5

Gunwalloe is a small fishing cove that lies to the south of Helston and 1.5 miles south of The Loe (see page 140). It has a church, pub and sandy beach, with lifeguards on duty in season and a beach cafe. Following the road to the sea brings you to Church Cove, where an intriguing little 15th-century church nestles close to the edge of eroded cliffs. North of the church is the noisily named Jangye-ryn, or Dollar, Cove and inland are extensive sand dunes.

If the beaches could talk, they'd tell lively tales of seafaring, smuggling and shipwrecks: the price of not giving the Lizard a wide enough berth was grief on Gunwalloe's shoreline. Dollar Cove saw the wreck of a Spanish treasure ship in the 1780s – if you have a metal detector, bring it here as much of the treasure was lost and is said to be in the bay. Halzephron and Gunwalloe fishing coves are just north of Church Cove and can be reached along the coast path. The waves are still heavy and threatening today, especially in the winter; to combat coastal erosion large blocks of granite have been tipped on to the beach. Parking is in the National Trust car park on the approach to Church Cove.

EAT AND DRINK
The Halzephron Inn
halzephron-inn.co.uk
TR12 7QB | 01326 240406
Perched high above Gunwalloe fishing cove, this 500-year-old stone inn has stunning views. across Mount's Bay. On sunny days grab a front bench and enjoy a pint of St Austell Tribute while looking out to St Michael's Mount. Everything is homemade, based around the best Cornish produce available, including plenty of fresh seafood.

▶ Gweek MAP REF 275 D5

The little village of Gweek, 3 miles east of Helston, is known to visitors mainly for its seal rescue centre, the saviour of many a rainy day in the area. The name, by the way, doesn't come from the noise an injured seal makes but is derived from the Cornish word 'gwig' meaning 'forest village'.

At the head of navigation of the Helford River, Gweek was an important port in Tudor times and has been active since Roman times. You will certainly see yachts and fishing boats pulled up on the bank at low tide today – try to imagine the scene in the late 19th century when Gweek had at least 200 boats working in the pilchard-fishing industry, as well as scores of boats importing timber, coal and limestone and exporting ore, corn and oysters. It must have been like Piccadilly Circus at rush hour – so very unlike this tranquil little spot today.

There's an annual summer fair and a fun band week each July, where the local Gweek silver band plays with two other local groups, and events include a pig roast, clay pigeon shooting, a tug of war and sheaf pitching.

MEET THE SEALIFE
Cornish Seal Sanctuary
sealsanctuary.com
TR12 6UG | 01326 221361
Open daily all year summer 10–5, winter 10–4
This small sealife centre exists to rehabilitate injured seals and home those that wouldn't be able to make it out in the sea today. Alongside a range of seals swimming in and around a large swimming pool, there are playful otters, comical penguins and happy ponies, goats and sheep. The rock-pool experience allows children to touch starfish and other marine life safely, and there is a small cafe and kiosks as well as a lovely walk in the woods to be had.

EAT AND DRINK
Black Swan
blackswangweek.co.uk
TR12 6TU | 01326 221502
This delightful inn, a stone's throw from the popular Cornish Seal Sanctuary, has become famous for its sirloin steaks, but also offers signature

dishes of steak and Guinness pie with creamy mash, and Cajun chicken breast. Beers include Cornish Doom Bar. If you'd like to stay over, the pub has four stylish bedrooms.

The Grange Fruit Farm
thegrangecornwall.com
TR12 6BE | 01326 221718
This fruit farm has a farm shop and a country kitchen restaurant. It's a great spot for Sunday lunch or a cream tea with fresh strawberries, and also has plenty to entertain the children, including pitch and putt, giant skittles and a sandpit.

▶ **PLACES NEARBY**
The tiny village of Mawgan is close to Gweek and has an interesting and ancient church.

St Mawgan in Meneage Church
Gear Hill, Mawgan, TR12 6BU
St Mawgan, who may have founded the church here in about AD 700, appears as a statue on the church tower, which also has carved shields of arms on it. The church dates from the 16th century and has a variety of Gothic window types. It also still has much of its original wagon roof, complete with bosses and angels.

▶ **Helford** MAP REF 275 D5
This pretty village on the Helford Estuary, east of Helston at the top of the Lizard Peninsula, gives you the chance to plunge into a romantic world of woodland and riverside paths. Nearby you'll find Frenchman's Creek, a winding inlet that inspired Daphne du Maurier's tale of the same name. Like many of the routes round here, it's best discovered on foot; parking is difficult. It's one of the many fine walks you can start in Helford; another path leads east to the coast at Dennis Head and to St Anthony and Gillan.

A passenger ferry sails to Helford Passage on the north bank from Helford Easter–Oct, giving you access to lush sub-tropical gardens. Glendurgan (see page 100), Trebah (see page 102) and Penjerrick gardens (see page 101) are the best known, where hydrangeas, camellias and rhododendrons flourish amid woodland on the estuary's banks and beyond.

EAT AND DRINK
The Ferryboat Inn
staustellbrewery.co.uk
Helford Passage, TR11 5LB
01326 250625
There are fabulous views over the Helford estuary from this waterside pub, which dates back 300 years. Whether it's a plate of oysters and a glass of fizz on the sunny terrace or Cornish rump steak and mash by the fire inside, this is a venue for all weathers. Everything is

▶ Aerial view of Helford river estuary (overleaf)

made on the premises and the Ferryboat burger is especially popular. Small plates of crabmeat, prawns and mackerel tacos are worthwhile. As the name implies you can hop on the ferry just outside.

▶ **PLACES NEARBY**

Helford is surrounded by beautiful countryside and is close to Helston. There is a golf course on the outskirts.

Budock Vean Hotel Golf Course
budockvean.co.uk
Helford Passage, Mawnan Smith, TR11 5LG | 01326 252100
Open daily all year
Set in 65 acres of mature grounds with a private foreshore to the Helford River, this 18-tee undulating parkland course has a tough par 4 fifth hole (456 yards) which dog-legs at halfway around an oak tree. The 16th hole measures 572 yards, par 5.

Manaccan
Just south of Helford, Manaccan is a pretty little village with a 12th-century church famed for the 200-year-old fig tree growing from its steeple wall. If you needed further proof of Cornwall's sub-tropical climate, there it is. As well as a church, the village has a pub, a cafe and a deli. Wooded lanes lead to Gillan Creek and Helford River. You can walk from here around Gillan harbour and to Gillan Cove, a sand/shingle beach.

▶ Helston MAP REF 274 C5

Helston is the true gateway to the Lizard – if you're on the way to the southernmost point of land in the UK, you'll certainly drive past it. It's the most southerly town in the UK and the second oldest town in Cornwall. The streets are lined with miners' cottages, Georgian houses, pasty bakeries and old pubs, and there are large supermarkets on the outskirts.

Helston was a port on the River Cober until the river silted up, and from the medieval period it was a thriving market town and the area's trading centre. The name of Coinagehall Street bears witness to the town's history as a centre of mineral mining and it's still a good shopping centre today. There is a great view down Coinagehall Street to the Gothic-style gateway of the bowling green and to the fields beyond. The Guildhall dominates the top of the street and the nearby Victorian Market House is a handsome building dating from the 1830s.

The town's annual Flora Dance, or Furry Dance, is held on 8 May and possibly dates from a pre-Christian time; it certainly has medieval links. This is when Helston-born people dance through the streets, and in and out of buildings and shops, from 7am to welcome the summer.

There is a folk museum in the Market House and Loe Pool, the largest freshwater lake in the county, is nearby. There's also a boating lake and a skate park. Goonhilly Satellite Station still functions as an important satellite communication teleport. Its visitor centre is currently closed but there are plans to reopen this section of the site as a Space Science Centre. Off the B3293 St Keverne road, located about 3.5 miles from Helston, is Trelowarren House. It has been the home of the Vyvyan family since the early 15th century and has a craft centre and restaurant.

VISIT THE MUSEUM
Helston Folk Museum
helstonmuseum.co.uk
Old Butter Market, Church Street, TR13 8TH | 01326 564027
Open Mon–Sat 10–4; check the website for reduced opening times
Behave yourself, children. This folk museum in the old butter and meat markets of Helston has a Victorian schoolroom, complete with a strict teacher, Mrs Crawford, to give modern children a taste of education in 1891. The collection here focuses on Victorian life and covers the whole Lizard Peninsula. In the loft there's a display on Bob Fitzsimmons, a boxer who in the 1890s won three world championships.

ENTERTAIN THE FAMILY
Coronation Park and Boating Lake
TR13 8SG | Open daily all year
Just below Helston is this popular flower-bedecked recreational area. There is plenty of safe boating fun for all the family with rowing boats and canoes and a special area for paddle boats for youngsters. There are also play amenities for kids, a skate park and a cafe. Facilities are good for wheelchair users and for people with visual impairment.

Flambards Theme Park
flambards.co.uk
Culdrose Manor, TR13 0QA
01326 573404 | Open late Mar–Oct from 10am, with more limited hours in winter
This family theme park delivers what it promises: something to do when it's raining on the Lizard. Undercover attractions include a life-size and authentic re-creation of a Victorian village, complete with cobbled streets, a Britain in the Blitz exhibition with a bomb shelter, and an indoor play park. Outside, rollercoasters, drop towers and merry-go-rounds cater for children of all ages.

GET OUTDOORS
Dan Joel Surf School
danjoelsurf.com
Poldhu Road, Mullion, TR12 7JB
07974 941575
Get into all that lovely surf at this popular venue. Located at the lovely National Trust beach of Poldubh, this is the ideal environment for learning how to

surf or to improve your skills. Well-qualified and friendly instructors are on hand to look after you and the youngsters are catered for at the Kids' Club.

Loe Pool

The Loe, the largest natural freshwater lake in Cornwall, is part of the Penrose Estate. Originally the estuary of the River Cober, over time it was cut off from the sea by a broad shingle bar created by rough Atlantic seas in the 13th century. It's a unique habitat with rare moths and woodlice, along with a number of rare plants, algae and other insects. It also attracts more than 80 species of bird and many more wildfowl in winter.

Local people would have you believe that the Loe is the place where Sir Bedivere cast Excalibur, King Arthur's sword, on his request. It's one of a number of lakes to have that story attached to it. There's a superstition that the Loe claims a victim every seven years and Cornish legend tells of the demon Jan Tregeagle (see also Bodmin Moor, page 62), who was doomed by his bad deeds to remove the sand from Gunwalloe to Porthleven. While doing so, he dropped a bag of sand at the end of Helston Harbour, forming the bar.

Penrose Estate

nationaltrust.org.uk
Penrose, TR13 0RD
01326 561407 | Accessible all year

Penrose Estate, surrounding Loe Pool, has beautiful woodland and farmland paths to explore. There is a convenient car park at the entrance. One way to see it is by bike; you could also strap on hiking boots and walk from here to the Southwest Coast Path. There is an outdoor gym trail and, in summer, the Stables cafe is open serving cream teas. Also within the estate is St Winwalloe Church, tucked into the rocky headland at Church Cove overlooking sandy beaches and clear aquamarine water. The Gunwalloe Valley is a good spot for birding. Penrose can also be reached from the Coronation Park and Boating Lake at the bottom end of Helston (see page 139).

Trelowarren Estate

trelowarren.com
Mawgan, TR12 6AF
01326 221224 | Open to non-residents Apr–Sep 11–5

This working estate, plus tourist accommodation, has spent 600 years in the hands of the Vyvyan family. With 1,000 acres of pasture and woodland down to the Helford River, rococo gardens, a restaurant using only local food, a Cornish art gallery and a mysterious Neolithic cave system, there's plenty to explore. Guests staying on the estate have access to everything, including tennis courts and a swimming pool. The 4-mile woodland walk takes in a Victorian folly, an Iron

Age Hill fort, an 18th-century garden and the highest point on the Lizard; a leaflet is available from the reception office detailing the route. Dogs are not permitted.

The pleasure gardens are open for estate guests only, and comprise 12 acres of 18th-century landscaping by Dionysus Willams. Funds are being raised to develop and extend the gardens in the future.

GO BACK IN TIME

Halliggye Fogou

english-heritage.org.uk
Trelowarren Estate, 5 miles southeast of Helston off the B3293

This mysterious place dates from the Cornish Iron Age and is a complex of well-preserved underground tunnels roofed and walled in stone. 'Fogou' in Cornish means 'cave' and nobody really knows what these were used for, though it has been suggested that they could have been refuges, storage chambers or shrines. The fogou is part of the Trelowarren Estate but it is free to enter and is under the care of English Heritage. You may have to pay their car park fee unless you're a member. Dogs on leads are welcome. Bring a torch.

EXPLORE BY BIKE

Porthleven Cycle Hire

porthlevencyclehire.co.uk
Commercial Road, Porthleven,
TR13 9JE | 01326 561101
Open all year

10 top beaches

- Kynance Cove, Lizard Peninsula
page 143
- Constantine Bay beach, near Padstow
page 194
- Gyllyngvase beach, Falmouth
page 97
- Polzeath beach
page 211
- Porthmeor beach, St Ives
page 239
- Harlyn Bay beach, Padstow
page 194195
- Porthcurno beach
page 214
- Perran Sands, Perranporth
page 208
- Watergate Bay, Newquay
page 183
- Sennen Cove
page 257

Hire bikes here to tour the quiet local roads down to the beach and estuary, or around the Penrose Estate and Loe Pool where there are cycle paths and woodland routes. Porthleven Cycle Hire offers free bike delivery to those staying in the local area and has road bikes, mountain bikes and trailer bikes for children. They also have a useful map and information on various accessible cycle trails.

EAT AND DRINK

New Yard Restaurant ◉◉

newyardrestaurant.co.uk
Trelowarren Estate, Mawgan,
TR12 6AF | 01326 221595

This restaurant has been carved out of the former stable yard of the 1,000-acre Trelowarren Estate, by the Helford River. With such class fish as hake, mullet and monkfish on the menu, foodies will definitely be at home here. On offer are a varied lunch menu, a fine wine list and Cornish craft beer, which all add to the appeal.

▶ PLACES NEARBY

As well as all the attractions of the Lizard Peninsula, the mining district of Wendron is close to Helston, complete with its independent mining attraction, Poldark Mine. In Constantine, you'll also find the Potager, a delightful garden and cafe.

Poldark Mine

poldarkmine.org.uk
Trenear, Wendron, near Helston,
TR13 0ER | 01326 573173
To check full details of underground tours, phone or see website

Though no longer a working mine, Poldark Mine is the only complete tin mine in Cornwall open for underground guided tours. A huge amount of refurbishment has been carried out in recent years and today Poldark Mine represents a beacon of Cornish mining history and is part of the Cornish Mining World Heritage site. As well as the famous underground tours, the site also has lovely gardens, a mining museum and a fascinating museum of Methodism. The on-site shop sells books, rock samples and mementos. The underground workings were used in the BBC's 1970s *Poldark* saga and again in the modern remake.

▼ Kynance Cove

The Potager

potagergarden.org

High Cross, Constantine, TR11 5RF

01326 341258 | Open Tue–Sun 10–5

Once an abandoned plant nursery, the Potager is now a beautiful garden with mature trees, hammocks, boules and badminton to play and an airy 100-foot glass house with table-tennis in an indoor garden. The Glasshouse Cafe, occupying a refurbished woooden greenhouse, serves homemade cakes, lunches, teas and ice cream. It's a unique, relaxing spot – and quite different from the other, more formal, garden delights that abound in the county.

▶ Kynance Cove   MAP REF 275 D6

The stunning beach at Kynance Cove is the cover star of many a Cornwall calendar. This is one of the best beaches in Cornwall and is reached by a long, steep walk down to where a pretty beach cafe serves delicious Cornish ice cream to greet you. Dramatic and historic, it's easy to imagine mermaids swimming in Mermaid's Pool, the part of the beach surrounded by boulders on three sides and only accessible at half tide. The legend goes that a local man living in Cury near Mullion found a sobbing mermaid here, cut off by the tide from the sea and her family. He helped her back to the sea, and she in return granted his wishes to break evil spells, become a healer and find stolen property.

It's not just an appealing place for mermaids and dreamers; Kynance was visited and much loved in the Victorian times by Prince Albert and Lord Tennyson, as it embodied the Romantic ideal of the picturesque in nature. Countless artists still paint scenes of the beach, which is submerged at high tide with gnarled monoliths of serpentine rock islanded in the deep sea. The largest of these is called Asparagus Island, with Steeple Rock and the Sugar Loaf lying between it and the mainland.

The cove and the cliff land to the east are in the care of the National Trust, which has a car park above Kynance, a cafe and a viewpoint for visitors with disabilities. Descent to the cove is steep, and the return is quite strenuous. Care should be taken if swimming off the cove – the tide comes in rapidly and the currents close to shore are dangerous. There are great rock pools to play in and caves to explore at low tide.

The Kynance area is of great biological importance. Rare species grow in the area, including sedges and tiny liverworts. Spiders, moths and even a rare European woodlouse are also found here. The mild climate and a maritime environment partly explain the richness of local wildlife.

▶ Lizard Point   MAP REF 275 D6

Starting at Lizard Village, where you can park the car, the walk down to Lizard Point is an easy one, next to the road and along a small path. You can also park at the Point, near an old lifeboat station. Breathe deeply and look out to sea: birds hang in the air, the water churns and you might see a dolphin or two. The air is mild here even in midwinter, and it's a key breeding ground for choughs, which have been breeding on the point since 2001, after an absence of 50 years. The RSPB runs a Chough Watchpoint in spring.

The coast path leads west above high cliffs. To the east it passes through a green, sheltered landscape above cliffs draped with the invasive Hottentot fig. The Lizard's position, jutting out into the Channel approaches, has made it dangerous to vessels. For a mile seaward off Lizard Point the sea tumbles in frightening overfalls during stormy weather. To the northeast lies the blunt promontory of Black Head and beyond here is the deadly Manacles Reef.

The fortress-like Lizard Lighthouse dominates the coast to the east. A warning light was first established here in 1612. Today's powerful light flashes every three seconds and can be seen in clear weather from up to 29 miles away. The fog signal is delivered by siren every 60 seconds on gloomy days. About 1.5 miles east of Lizard Point is Church Cove and its attractive little church of Landewednack. The cove is reached on foot from the car park past thatched cottages. A short walk south along the coast path leads to the remarkable cliffside site of the Lizard-Cadgwith lifeboat house.

EAT AND DRINK

Housel Bay Hotel ◉
houselbay.com
Housel Cove, TR12 7PG
01326 290417
Perched on a blustery clifftop on the Lizard, Housel Bay is a late Victorian hotel with many original features and dramatic views over the gardens and the Channel. The kitchen offers a modern British repertoire with some Italian influence that is particularly strong on fine Cornish fish. The staff will engage you with charm and as well as efficiency.

Polpeor Cafe
Lizard Point, The Lizard, TR12 7NU
01326 290939
At Britain's most southerly cafe, perched high on the cliffs on Lizard Point, you can watch waves crashing onto the rocks and choughs wheeling around the cliffs while you tuck into a local crab salad and sandwiches or a traditional cream tea. On fine summer days, the suntrap terrace right on the cliff edge is the place to eat.

▶ The Manacle rocks

▶ Mullion MAP REF 274 C6

On the west coast of the Lizard, between Gunwalloe and Lizard Point, Mullion is a bustling community full of shops, restaurants and tea rooms. The Church of St Melanus in the village has a remarkable collection of bench ends depicting characters, including a jester and a monk. The biggest attraction here is Mullion Cove, the 19th-century harbour a little way from the village, reached by road. Pass through Mullion Meadows, an area of craft galleries, workshops and tea rooms, on the way there.

GET OUTDOORS

Mullion Cove

The dramatic sight of Mullion Cove and harbour tells you plainly why there are so many artists in the area. Built in 1893 to help the ailing pilchard fishing industry, it's still in use today and is maintained by the National Trust. Big cliffs and sea stacks, gold-leafed with yellow lichen, enclose the narrow inlet and its substantial piers, while offshore the bulky mass of Mullion Island lies flickering with seabirds.

The coast to the south is pleasantly remote, especially around Predannack Head, where you'll find rare wildflowers, and Vellan Head, with delightful coast walks to either side of the cove. Just to the north of Mullion is Polurrian Cove where there is a large sandy beach, and further north again is the popular Poldhu Cove with its sandy dunes.

HIT THE BEACH

The large sandy beach at Poldhu Cove is a big draw for local holidaymakers. With lifeguards in the summer, a beach cafe and a shop, it's one of the largest beaches on the peninsula with some of the best facilities. In the summer, the cafe serves pizza in the evening too. It's a safe beach for swimming.

PLAY A ROUND

Mullion Golf Club

mulliongolfclub.co.uk
Cury, Helston, TR12 7BP
01326 240276 | Open daily all year
Founded in 1895, Mullion Golf Club's clifftop and links course with panoramic views over Mount's Bay is the most southerly course in England. A steep downhill slope on the sixth and the tenth descends to the beach with a deep ravine alongside the green.

SADDLE UP

Newton Equestrian Centre

newton-equestrian.co.uk
Newton Farm, Polhorman Lane, TR12 7JF | 01326 240388
For beach rides, countryside hacks, horse-riding holidays and yoga, this equestrian centre on the Lizard caters for all levels of experience

and also has accommodation on site. Deals and offers can be found on their website; their spa, gym and yoga facilities are not just for horse-riders. Contact direct for beauty treatment details.

EAT AND DRINK
Mullion Cove Hotel ⊚⊚
mullion-cove.co.uk
Mullion Cove, Lizard Peninsula,
TR12 7EP | 01326 240328

The hotel's location could hardly be bettered: it's perched on the top of cliffs overlooking Mullion's harbour, with spectacular coastal views. There's a timeless elegance to the restaurant, where window tables are inevitably at a premium, with menus changing daily and plenty of seafood choices thanks to the local fishing boats.

▶ Porthallow   MAP REF 275 D5

The small fishing cove of Porthallow, between St Keverne and Roskorwell on the east coast, was known for its pilchards, hence the name of the local pub, the Five Pilchards. These days it's known for being the midway point on the South West Coast Path – there's a waymarker on the beach acknowledging it – and to geologists as the geological boundary fault line separating The Lizard from the rest of Cornwall. The village has a small, shingly beach, once popular with divers heading out to the Manacles, where you can now park and peacefully watch the waves in winter. The village beach committee organises events through the year, including Easter egg hunts, duck racing and summer beach parties. There are lovely coastal walks from the village to Nare Head and beyond to Gillan Creek.

ENTERTAIN THE FAMILY
Chocolate Factory and Craft Centre
the-chocolatefactory.co.uk
Mullion Meadows, TR12 7HB
01326 241311 | Open daily 10–5
Get your taste buds out for a visit to this lip-smacking venue, home of Trenance Chocolate. Also on site is The Gallery Anthony with resident artists, a wood turner and a glassmaker, and Honey Cosmetics, who produce skincare products made from local Cornish honey.

EAT AND DRINK
Fat Apples Cafe
The Old Vineyard,
TR12 6QH | 01326 281559
This friendly, community-run cafe welcomes walkers, dogs and holidaymakers as well as locals catching up on the village gossip. Serving homemade cakes, pies, coffee, lunches and snacks, it's just a short walk from the beach and also has a wild camping spot in the orchards.

▲ Loe Bar

▶ Porthleven MAP REF 274 C5

Porthleven centres around the harbour, as it has done for centuries. It was a notable fishing and shipbuilding village in days gone by and those industries still survive today, with concessions to the tourist trade including an interesting mix of galleries, shops, pubs and restaurants around the inner harbour and quays. At low tide you can see Giant's Rock, a huge boulder on the north side of the outer harbour. It is believed to be a glacial 'erratic' carried here while probably embedded in an ice floe during the last Ice Age.

It's a pleasant place to visit, with grand Victorian villas on the south quay and a bustling quayside. To the southeast, a road lined with cottages leads along the cliff edge and Loe Bar Road leads to a car park, for the short walk to Loe Bar and the Penrose Estate (see Helston, page 138).

Be warned that the outer end of Porthleven Harbour is very exposed to high tides and you should never walk along the outer piers. Swimming in this area is dangerous. Porthleven Beach is very popular with surfers, but Praa Sands, a beautiful, long, sandy beach just 4 miles away, is a much better bet for families.

EAT AND DRINK
Kota Restaurant ⊛⊛
kotarestaurant.co.uk
Harbour Head, TR13 9JA
01326 562407

Perched on the waterfront, Kota takes its name from the Maori word for seafood, the linguistic reference giving a clue to one element of chef-patron Jude Kereama's ethnicity. In a spacious beamed room with a tiled floor and unclothed tables, an inspired spin on marine-based fusion food wins many converts.

The Ship Inn
theshipinnporthleven.co.uk
Mount Pleasant Road, TR13 9JS
01326 564204

Dating from the 17th century, this smugglers' inn is built into the cliffs, and is approached by stone steps. In winter, a log fire warms the interior, while the flames of a second flicker in the separate Smithy party room. Expect a good selection of locally caught fish and seafood, all smoked in Cornwall. Bookings are not taken.

▶ PLACES NEARBY

A short drive along the coast takes you to one of Cornwall's finest sandy beaches; Helston and the other delights of the west coast of the Lizard are also close by.

Praa Sands
TR20 9TF

Four miles from Porthleven, Praa Sands is a wide swathe of golden sand beloved by families, swimmers and surfers alike – and there's room for all of them in a mile and a half of beach, dunes and natural habitats. It's in a sheltered position on Mount's Bay and has cafes and lifeguards in season. Dogs are banned Easter to September. There's parking by the beach.

Pengersick Castle, said to be one of the most haunted buildings in the UK, is in the village nearby. Interestingly, the Cornish name for Praa Sands, *Poll an wragh*, means 'witches' cove'. The castle is open for guided tours by appointment (tel 01736 763973).

▶ St Keverne MAP REF 275 D6

Just north of Coverack on the southeast coast of the Lizard Peninsula, St Keverne is a village full of character with a prominent and striking church. St Keverne's church was important for more than spiritual reasons: as the tallest landmark roundabout, highly visible from the sea, its spire was a key sight for local fishermen and aided navigation. The Manacles, a series of vividly named treacherous rocks, lie offshore; their Cornish name, *Maen Eglos*, meaning 'the Church Stones', seems even more menacing.

St Keverne Church is one of Cornwall's largest and most intriguing churches architecturally. It dates mostly from the

15th century, with some pillars from the 13th century. Parts of the church were rebuilt after the spire was struck by lightning in 1770. As well as an interesting interior, the church's graveyard is worth a look, full as it is of memorials to drowned sailors.

As well as the church, there are a number of welcoming pubs in the square, and for children, families and ice-cream lovers, a visit to Roskilly's farm can't be beaten.

SEE A LOCAL CHURCH
St Keverne Church
North end of High Street,
TR12 6NE
As mentioned, St Keverne Church was important spiritually to the local area, and also as a navigational tool when sailing off the south coast, and the church's stained-glass windows remember shipwrecks and lives lost at sea over the past centuries. Remarkably, the 13th-century pillars are not made from local stone and it is thought that they might have originated in Brittany. The 15th-century font is another interesting feature, with angels at each corner and AM, for Ave Maria, and IHS, for Jesus, carved into it.

▼ St Keverne Church

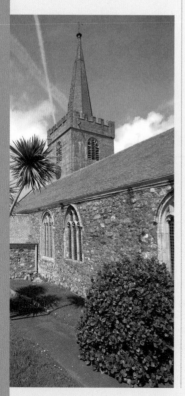

EAT AND DRINK
Roskilly's
roskillys.co.uk
Tregellast Barton Farm, TR12 6NX
01326 280479 | Check the website or call for opening times
Roskilly's is a family-run, working organic farm where they make one of Cornwall's much-loved ice creams, as well as clotted cream, fudge, preserves, jams and juices. A great family day out on the farm can culminate with a homemade lunch, tea and cake, or a delicious cream tea with warm scones and their famous clotted cream and fruity jams, all washed down with apple juice or cider made on the farm. There's a viewing gallery so you can watch the cows being milked (at 5am or 4.30pm, depending on how keen you are).

▲ The harbour at Looe

▶ Looe MAP REF 277 D6

Looe is a vibrant and bustling seaside town on the south
coast of Cornwall. As with any popular resort, it can get quite
busy in high season; the harbour is a magnet for children
looking for the best spot to go crabbing, while families can be
relied on to flock to East Looe beach, as well as several other
beaches in the area (see page 153). But that's not all that Looe
has to offer: when you look a little closer, there are some
interesting places to visit, including ancient woodlands and a
beautiful estuary.

The railway was mainly responsible for the development of
Looe as a holiday destination. Popular with tourists since the
early 19th century, when war with France sent the leisured
classes to southwest England in search of a home-grown
alternative to the French resorts, the bathing machine arrived
at Looe beach in 1800, and when trains came to the area there
was no stopping them. Incidentally, the train line linking
Liskeard to Looe is a real delight, running on a track beside the
estuary overhung with trees.

Looe divides into East Looe and West Looe; West Looe is the
more upmarket side, with a few souvenir shops leading through
to a shingle beach with a view of Looe Island – and free parking
beside the road – while East Looe is where you'll find the town
centre, shops, restaurants, sandy beach and harbour.

A walk round to the far end of East Looe's beach takes you to a cave used by smugglers. The old pilchard-curing cellars by the quay here are built from unadorned stone and many of the cottages have an outside stone staircase, showing that the ground floors were used as pilchard-processing cellars and net stores. Looe is Cornwall's second largest fishing port and you can sit and watch the boats go by, with a crab line or ice cream in hand, on the quay. Looe's viewpoint, Banjo Pier, can be reached from the quay.

Access to Looe
The main car park for East Looe is at Millpool and there's another car park in the town. Both are pay-and-display; the Millpool car park has a children's playground and a small pleasure boating lake beside it.

The delightful Kilminorth Woods are reached easily from the Millpool car park. Waymarked walks lead through a splendid oak wood and alongside the West Looe River. The woods and river are rich in plant, insect and bird life, including herons, which nest in the trees on the opposite bank. Further information can be obtained at the Discovery Centre.

VISIT THE MUSEUMS AND GALLERIES
Old Guildhall Museum
eastlooetowntrust.co.uk/
looe-museum.php
Higher Market Street, East Looe,
PL13 1AA | 01503 263709 | Open
late Mar to mid-Oct daily 11–4
This small, local museum gives a flavour of the history of Looe and its smuggling, fishing and boatbuilding past. The building itself was once East Looe's Town Hall and Magistrates Court and has ancient cells and 18th-century domestic items, plus a genuine cat o' nine tails.

South-East Cornwall Discovery Centre
Millpool, West Looe, PL13 2AF
01503 262777 | Open summer daily 10–5, winter 11–3
This small visitor centre promotes green tourism in southeast Cornwall and has a shop and a booking service.

MEET THE MONKEYS
The Monkey Sanctuary
monkeysanctuary.org
Murrayton House, St Martins,
PL13 1NZ | 01503 262532
Open Apr–Sep Sat–Thu 11–4.30,
Mar, Oct weekends only
Wild Futures' Monkey Sanctuary cares for unwanted and former pet monkeys. Visitors can meet some of these characters – Capuchin monkeys, woolly monkeys and Barbary macaques – dependent on the stage of their rehabilitation, and keepers are on hand to talk about the sanctuary's rescue work, as well as the charity's wider work.

GET OUTDOORS
Kilminorth Woods
Millpool car park | 01503 262777
This glorious nature reserve and woodland area is within easy reach of Looe. The valley traces the West Looe River and is a pretty backdrop for it. Also here is a huge sixth-century earthwork, the Giant's Hedge, which runs 9 miles from Lerryn to Looe.

Looe Island
Also known as St George's Island, Looe Island is just offshore and is open to day visitors in the summer. It has a lovely history – in the 1960s, a pair of sisters were determined to own their own island and bought this beautiful place, living on it until they died. Now under the care of the Cornwall Wildlife Trust, it's a natural sanctuary for seabirds and seals and was a known smuggler's haunt. It also has the ruins of a 12th-century Benedictine chapel on it. The ferry service for visitors runs in the summer, tides permitting, taking 20 minutes and allowing visitors two hours on the island. Look for The Islander board on the quay near the lifeboat station in East Looe.

For the Looe Valley Line
see **Liskeard**, page 127

HIT THE BEACH
East Looe beach is the most obvious and closest choice to the town. Plaidy Beach, less than a mile from East Looe, is also a good option, with concrete steps leading down to the sandy beach, which also features rock pools. Hannafore Beach, in West Looe, is shingly with some sand and is good for rock pooling at low tide. There's a walk along the promenade on West Looe from here too, with views of Looe Island. East up the coast from Plaidy Beach, Millendreath Beach is in a sheltered cove with rock pools at high tide and some sand, just under a mile up the coast towards Whitsand Bay on the Southwest Coast Path.

TAKE A BOAT TRIP
Looe's seafaring and fishing history means that there are plenty of sea cruises and fishing trips available from the harbour. The Islander Ferry takes visitors to Looe Island in season (see left) and charter boats even take visitors out shark fishing. A good evening trip is up the West Looe River to the Watergate, where you can see herons and other riverbank wildlife. Check the boards in East and West Looe for both sea and river trips, which all depend on weather and tides.

Glass Bottom Boat trips
01503 263747/07771 798339
A great way to get under the ocean's 'skin' without getting wet, the *Aquarius* offers trips around Looe Island with a chance of spotting seals playing in the clear water. Check out your knowledge of marine plant life as well.

HIRE A BIKE

Cornish Cycle Hire

cornishcyclehire.co.uk

Pensilva, PL14 5PJ | 07976 450462

Cornish Cycle Hire delivers mountain bikes in the Looe area direct to your accommodation so you can spend a day cycling along the shore, exploring the country lanes and woodlands around the town. Adult and child bikes plus trailers and HD cameras are available.

GO FISHING

Looe Chandlery

looechandlery.co.uk

Millpool Boatyard, West Looe, PL13 2AF | 01503 264355

East and West Looe Rivers both have a trout and salmon fishing season from 1 April to 15 December. You need a permit to fish, available from Looe Pet Supplies (see above). There are also plenty of sea-fishing trips on offer from Looe Quay. Check the boards for details – mackerel is the catch of the day typically, but some operators promise shark fishing too. Looe Chandlery also sells fishing supplies.

Looe Pet Supplies

Buller Street, PL13 1AS

01503 263535

Out The Blue

The Quay | 07855 033155

The *Out The Blue* charter boat runs wreck-fishing trips on which you can catch hefty cod, pollack and conger, or try your luck for such prized species as bass, turbot, or even shark.

PLAY A ROUND

Looe Golf Club

looegolfclub.co.uk

Bindown, PL13 1PX

01503 240239 | Open daily all year

Designed by Harry Vardon in 1935, Looe Golf Club's downland and parkland course commands panoramic views over southeast Cornwall and the coast. It's an easy-walking course with views across to Dartmoor to the east, countryside and moors to the west and north, and Looe Island to the south.

EAT AND DRINK

Daisy's Cafe

Castle Street, PL13 1BA

07988 803315

Rekindle old memories of seaside trips in the delightfully retro interior of this friendly little cafe with its all-day breakfasts, lunchtime treats – there are even gluten-free pasties on offer – sandwiches and soups.

Larsson's Coffee House and Creperie

larssonscoffeehouse.com

7 Buller Street, East Looe, PL13 1AS

01503 265368

Nicely modelled interiors based on the paintings of Swedish artist Carl Larsson add a charming Continental flavour to the sweet and savory crepes, tasty paninis and cakes in this cosy little licensed place. The German cheesecake is a speciality. There are regular music evenings featuring local musicians and songwriters.

The Ship Inn
staustellbrewery.co.uk
Fore Street, PL13 1AD
01503 263124
This lively pub stands on a corner a minute's walk from the working harbour. The menu includes burgers and hot baguettes, steak and ale pie and hunter's chicken. Tribute is on tap. A quiz is held on Mondays throughout the year and live bands play regularly.

Trelaske Hotel & Restaurant ◉◉
trelaske.co.uk
Polperro Road, PL13 2JS
01503 262159
In a rural location between Looe and Polperro, this small-scale hotel is surrounded by 4 acres of peaceful grounds. In the spacious restaurant, daily-changing menus are dictated by availability. Vegetables straight from the garden get the thumbs up for their stunningly fresh flavours, as do breads, while puddings hit the same consistently high standards.

▸ **PLACES NEARBY**
The small village of Duloe is set in deep Cornish countryside, a quiet getaway midway between the bustling towns of Liskeard to the north and Looe to the south. Duloe is also home to the Cornish Orchards company, renowned for its ciders and juices. Seaton Beach and nature reserve are easily reached. Port Eliot (see page 116) is also worth a visit.

Cornish Orchards
cornishorchards.co.uk
Duloe, PL14 4PW
01503 269007
Based at Duloe, Cornish Orchards produce a great range of ciders and other delicious products, including vintage ciders, pear cider, pressed apple juice, ginger beer and other sparkling flavours. Visit the farm shop for a taster and to discover more products.

The Plough
Duloe, near Looe, PL14 4PN
01503 262556
Set in deep Cornish countryside midway between Liskeard and Looe, Duloe is home to the Cornish Orchards Company, so it's no surprise to find its ciders on tap alongside St Austell ales in The Plough's bar. The use of local produce extends when possible to the menus.

Seaton Beach
Four miles east of Looe on the South West Coast Path, the village of Seaton has a sand and pebble beach, a divers' centre and a beach cafe. It's popular with families, with a car park adjacent to the beach. There are no lifeguards and dogs are welcome year round. Take care in the sea as the current can be unpredictable. Nearby, Seaton Valley Countryside Park is a former caravan park turned nature reserve with otters and kingfishers, and has a sensory garden, cycle paths, play area and woodland walks.

▶ Lostwithiel MAP REF 276 C5

John Betjeman reputedly said that there is history in every stone of Lostwithiel – he wasn't wrong, but he didn't mention that you'd find it in every shop too. Located between St Austell and Liskeard in east Cornwall, Lostwithiel is the county's antiques capital. Crammed with antiques shops and with an antiques market running on alternate Fridays in the community centre, it's the place to come to find vintage items, furniture, militaria, silver and more.

In medieval times, the town was a busy port, but the silting up of the river put a stop to that. It has a beautiful 13th-century bridge with five pointed arches spanning the river and the ruined Restormel Castle nearby, also 13th-century, is considered the best-preserved military building in Cornwall.

Further history can be seen today alongside independent shops, antiques shops and delis, in the arches and buttresses of the Duchy Palace on Quay Street and the 13th-century tower and 14th-century spire of the Church of St Bartholomew. Guided historic walks of the town take place on Thursdays in the summer from outside the Tourist Information Centre. There is a town museum in Fore Street. Coulson Park is by the River Fowey and there are pleasant riverside walks.

TAKE IN SOME HISTORY
Restormel Castle
english-heritage.org.uk
Near Restormel Road,
PL22 0EE | 01208 872687
Open Jul–Aug daily 10–6, Apr–Jun,
Sep 10–5, Oct 10–4
A mile upriver from Lostwithiel, Restormel Castle was built during the Norman period on the site of a wooden fortification and was twice visited by Edward the Black Prince. Today the impressive ruins of the circular keep have fabulous views and make a good picnic spot. You can climb the castle steps for views and look down on the remains of the rooms. In the woodlands around it, you might see black pheasants and beautiful wildflowers. In the summer, theatre performances take place here; in the spring the bluebells and daffodils are worth seeing.

VISIT THE MUSEUM
Lostwithiel Museum
museumsincornwall.org.uk
Fore Street, PL22 0BW
01208 873005 | Open Apr–Oct
Mon–Sat 10.30–4.30
This small town museum celebrates the history of Lostwithiel with artefacts and photographs spanning the past 200 years. It's very small – in 2007 it became the smallest museum in the country to have Museums and Galleries Commission accreditation – and is much used by those wanting to find out more about their family history.

▲ Restormel Castle

PLAY A ROUND
Lostwithiel Hotel, Golf and Country Club
golf-hotel.co.uk
Lower Polscoe, PL22 0HQ
01208 873550 | Open daily all year
The 18-hole course at the Lostwithiel Hotel is one of the most varied in the county, designed to take full advantage of the natural features of the landscape, combining two distinct areas of hillside and valley. The challenging front nine has magnificent views, while the picturesque back nine runs through parkland flanked by the River Fowey.

EAT AND DRINK
Asquiths Restaurant ◎◎
asquithsrestaurant.co.uk
19 North Street, PL22 0EF
01208 871714
Its black and white decor, exposed stone walls, modern artwork and smartly set tables combine to create a positive first impression of this restaurant opposite the church. Food is taken seriously too, as confirmed by a glance at the sensibly short menu, with thoughtfully composed dishes including venison from the local Boconnoc estate.

▶ **PLACES NEARBY**
Cornwall's biggest exotic animal sanctuary, Porfell Animal Land, is in Lanreath, just outside Lostwithiel.

Porfell Animal Land and Wildlife Park
porfell.co.uk
Lanreath, near Lostwithiel, PL14 4RE | 01503 220211
Open mid-Feb to Mar daily 11–5, Apr–Oct 10–6
This wildlife sanctuary looks after more than 250 animals from around the world that otherwise would be neglected or no longer wanted. Including lemurs, meerkats, emus and coatis, they are an unusual and exotic bunch. It takes about half a day to explore the woodlands, African area and children's farm. There's also a cafe.

▶ Marazion MAP REF 274 B5

It's impossible to mention Marazion without first mentioning St Michael's Mount. This distinctive and beautiful part-time island lies just off the coast, connected to the town twice a day when the tide is low. The romantic twin to Mont St Michel in Normandy, this former monastery, prison and castle-under-siege has been reached by pilgrims via its cobbled causeway for centuries, and we're still visiting today. But more of that later – there's a little more to Marazion than the Mount.

Marazion Marsh is an important breeding ground for birds and is looked after by the RSPB; whatever time of year you visit, there's something to watch here. The wide sandy beach is safe for bathers and attracts watersports fans. The town has several pubs, restaurants, cafes and shops to browse through.

Formerly the main trading port of Mount's Bay, Marazion was upstaged when Penzance developed its own market and port in the 16th century but Marazion has retained its status as a 'town' – beware of calling it a 'village' in front of locals. There are several art galleries – if you're looking to bring home a scenic painting of a Cornish harbour or romantic windswept headland, look no further.

Nearby, the quiet village of Perranuthnoe, a short distance southeast, has a south-facing beach that provides reasonable surfing. A few miles further east lies Prussia Cove, a secluded rocky inlet of great charm reached most rewardingly by a pleasant 2-mile walk along the coast path. The whole Mount's Bay area was a prime smuggling district and walks around the coast uncover secret coves and inland paths with a dark history.

▼ Marazion Causeway

▶ **St Michael's Mount** MAP REF 274 B5

stmichaelsmount.co.uk

TR17 0HS | 01736 710265 | Island accessible daily all year on foot at low
tide; also by boat in the summer at high tide

You don't have to be visiting on a misty day to see the magic, myths and legends swirl around St Michael's Mount. According to Cornish legend, in the fifth century AD a group of fishermen saw the Archangel St Michael perched on a ledge of rock on the western side of the Mount, and it has been called St Michael's Mount ever since. Whether that was a seal, a hardy swimmer or a trick of the light, it really doesn't matter – this is a magical place.

It was also said that the giant Cormoran lived on St Michael's Mount and waded across to the mainland to feast on cows and sheep. He was supposedly felled by a local lad named Jack and the story has become the Cornish folk tale of Jack the Giant Killer.

Atop the island, and reached by winding steps and a cobbled pathway, there's a 12th-century castle. The lower part of the island has beautiful sub-tropical gardens although these have distinct opening and closing times. The island can be visited year round, and has pubs, a shop and a harbour with charming whitewashed cottages.

History

Bronze Age finds on the island, including an axe head and a dagger, show that the mount was an important place long before the religious vision gave it its name. The castle was built in 1135 by the Abbot of Mont St Michel in Normandy, but the original building was destroyed by an earthquake in 1275. Rebuilt, it has been used as a church, priory, fortress and private home over the past 700 years and it was seen as a strategically important place during the Wars of the Roses, the Prayer Book Rebellion, the attack of the Spanish Armada – the first of the beacons that warned London of its approach was lit here – and the English Civil War, when in 1646 it was a Royalist stronghold forced to surrender to Parliament.

In the 18th century, the St Aubyn family made it a permanent family residence, in due course constructing a new wing and Victorian apartments complete with armour, oil paintings and Chippendale furniture. The John St Aubyn of the day was made Lord St Levan on his retirement for his services to politics.

Today, most of St Michael's Mount is in the care of the National Trust although the current Lord St Levan, James St Aubyn, and his family occupy private quarters on the top floors of the castle, enjoying what is probably the finest viewpoint in Cornwall.

▲ St Michael's Mount castle

The castle

Open mid-Mar to Jun, Sep–Oct
Sun–Fri 10.30–5, Jul–Aug Sun–Fri
10.30–5.30

With everything from suits of
armour to a Samurai warrior
and a mummified cat to see, the
castle is a great place to start.
Used as a family home since
the 18th century, there's plenty
of family history to view,
including oil portraits of the
former owners, a beautiful
library and a historic tidal clock
made in the 1780s, enabling the
family to plan their crossings to
the mainland. The Priory
Church includes 500-year-old
alabaster panels, and in the
map room there's a model of
St Michael's Mount made by the
butler from Champagne corks
in 1832. Best of all, on a sunny
day, are the views from the
terraces of the gardens.

The gardens

Open mid-Apr to Jun Mon–Fri
10.30–5, Jul–Sep Thu–Fri
10.30–5.30

The tiered gardens clinging to
the steep granite slopes of the
mount are exotic in the extreme
– the granite holds heat well so
plants from Mexico, South
Africa and the Canary Islands

have flourished in the sea breeze. There are lawns to picnic on, a children's trail and a free map. Access to the gardens is restricted to particular days because of their fragile nature, but they look just as good viewed from the castle.

Visiting

You should allow around 3–4 hours to experience the whole island on a day when all the attractions are open. On Tuesdays and Fridays there are free guided walks around the village and harbour side of the island, which are led by a local resident and focus on island daily life.

EAT AND DRINK
**Island Cafe and
Sail Loft Restaurant**
nationaltrust.org.uk
The Harbour, St Michael's Mount,
TR17 0HS | 01736 710748
This excellent tea room in a converted laundry is welcoming and cheerful, with a mouthwatering array of treats and six varieties of tea. As well as traditional teas, the Island Cafe offers light lunches and snacks, with local Cornish pasties as a speciality. The Sail Loft, in the island's old sail loft on the edge of the village, serves Newlyn crab, Cornish cheeses, local fresh fish and homemade breads and cakes.

VISIT THE MUSEUM
Marazion Town Museum
marazion.info/marazion-museum
Town Hall, The Square, TR17 0AP
01736 711061 | Open Easter, Jun–
Oct Mon–Fri 10–4

Marazion's museum is in the town hall, with plenty of quirky touches including a re-creation of a gaol cell and a unique exhibition devoted to HMS *Warspite*, which was wrecked off the nearby coast in 1947. It also includes a host of memorabilia about the town and its history.

HIT THE BEACH
For the best views of St Michael's Mount, Marazion beach is spectacular. It's wide, sandy and exposed, and attracts windsurfers, kite surfers, jet skiers and sailors. There's a lifeguard here in season and a windsurfing school at the end of the beach. Dogs are banned from Easter to September.

Praa Sands (see page 149) is another much-loved beach just down the coast at the start of the Lizard Peninsula.

GET OUTDOORS
Marazion Marsh
rspb.org.uk

Marazion Marsh is a key birding area, described by the RSPB as one of the best wildlife areas in the UK. It's open year round and is free; dogs must be kept on leads.

▼ St Michael's Mount viewed from Marazion

More than 250 bird species and 18 mammal species have been recorded here in Cornwall's largest reed bed, including heron and egret. Check the RSPB website for further information on seasonal spotting and their work here.

EAT AND DRINK
Ben's Cornish Kitchen ⊛⊛
benscornishkitchen.com
West End, Marazion,
TR17 0EL | 01736 719200
Behind its shop-front facade, the Kitchen extends over two wooded floors furnished with plain tables and raffia chairs, with some local artworks for sale. Contemporary-styled cooking with a classical background features perfectly constructed dishes with prime ingredients receiving due prominence. Don't miss the excellent breads.

Mount Haven Hotel & Restaurant
mounthaven.co.uk
Turnpike Road, Marazion,
TR17 0DQ | 01736 710249
St Michael's Mount forms a dramatic backdrop at this boutique hotel near the South West Coast Path. Inside, the furnishings and decor are a mixture of East and West, while a team of therapists is on hand for mind, body and spirit treatments. What's on offer in the restaurant, however, is of a thoroughly contemporary British flavour, with the kitchen showing an unassuming respect for its ingredients.

▶ **PLACES NEARBY**
Perranuthnoe, a short way along the coast, southeast, is a charming seaside village. St Hilary, a couple of miles inland, has a church of the same name, with an intriguing history going back to Roman times.

Perranuthnoe
The fine sand and shingle beach here has the best surfing potential on Mount's Bay. There are toilets at the car park above the beach and a pleasant little complex of art shops, galleries and cafe just up the road. There's a lovely, easy walk of about a mile and a half along the coast path to Prussia Cove, passing the knuckly little headland of Cudden Point.

St Hilary's Church
St Hilary, reached off the
B3280 beyond St Hilary School,
TR20 9DQ
Dedicated to a fourth-century French bishop, the churchyard's shape suggests that it may have originally been a Roman fort guarding the tin mines that attracted traders to Cornwall for more than 2,000 years. Two stones here mark its remarkable history: one is a Roman milestone, dating from AD 306; the other is a stone inscribed 'Noti Noti', possibly a memorial to 'Not son of Not', dating from the 6th or 7th century.

The church was almost entirely destroyed by fire on Good Friday 1853, with only its ancient spire, a shipping landmark for Mount's Bay and St Ives Bay, surviving, and was rebuilt in 1854 by architect William White of Truro, who retained as much as he could from the old church. A later vicar commissioned decorations by local artists, but many were sadly vandalised in 1932 by 'extreme Protestants'.

▶ Mawgan Porth MAP REF 275 E2

This lovely cove between Padstow and Newquay is linked to both via the South West Coast Path and is good for swimming, sandcastle-building, cave exploring and coasteering.

Overlooked by Cornwall's top eco-friendly hotel, the Scarlet, and its sister hotel, the award-winning family-friendly Bedruthan Steps Hotel, it has a pub and cafe and both the restaurants plus Scarlet's spa are open to non-residents. Just up the coast towards Padstow is Bedruthan Steps itself, a National Trust beach and clifftop area (see page 56).

GO ROUND THE GARDENS
The Japanese Garden
St Mawgan, TR8 4ET
Open daily 10–6
This is the ideal outing for fans of bonsai and Japanese gardening, or for anyone looking for a break from busy sightseeing. The fascinating garden boasts a wealth of exotic plants, a koi pond, Buddha shrine, garden sculptures and gentle walkways, all with a soothing background noise of gently running water.

HIT THE BEACH
Mawgan Porth's award-winning beach has a lifeguard from April to September and is dog friendly. Rock pools and caves are exposed at high tide.
A beach shop and cafe are nearby, and surf hire can be found at Bedruthan Steps Hotel – follow the path up from the beach to the back of the hotel to find its surf shack.

BOOK BEAUTY TREATMENTS
The Scarlet
scarlethotel.co.uk
The Scarlet, Tredragon Road, TR8 4DQ | 01637 861800
This luxury spa focuses on tailor-made Ayurvedic treatments and has relaxation pods that are in tented rooms, swimming pools and a scarlet-coloured outdoor hot tub for seaweed treatments. There's also a rhassoul mud treatment therapy. Everything is designed to preserve the environment.

PLAY A ROUND
Merlin Golf Course
merlingolfcourse.co.uk
St Eval Road, TR8 4DN
01841 540222
Open daily all year
The Merlin Golf Course is a heathland course, which has superb views of the coast and the surrounding countryside. Designed for all standards of golfer, it's fairly easy

walking. The most challenging hole on the course is the par 4 18th, with out of bounds on the left and ponds on either side of the green.

EAT AND DRINK
The Park Cafe
mawganporth.co.uk
TR8 4BD | 01637 860594
This family-friendly cafe has won multiple awards and serves wholesome food with an emphasis on the slow food movement. Expect the likes of dippy eggs, homemade fish fingers, and delicious and inventive home-baked cakes. It's part of The Park, a holiday complex, but non-residents are welcome.

The Scarlet Hotel ⚛⚛
scarlethotel.co.uk
Tredragon Road, TR8 4DQ
01637 861800
Huge windows opening on to the terrace, with wonderful views of the beach, sea and headland, dominate the restaurant at this modern hotel, with its miles of glass and trendy furnishings. It also has impeccable eco credentials. The kitchen's larder has been 'grown, reared, caught or foraged to taste as it should', according to the hotel, and the freshness of the ingredients shines through. Vegetarians are properly catered for, and desserts are not lacking the wow factor.

▶ Mevagissey MAP REF 275 F4

This lovely, traditional fishing village is one of south Cornwall's most charming, with narrow streets lined with cafes, pubs and gift shops leading down to a harbour bobbing with colourful boats. Fishing was always a major part of the village's history: today boats bring in pilchards – now known as 'Cornish sardines' in a bid to move upmarket – mackerel, crab and lobster. You can walk past the boats unloading their catch and round the quay to the point, where there's a small shingle beach to the left and a coast path.

The village dates from at least 1313, and was a major pilchard-fishing port in Tudor times. Like many Cornish fishing villages, Mevagissey has great character, especially in the old part of the village between the Fountain Inn and the Battery on the eastern side of the harbour. Many of the houses are colour-washed, and despite the fact that the harbour area has seen some rather brutal modern development, the village has retained its Cornish charm. A Feast Week is held in the village in June every year, with dances and music during the week and a grand carnival with fireworks to close it.

The aquarium at the old lifeboat house on the South Quay gives an insight into life in deeper waters – profits go to the upkeep and improvement of Mevagissey harbour – and there is a little museum of local history on the East Quay. The biggest draw, apart from dinner in a Mevagissey restaurant followed by a moonlit stroll around the quay, is the Lost Gardens of Heligan, which are found on the cliff above the village and reached by the B3273 St Austell road.

VISIT THE MUSEUM
World of Model Railways
model-railway.co.uk
Meadow Street,
PL26 6UL | 01726 842457
Open mid-Mar to Oct daily 10–5;
check website for other times
This model railway museum is a bit out of step with the rest of the seafaring town, but if you're into trains, if it's raining or if you're with a transport-mad toddler, it's a neat place to spend half an hour watching the large model train collection go round and round in circles. Highlights include a set reflecting the local scenery, and steam and diesel trains.

MEET THE SEALIFE
Mevagissey Aquarium
South Quay, PL26 6QU
01726 843305 | Open Apr–Sep daily 10–5
Housed in the old RNLI lifeboat house on the quay, this small aquarium holds local Cornish sealife, including crabs and lobster, and has a film on the pilchard-fishing industry. It's a bolthole in the rain, and all proceeds support the harbour.

TAKE A BOAT TRIP
Mevagissey Ferries
mevagissey-ferries.co.uk
07977 203394 |
Open end Apr–Sep

There are plenty of boat trips to take from this little harbour in the summer. Boards and booking offices at the harbour provide full information. You could also take a ferry from Mevagissey to Fowey and back again. The trip lasts 35 minutes with views of the contrasting harbours, and hopefully sight of a seal or dolphin along the way. All sailings are weather and tide permitting.

GO SEA FISHING
Mevagissey Shark Angling Centre
mevafishingshop.co.uk
West Quay, PL26 6UJ
01726 843850
Whether you're looking for an hour's mackerel fishing or a full day's charter with spear fishing, there are plenty of options in Mevagissey. The Shark Angling Centre on the quay sells fishing tackle and bait, and offers a booking service and advice. They offer 2-, 4- and 8-hour fishing trips from April to September for 8 to 12 people with various different skippers; call for more information.

EAT AND DRINK
The Ship Inn
theshipinnmeva.co.uk
Fore Street, PL26 6UQ
01726 843324

With a location just a few yards from Mevagissey's picturesque harbour, the great choice of fish dishes at this traditional inn should be no surprise. Low-beamed ceilings and flagstone floors enhance the colourful nautical atmosphere, while music nights with local musicians add to the cheerful ambience.

▲ Fishing port at Mevagissey

▶ PLACES NEARBY

On the hill above Mevagissey is one of Cornwall's best-known gardens, the Lost Gardens of Heligan. And nearby you'll also find a small local vineyard that makes the best of the area's sunshine.

The Dodman

Dodman Point, south of Gorran Haven, is the highest headland on the southern coast of Cornwall. The headland, known locally as the Dodman, is enclosed by a massive Iron Age earthwork nearly 2,190 feet long and 20 feet high, which it is thought could have housed a promontory fort. There is a circular path around it leading to the South West Coast Path. The point also has an 18th-century watchtower with a large granite cross on it, visible from several miles away, which was created to help navigate the coastline from the sea.

Gorran Haven

This unspoilt coastal village clusters around a small cove with fishermen's cottages arranged around it. It's a sheltered spot with two safe, sandy beaches good for swimming. Walkers on the South West Coast Path pass here. Steep lanes and passageways climb from the harbour and there's an intriguing little chapel dating from the 15th century built on solid rock. The village has several food outlets as well as beach shops.

Polmassick Vineyard

polmassickvineyard.co.uk
St Ewe, near Mevagissey, PL26 6HA
01726 844427 | Open late May–Sep
Wed–Sun 12–5 or on request
Cornwall's oldest vineyard has run guided tours since 2014 and offers 'cellar door' tasting sessions. They also sell their wines here and have a pretty and peaceful wine garden where they invite you to bring a picnic and enjoy wine by the glass. There's a free car park, no admission fee and dogs on a lead are welcome.

The Lost Gardens of Heligan

See highlight panel overleaf

▶ The Lost Gardens of Heligan

MAP REF 275 F3

heligan.com

Pentewen, St Austell, PL26 6EN | 01726 845100 | Open Apr–Sep daily 10–6
(late Jul–late Aug till 7.30), Oct–Mar 10–5

With one of the most romantic back stories of all of Cornwall's lush
gardens – and that's saying something – the Lost Gardens of
Heligan are *the* gardens to see. Even the least green-fingered will
enjoy this one – it's not just about tropical plants that make you feel
as if you're in an exotic rainforest, there's also a sculpture trail and
a neatly planted Victorian garden complete with a pineapple pit.

The story goes like this: Heligan was the seat of the Tremayne
family from the mid-18th century. At the end of the 19th century, its
thousand acres were at their zenith, with 22 gardeners tending the
trees, rhododendrons and melons. When World War I struck,
everything changed. Sixteen of the gardeners went to war and
never returned. Jack Tremayne, the family heir, left England for
Italy and settled there, leasing out the estate. Only a few years
later, the once well-tended estate fell into a deep sleep.

Upon Jack's childless death, the estate passed to a trust. A member of the extended Tremayne family introduced then-record producer Tim Smit to the gardens and he was, forgive me, smitten. Along with a group of other enthusiasts, Smit brought the gardens back to life in a process filmed by Channel 4. He remains involved here and, after bringing the gardens back to life, he went on to create the Eden Project; if you visit both attractions you get a discount as a thank you.

Today, Heligan is an exciting place to visit, with 200 acres including the Lost Valley, the Jungle, where visitors are overshadowed by enormous ferns, and more delicate and precise Italianate gardens. There are also productive gardens, pleasure grounds, sustainably managed farmland, wetlands, ancient woodlands and a pioneering wildlife project.

Check the website for regular events, walks and talks, which all enrich a visit. Well-behaved dogs on leads are welcome all year. Allow a good half day or longer for a visit. There's a tea room, a shop and a plant centre, and you can bring a picnic.

▶ Morwenstow MAP REF 277 D1

The parish of Morwenstow lies at the northern extreme of Cornwall near Bude (see page 70) on the Devon border. Its coastline is awesome, yet unexpected: dramatic ravaged and twisted slabs of rock and 300-foot cliffs bordered by flat green fields. This is the land of the famous Culm Measures, great pieces of layered shale that rise from boulder-strewn beaches striped with dark rock. At times, with a boiling sea, it looks otherworldly.

Its natural beauty apart, Morwenstow owes much of its fame to the reputation of the Victorian parson, eccentric and unsuccessful poet, Robert Hawker, who was vicar at the Church of St Morwenna for many years – see opposite.

Southwards from Morwenstow is the hamlet of Coombe, set in a shady, wooded valley. The river reaches the sea at Duckpool where the pebble beach has built up to dam a small pool of fresh water. Just north of Coombe, the coast path passes above Lower Sharpnose Point, where spectacular natural piers of rock jut out into the sea like the massive walls of ruined temples. Inland, the smooth satellite dishes of the Cleave Camp Satellite Station strike an incongruous note amidst such raw natural beauty, and dominate the view for miles around.

Cliff-path walks and beach visits are a must-do in the area.

▼ Hawker's Hut

GET OUTDOORS
Tamar Lakes Country Park
swlakestrust.org.uk
Cornwall, EX23 9SB
01288 321712 | Open Apr–Sep
You can catch a Cornish or a Devon fish in the Tamar Lakes, depending on which side of the county border you are on. The border runs right through the middle of these two handsome lakes that lie a few miles inland from Morwenstow. The Upper Lake is the bigger of the two; the smaller Lower Lake is more of a birdwatchers' enclave. You can walk or cycle round the Upper Lake. For watersports

enthusiasts there's sailing, windsurfing and kayaking, including tuition if desired. There's also a cafe and an adjoining campsite.

GO BACK IN TIME
Hawker's Hut
robertstephenhawker.co.uk

A 3-mile circular walk from Morwenstow church takes you to this tiny wooden cabin built overlooking the cliffs from timbers of wrecked ships. It's a National Trust-owned place, and is much frequented by passing walkers, who over the years have carved their initials in the driftwood planks.

Morwenstow's Victorian vicar, Robert Stephen Hawker, was a rather eccentric figure who was dedicated to recovering the bodies of drowned sailors – in no short supply along this treacherous coast. He's said to have smoked opium and dressed up as a mermaid, and lives on as one of Cornwall's most colourful characters. Sitting here, overlooking the waves, it's impossible not to think of him watching ships wrecked on the rocks, and saving those who he could. Some less fortunate were buried in the graveyard of his church.

SEE A LOCAL CHURCH
St Morwenna Church
EX23 9SR

Hawker's church lies at the head of a shallow combe that leads towards the cliffs. Inside, it's pleasantly melancholic, especially at dusk, when there is a wonderful feeling of isolation. From 1835–37, Robert Hawker was the vicar of the parish here. In the graveyard is a preserved figurehead from a ship wrecked on the rock nearby. Reverend Hawker is credited with reintroducing Harvest Festival celebrations into the church, and wrote the *Song of the Western Men*, now Cornwall's anthem, especially at rugby matches. Hawker built a new vicarage – three of its chimneys were modelled on the towers of favourite churches, another on the tower of an Oxford college. The kitchen chimney was a replica of his mother's tomb.

The land around the church and the stretch of cliffs to the west are owned and conserved by the National Trust.

EAT AND DRINK
Rectory Tea Rooms
rectory-tearooms.co.uk
Rectory Farm, EX23 9SR
01288 331251

This 13th-century farmhouse, just 10 minutes from the spectacular Cornish cliffs, is full of atmosphere. Heavy oak beams salvaged from wrecked ships, ancient flagstone floors worn by countless feet, and large, open fireplaces all help to make a memorable visit. Freshly prepared food includes ploughman's platters, soups and pasties, as well as light, home-baked scones served warm with jam and copious amounts of clotted cream.

▶ Mousehole MAP REF 274 B5

Named for its small harbour and tight harbour mouth, Mousehole, pronounced 'Mouz'l', is a picturesque fishing village with evocatively narrow streets, tempting alleyways and passages, and brightly painted boats in the harbour. The far end of Mousehole's tiny harbour has a splendid inner wall of irregular granite blocks, a perfect subject for imaginative photography or sketching, and some 450 yards off the harbour there's a little island, St Clement's Isle, named after a hermit who lived there and lit the hazard light for ships. When the tide is low, there's a sandy beach in the harbour; just east of the harbour wall, visitors can access a shingle beach too.

While any time of year is good for exploring the town's harbour, craft shops, galleries, cafes and pubs, it is particularly special in November and December. On 23 December, the town celebrates Tom Bawcock's Eve, a night commemorating a local hero from the 16th century who ventured out into stormy weather to bring back fish for the starving town. Stargazey pie, a pastry-topped pie with fish heads poking out, is the traditional dish of the day. Around the festive period, the town goes into Christmas lights in a big way, with floating lights in the harbour and beautiful displays around the town.

Dylan Thomas visited the town, as he had a friend living here, and it supposedly inspired *Under Milk Wood*. A more recent inspiration was the terrific bravery of the *Solomon Browne* lifeboat crew, which folk singer Seth Lakeman used as an inspiration for his RNLI benefit song. In 1981, eight volunteer lifeboat men died while repeatedly attempting to save eight people on the wrecked cargo ship *Union Star* on a stormy night with hurricane force 12 winds. There is a memorial to the crew in the Church of St Pol de Leon, on the steep hill leading inland to the village of Paul.

▼ Mousehole

The road out of Mousehole to the west leads up the dauntingly steep Raginnis Hill. Partway up is the famous Mousehole Bird Hospital, a refuge for countless injured birds, many of which are the victims of oil pollution.

A word of warning: Mousehole's narrow streets are not built for cars. Park outside the village on the road from Newlyn as the harbour car park is often full.

MEET THE BIRDLIFE
Mousehole Bird Hospital
mouseholebirdhospital.org.uk
Raginnis Hill, TR19 6SR
01736 731386 | Open all year
This small independent bird hospital is set up to help birds in distress, receiving and rehabilitating wild birds where possible, and with a number of permanent and unusual residents in their aviaries. They are open daily and ask for a donation rather than admission fee; every year on average 1,500 birds pass through their doors.

SEE A LOCAL CHURCH
St Pol de Leon
Very much part of Mousehole's history is the village of Paul with its parish church of St Pol de Leon. It's a steep climb uphill from the harbour but the church is worth visiting for its historic architecture and for the stirring memorial to the lost lifeboatmen of the *Solomon Browne* (see left). The church's name derives from a 5th-century Welsh missionary who also founded the cathedral of Pol de Leon in Brittany. In the wall of the churchyard is a monument to Mousehole fishwife Dolly Pentreath who died in 1777 at the alleged age of 102. Dolly was said to be the last person to speak the old Cornish language as well as English.

GET ON THE WATER
In the summer months, charter boats are available from the harbour, offering pleasure trips and short fishing trips for mackerel, dab and other local fish. Dolphins, seals and

10 top fishing villages

basking sharks are occasional visitors nearby and the town looks even prettier viewed from the sea. All trips are weather and tide dependent.

EAT AND DRINK
The Rock Pool Cafe
rockpoolmousehole.co.uk
The Parade, Mousehole,
TR19 6PR | 01726 732645
Overlooking Mousehole's tidal rock swimming pool, from which it takes its name, this bright and colourful place has a lovely atmosphere to go with its fabulous views of Mount's Bay from the outside terrace with its little summerhouse and cheerful bunting. This is a great place for coffee and cakes, cream teas, lunch – the crab sandwiches are delicious – cocktails for later, light meals and delicious platters.

▶ Mylor   MAP REF 275 E4

Dense with trees and bordered by tidal creeks, the parish of Mylor lies between Truro and Falmouth. A network of country lanes north of Falmouth links Mylor Bridge, Restronguet Passage, Mylor Creek and Mylor Churchtown, where there was once a royal dockyard. The Church of St Mylor has some unique features – a turret rises from its west gable and it has Norman doorways. Look out for the headstone of Joseph Crapp with its lyric epitaph, near the east window, and that of Thomas James, a smuggler, near a fork in the churchyard path. South of Mylor Bridge, the village of Flushing faces Falmouth across the river and a passenger ferry links the two.

Restronguet Creek was an important port for the export of tin and copper until the 20th century, and it has a character-packed 13th-century pub, The Pandora Inn. Named after the ship sent to Tahiti in 1790 to bring back the mutinous crew of Captain Bligh's HMS *Bounty*, a ship that sank on the Great Barrier Reef with great loss of life, the inn was owned by the captain of the *Pandora* who returned to Cornwall after being court martialled. It was badly damaged by fire in 2011, but has been restored using traditional materials and methods.

GET ON THE WATER
Mylor Sailing School
mylorsailingschool.co.uk
Mylor Yacht Harbour,
TR11 5UF | 01326 377633
Open all year
As well as sailing courses, this school runs open days, half-term activity days and pirate adventures aboard pirate ships. Family holidays are on offer for those aged seven and up; individual tuition and Sunday-morning sessions for those who can already sail is also an option.

EAT AND DRINK

The Pandora Inn

pandorainn.com

Restronguet Creek, TR11 5ST

01326 372678

This award-winning 13th-century inn has Cornish Rattler ciders and St Austell Brewery ales on tap and a colourful history (see opposite). Today, despite a scorching in a fire in 2011, the thatched roof, low-beamed ceilings and flagstone floors, along with the wood-pegged green oak beams of the dining room retain their character. Food is served all day, from coffee and cake to local fish and home-smoked chicken breast and mackerel.

▶ Nare Head MAP REF 275 E4

This stretch of south-coast Cornwall between the Roseland Peninsula and Dodman Point includes small villages, the parishes of Gerrans, Veryan and St Michael Caerhays, rocky and sandy beaches, and the 19th-century estate of Caerhays, known particularly for its magnolias. There aren't many sights as such, but it is wonderful walking territory, particularly around the coast path, and feels like a hidden part of Cornwall. The best way to get there is to use the A3078, then follow signs to Veryan, a village with remarkable round thatched cottages and a large, dark church.

The best beaches are at Pendower and Carne, where there is parking available and easy access to Nare Head. There are beaches all the way along the shores of Gerrans Bay and Veryan Bay, and there's also a beach at Porthluney Cove below Caerhays Castle.

Walks around Nare Head itself are highly recommended. On a good day you can see miles out to sea, and the headland includes a Bronze Age barrow, Carne Beacon, a World War II decoy bunker, an Iron Age earthwork, wooded valleys and views over to St Agnes Beacon.

For other attractions in the nearby area, see Roseland Peninsula, page 222.

TAKE IN SOME HISTORY

Caerhays Castle

caerhays.co.uk

Gorran, St Austell, PL26 6LY

01872 501310 | Gardens open mid-Feb to mid-Jun daily; castle open mid-Mar to mid-Jun Mon–Fri

This 19th-century Gothic castle, designed by famed Regency architect John Nash, and estate is famed for its magnolias and a visit in springtime when they are in bloom is highly recommended. Caerhays holds the largest collection in England and is one of four gardens in the National Magnolia Collection.

John Charles Williams created the gardens here in the

19th century and financially supported plant hunters to amass this beautiful collection. As well as creating this unrivalled collection of magnolias and shrubs, he specialised in the cultivation of daffodils, another good reason for a springtime visit.

There are four marked routes through the 120-acre estate, red, yellow, blue and green, and guided tours with the gardeners, lasting 1–2 hours, can also be booked. The red route takes in magnolias, rhododendrons and azaleas just to the west of the castle; the yellow route traces round the hill at the back of the castle, behind Mr Roger's Quarry, where you can admire the best variety of *Magnolia campbellii* at Caerhays, *mollicomata* 'Lanarth', which produces cyclamen-purple flowers; the blue route is a long circuit around the back of the castle and hills and the estate's two quarries; and the green route skirts around the outside of the estate from the main drive to the Japanese hydrangea planting, the fernery and the old cart road. There's a lot to see, including *Rhododendron arboreum* hybrids that are more than a century old, and an oak that was probably sent to Caerhays from Louisiana by the great plant collector Professor Charles Sprague Sargent.

The beautiful castle is open for guided tours on weekdays only mid-March to mid-June and is still inhabited by the

Williams family. Expect to see gilded frames holding oil paintings, a Georgian hall, and lavish furnishings and fixtures. Book in advance for tours and check the website's events listings if you're interested in gardening, as they run popular lectures in association with the Royal Horticultural Society in the spring, and various events and fairs.

EAT AND DRINK
The New Inn
newinn-veryan.co.uk
Veryan, TR2 5QA | 01872 501362
This unspoiled, part-thatched pub in Veryan has open fires, a beamed ceiling, a single bar serving St Austell ales and a warm, welcoming atmosphere. Sunday lunch is a speciality. On other days expect superior pub grub including local seafood, Sunday roasts and traditional puddings, plus Cornish craft beers. Vegetarian choices also.

The Quarterdeck at The Nare ◉◉
quarterdeckrestaurant.co.uk
Carne Beach, Veryan-in-Roseland, TR2 5PF | 01872 500000
The Quarterdeck is a yachtie-themed setting of polished teak, gingham seats and square rails with vast full-length windows offering sea views. The kitchen produces confident modern dishes including local Portloe crab and lobster and Fowey mussels and oysters on the lunch and dinner menus.

▼ Nare Head

▶ Newquay

MAP REF 275 E2

▲ Surfers at Watergate Bay

Chances are you've heard of Newquay. It's Cornwall's best-known tourist town, a place alive in the summer with parties, clubs, and teens and twentysomethings. It's also the UK's surf capital, where international surfers battle it out on Fistral Beach every year in the country's only top-rated surf championships. Run to the Sun takes place here every May, a festival of music, mods and VWs. Teenagers camp and celebrate or commiserate after their exam results come in; packs of stag nighters roam the streets, hen nighters drink cocktails and shots in beach bars, and families build sandcastles on the beach and play ankle-deep in the sea. There's a lot to this town – you couldn't ever write it off as boring.

The beach is the big draw no matter who you are – mod or tot, surfer or drinker. Fistral is the best-known beach, a surf beach where in the summer months the water is packed with the yellow and blue foam boards of learners and the waves are

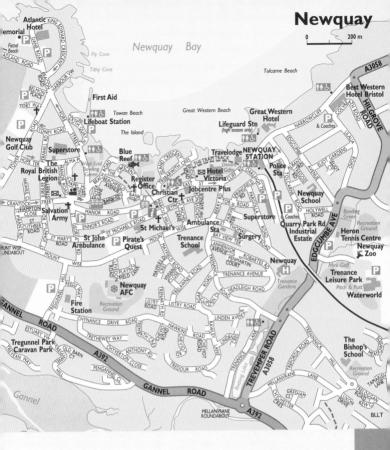

Newquay

0   200 m

nearly always lacklustre. A word of warning: if you want to
learn to surf, there are less crowded spots, and the local
residential surf schools will probably take you there, rather
than Fistral Beach, so you have a fair shot at riding a wave
rather than running over other learners. As well as Fistral
Beach, there are four other beaches walkable from the town
centre, and the watersports centre at Watergate Bay just up the
coast is a good bet for activities.

Despite Newquay's reputation as a party town, it's also a
good place for a family holiday, with the aforementioned
beaches plus attractions such as a zoo, an aquarium and a
swimming pool. Check that you're not staying in a party hotspot
before you book your accommodation, though: some campsites
have banned large single-sex groups for this reason, because
they want family visitors.

Near to the town you'll find the Elizabethan manor house
Trerice, a National Trust property, while up the coast there's
Rick Stein's empire at Padstow.

◀ Towan beach island bridge

ENTERTAIN THE FAMILY

Newquay Zoo,
Trenance Gardens

newquayzoo.org.uk

Newquay, TR7 2LZ

01637 873342 | Open daily all
year 10–5

Set within exotic lakeside
gardens and with more than
130 species, Newquay Zoo is
one of Cornwall's most popular
attractions. The Madagascar
Walkthrough features crowned
lemurs, vasa parrots, striped
mongoose and more. Animal
feeds and informative talks run
throughout the day. Children
can also enjoy the Tarzan Trail
and Dragon Maze. Other
highlights include the Tropical
House, Oriental Garden,
Penguin Pool, Village Farm and
lots more.

Pirate's Quest

piratesquest.co.uk

22 St Michael's Road, Newquay,
TR7 1RA | 01637 873379

Open Apr–Oct daily 10.30–3

It's not a swashbuckling holiday
in Cornwall without a glimpse
of some real live pirates, me
hearties, so get ye down to
Pirate's Quest to meet 'em.
Visitors join an hour-long tour
led by a 'pirate crew' and
negotiate their way past
thrilling locations such as Ne'er
Do Well's Passage, the Wreck of
the Royal Anne and the Lost
Land of Lyonesse. Children can
follow a treasure map to reveal
a secret code and claim their
own pirate booty.

MEET THE SEALIFE

Blue Reef Aquarium

bluereefaquarium.co.uk

Towan Promenade, Newquay,
TR7 1DU | 01637 878134

Open daily all year 10–6

Discover Cornish marine life
from native sharks and rays to
the intelligent and playful
octopus in this large aquarium.
From here, journey through
warmer waters to watch the
magical seahorses, unusual
shape-shifting, jet-propelled
cuttlefish and the vibrant,
swaying tentacles of sponges
and anemones. The safari
continues through the
underwater tunnel below a
tropical sea. Daily talks and
regular feeding demonstrations
bring the experience to life.
Check the website for special
events. The aquarium is right
next to Towan beach.

HIT THE BEACH

There are plenty of beaches to
choose from in the Newquay
and Watergate Bay area – good
to know when it's busy in high
season. Dogs are banned from
Easter to September and
lifeguards patrol in peak
season. See also St Agnes
for other nearby sandy spots
(see page 224).

Fistral Beach

For more information on events,
visit fistralbeach.co.uk

This large sandy beach is
Newquay's best-known beach,
the site of the annual

▶ Beach from cliff, Whipsiddery

Boardmasters international surf contest and festival and the host space for a number of big family events in the summer months. It's a world-class surf beach and there are surf hire companies and a BSA-registered surf school just off the beach, next to beach bars and shops. Lifeguards patrol in peak season. Little Fistral, a cove at the north end of the beach, is only accessible at low tide and has no lifeguard cover.

Great Western Beach

One of the four beaches accessible on foot from the town centre, Great Western is a sandy beach with rock pools and caves to explore at low tide, when it combines with Lusty Glaze, Towan and Tolcarne Beaches to become a mile-long stretch of sand. Access is via a steep cliff path at high tide, or via the other beaches at low tide. It's a popular family and surf beach, with cafes, surf hire and surf tuition, and a lifeguard from May to September. The nearest car park is in town.

Lusty Glaze

For full event details, see lustyglaze.co.uk

This horseshoe-shaped beach, backed by cliffs, has a restaurant and bar, regular events and Sundowner Sessions in summer, a programme of free evening gigs on the beach. The name derives from the Cornish for 'a place to view blue boats' – but there's not much

fishing going on these days. There's a surf school and the Adventure Centre, which offers children's activities, abseiling, a 750-foot zip wire and jet-ski adventures. There are lifeguards on the beach in peak season and the beach is home to the National Lifeguard Training Centre. It's a decent family and surf beach.

Porth Beach

This large, sandy beach is safe for swimming and is sheltered at its mouth by Porth Island, which can be walked round at low tide. At mid-tide on a windy day there's a blowhole just at the end of the island for added drama. It's narrow, family friendly and easily accessed, with a pub on the beach and cafes across the road. Surfing is banned here in the summer season.

Tolcarne Beach

Tolcarne is the largest of Newquay's beaches, a stretch of sand between Great Western and Lusty Glaze surrounded on three sides by cliffs. Access is via the steep steps in the cliffs or at low tide from Newquay's other beaches. There is no car park nearby. The beach has all the usual facilities, including a surf school and surf hire, and it's safe for swimmers. There are rock pools at low tide, caves in the cliffs, and the Tolcarne Wedge, a punchy high-tide wave that attracts the UK's top bodyboarders.

Towan Beach

The westernmost of Newquay's beaches, Towan is the closest one to the town centre. It is notable mostly for its private island, connected by a bridge to the mainland, which has a luxurious holiday home that is available to rent. The beach is sandy and safe for swimmers. Parking is in the town and there are plenty of cafes and beach shops nearby. The Blue Reef Aquarium is right by the beach.

Watergate Bay

extremeacademy.co.uk
Extreme Academy, Watergate Bay, TR8 4AA | 01637 860840
Open daily all year 9–5
This large, west-facing beach is home to the Extreme Academy and is a great place to go if you want to learn to surf or kite surf, wave ski or stand-up paddleboard, depending on the weather. Last-minute lessons are usually available. It can be breezy. There's a lifeguard here in season and a great beach cafe, The Beach Hut. Jamie Oliver's restaurant (see page 186) and the Watergate Bay Hotel are just beyond the beach.

GO ON A BOAT TRIP

Newquay Harbour Boatmen's Association
newquay-harbour.com
South Quay, The Harbour, TR7 1HR | 01637 876352
Open May–Sep daily 10–6, weather and tides permitting

10 top surf beaches

▶ Watergate Bay, see left
▶ Fistral Beach, page 180
▶ Constantine Bay, page 194
▶ Gwenver Beach, page 257
▶ Polzeath Beach, page 211
▶ Harlyn Bay, page 194
▶ Widemouth Bay, page 75
▶ Porthmeor Beach, page 239
▶ Gwithian Beach, page 109
▶ Lusty Glaze, see opposite

A variety of boat trips are on offer, including speedboat hire, pleasure cruises and deep-sea angling trips. Mackerel fishing trips involve trolling a few lines and taking the catch home. The seals are often in the harbour, and you'll see beautiful craggy cliffs and headlands, Newquay from the sea and perhaps a dolphin. Call in advance.

EXPLORE BY BIKE

Cycle Revolution
7 Beach Road, TR7 1ES
01637 872364
There are some lovely routes along the golf course and the cliffs and around Newquay, which is on National Cycle Route 32 running from Land's End to Bodmin (see sustrans.org.uk). The Camel Trail is also within reach of the town. Cycle Revolution hires out bikes from a base near Crantock, just outside the town centre.

▶ Lusty Glaze beach, Newquay (overleaf)

GO FISHING
Porth Reservoir
swlakestrust.org.uk
near Newquay
01209 860301

For coarse fishing, Porth Reservoir near Newquay is a good bet. As well as being a coarse fishery, it's also a bird reserve with specialist hides. The reservoir is stocked with carp and has some large fish, with 32lb carp, 24lb pike and 10lb bream being caught. Call for details on permits.

GO SWIMMING
Waterworld
tempusleisure.org.uk
Trenance Leisure Park,
TR7 2LZ | 01637 853828
Open daily all year; check website for exact hours

Good to know about for a rainy day with children, Waterworld is a large swimming pool with a six-lane 80-foot pool and a tropical fun pool with two waterslides, a waterplay hut, an erupting volcano and a snake fountain. There's also a gym and exercise classes.

PLAY A ROUND
Newquay Golf Club
newquaygolfclub.co.uk
Tower Road, TR7 1LT
01637 874354 | Open daily all year

One of Cornwall's finest seaside links courses with magnificent views over Fistral Beach and the Atlantic Ocean. Open to the unpredictable nature of the elements and possessing some very demanding greenside bunkers, the prerequisite for good scoring at Newquay is accuracy.

EAT AND DRINK
Fifteen Cornwall ⊛
fifteencornwall.co.uk
On The Beach, Watergate Bay,
TR8 4AA | 01637 861000

This beachside outpost of Jamie Oliver's London and Amsterdam restaurants opened in 2006. Apart from serving good food, the ethos of Fifteen is to give unemployed young people, some of whom have difficult backgrounds, a solid grounding in kitchen skills and experience. The venue of Fifteen is in a large, contemporary space whose floor-to-ceiling windows serve up a glorious Watergate sea view. Italian-Cornish fusion results in the likes of the imaginative brill and monkfish dishes, while there are also some tasting and sharing menus available.

Lewinnick Lodge
hospitalitycornwall.com
Pentire Headland,
TR7 1QD | 01637 878117

Lewinnick Lodge perches on the cliff top of the Pentire Headland, enjoying a timeless panorama of sea views. This is a destination eatery, but real ales, local cider, crisp wines and premium lagers are also all on offer in the bar. Wraps, baps and gourmet burgers can be ordered, but fresh seafood, much of it from Cornish waters, is the menu's key attraction. Meats from the county include slow-roasted lamb and beef.

Trenance Cottage Tea Rooms and Gardens

trenancecottagesnewquay.co.uk
Trenance Lane,
TR7 2HX | 01637 872034

The perfect way to escape the bustling beach is at this award-winning Georgian tea room. You can lunch on the tasty fresh local crab, home-baked pasties and ploughman's lunches, which include local cheese, or simply peruse the extensive tea list, which offers a brew that matches your meal or one of the tea room's delicious homemade cakes.

▶ **PLACES NEARBY**

Newquay is surrounded by tourist attractions as well as beautiful beaches, a steam railway and the Elizabethan estate of Trerice.

DairyLand Farm World

dairylandfarmworld.com
Summercourt, near Newquay,
TR8 5AA | 01872 510246
Open late Mar–Oct daily 10–5;
check for other opening times

Visitors can watch while the cows are milked to music on a spectacular merry-go-round milking machine. The life of a Victorian farmer and his neighbours is explored in the Heritage Centre, and a Farm Nature Trail has informative displays along pleasant walks. Children will have great fun getting to know the farm animals in the Farm Park. They will also enjoy the playground, assault course and indoor play areas.

Holywell Bay

Six miles west of Newquay, this mile of sandy beach with dunes is popular with families and surfers, and is usually less packed and more friendly than those in the town. There are streams and rock pools at low tide; dogs are welcome and it's safe for swimmers. The twin rocks offshore are called Gull Rocks or Carter's Rocks. There's said to be a holy well in one of the caves at the northern end of the beach, which is only accessible at low tide; it certainly has an unusual rock formation inside it. There are facilities nearby and a car park.

Holywell Bay Fun Park

holywellbayfunpark.co.uk
Holywell, TR8 5PW
01637 830095 | Open Easter
holidays, mid-May to mid-Sep daily
from 10.30am, mid-Apr to
mid-May, mid-Sep to mid-Oct
weekends only; enquire for other
opening times

This is a family fun park with rides, water attractions, pitch-and-putt, trampolines and plenty more rides, all paid for individually. There is free car parking and free entry. Check the website for full opening hours – it's open late in July and August, and at various times depending on the season.

Holywell Bay Golf Park

holywellgolf.co.uk

TR8 5PW | 01637 832916

Open daily all year

Situated beside the family fun park, this is an 18-hole short course with great sea views. Fresh Atlantic winds make the course hard to play and there are several tricky holes, particularly the 18th over the trout pond. The site also has an excellent 18-hole pitch-and-putt course for the whole family to enjoy.

Lappa Valley Steam Railway

lappavalley.co.uk

St Newlyn East, near Newquay

01872 510317 | Open late Mar–Oct Sun–Fri 10–5.15

This little Lappa Valley attraction has three miniature railways in its grounds plus a steam railway running on a track dating from 1849. More for families than for serious rail enthusiasts, there's also a boating lake, crazy golf, pedal cars and play areas. There are two stations; Benny Halt is where the ticket office and car park are. All other activities are at East Wheal Rose. There are special events held all year, including Santa Specials at Christmas.

The Smugglers' Den Inn

Trebellan, Cubert, near Newquay, TR8 5PY | 01637 830209

This thatched 16th-century pub, which is just 15 minutes from Newquay, is popular with locals and visitors alike, with a long bar, family room, children's play area, courtyards and huge beer garden. Local ingredients are the cornerstone of the family-friendly menu, which features staples such as homemade fish pie, chicken curry and wild mushroom Strogonoff.

Trerice

nationaltrust.org.uk

Kestle Mill, near Newquay, TR8 4PG | 01637 875404

Open mid-Feb to Oct daily 10.30–5, Nov–20 Dec Sat–Sun 11–4

This glorious Elizabethan manor, surrounded by Tudor gardens, was Winston Graham's inspiration for Trenwith, Poldark's family home, and is a lovely place to visit. The architecture dates from the 1570s, and the plaster ceilings of the Great Hall and Great Chamber are a particular delight. Outside, you can try your hand at the Cornish form of bowls, with games known as kayling or slapcock, and wander through an orchard of Cornish apple trees. There are regular events held here such as Tudor banquets – see the website for full details – and the National Trust has put in a lot of work to make this place come alive, with Tudor music drifting out into the gardens, and old-fashioned purple carrots and salad leaves planted in the cottage garden. The Elizabethan knot garden is composed of 800 young yew trees, which are interspersed with white roses, lavender and oregano.

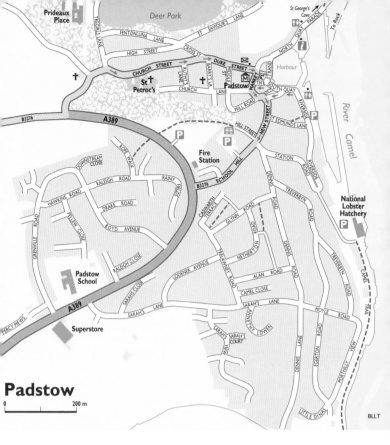

▶ Padstow MAP REF 276 B4

On the Camel estuary north of Newquay, Padstow has acquired
the nickname 'Padstein' for its celebrity chef connection.
Mr Stein has not one but three restaurants in the small town,
plus a fish and chip shop, and he's been the driving force that
has made this working harbour an attractive prospect for
holiday visitors. It's a delightful place to visit, with art shops,
boutiques and cafes in the maze of narrow streets around the
harbour, and an easy place to spend a morning or afternoon
and a lot of money, if you're keen to shop.

Shoppers and foodies should note, though, that Padstow has
a lot more to it than sublime fish and seaside knick-knacks
– it's been a significant town in Cornwall for a long, long time.
Padstow was a busy trading port from the earliest times, and
Welsh and Irish saints of the Dark Ages landed here. St Petroc
arrived from Wales in the sixth century and stayed for 30 years,
founding a monastery which thrived until 981 AD when it was
destroyed by marauding Vikings.

The town has a couple of interesting local traditions,
including Obby Oss, a festival on May Day, and Mummers' Day,

a celebration on Boxing Day that can be traced back to an ancient midwinter party.

Along with boat trips and the National Lobster Hatchery, the town has three significant walking trails. The Saints Way, Forth an Syns in Cornish, is a 28-mile route from Padstow to Fowey. It can be walked in 2 days and is best started at the Church of St Petroc, Padstow. The first part of the walk to Little Petherick, 2 miles south of Padstow, is worth doing for its own sake. The Camel Trail runs along a disused train line from Padstow to Wadebridge (see page 268) and can be cycled or walked, and the South West Coast Path winds along the cliffs here with lovely views of the estuary and its mussel and oyster farms.

TAKE IN SOME HISTORY
Prideaux Place
prideauxplace.co.uk
PL28 8RP | 01841 532411
House open Easter Sun–early Oct Sun–Thu 1.30–4; grounds and tea room 12.30–5. Also open through the year by appointment.
This Elizabethan house and its 40 acres of landscaped gardens overlook Padstow and date from 1592. The house is still occupied by the Prideaux family, which can trace its ancestry back to William the Conqueror. Overlooking a deer park, this splendid house contains a wealth of family and royal portraits, a fine porcelain collection, a growing teddy bear collection and a magnificent 16th-century plaster ceiling in the Great Chamber, which has some marvellous views across countryside to Bodmin Moor. There's plenty of opportunity for walking in both formal gardens and woodland, and there is also a peaceful tea room. The house has been featured in many film and TV productions, including Trevor Nunn's *Twelfth Night*.

Of the house's 81 rooms, 46 are bedrooms and only six of those are habitable; the remaining rooms are as US army personnel, who were billeted there, left them after World War II.

MEET THE LOBSTERS
National Lobster Hatchery
nationallobsterhatchery.co.uk
Padstow, PL28 8BL | 01841 533877
Open Apr to mid-Jul, mid-Sep to Nov daily 10–5, mid-Jul to mid-Sep 10–7.30, Nov–Mar 10–4
This pioneering marine research facility is on the quay by the car park and provides an interesting insight into the country's vulnerable lobster populations and the situation facing them in the sea. Its main aim is to preserve the species and conserve vulnerable populations, and it focuses a lot of attention on the issue of biodiversity and sustainable fishing. The visitor centre is an interesting way to learn more about the issue, get up close and personal with lobsters and local sealife in the mini

aquarium, and find out why you should be picky about where you buy your fish and chips.

HIT THE BEACH

Padstow's beaches are at the north of the town and accessed by the South West Coast Path. The walk takes about 10 minutes to St George's Cove, and on to Harbour Cove and Hawker's Cove. You can also walk to the headland and Stepper Point (the sleeping dragon) with views across to Rock. There is a ferry running to Rock (see page 221) at high tide and a lovely beach there too. The beaches are all sandy with rock pools at high tide and some strong currents. Dogs are banned Easter to September.

EXPLORE BY BIKE
Padstow Cycle Hire
padstowcyclehire.com
South Quay, PL28 8BL
01841 533533 | Open daily all year 9–5
Cycle along the coast, around the town or along the Camel Trail, which runs from Padstow to Wadebridge. Padstow Cycle Hire rents men's, women's and children's bikes, trailers, tandems, baby bike seats and tagalong bikes, and runs evening cycle rides in the summer. Part-day hires, after 3pm, are also possible.

TAKE A BOAT TRIP
Padstow Sealife Safaris
padstowsealifesafaris.co.uk
North Quay, PL28 8AF
07754 822404

Padstow Sealife Safaris runs nature-focused boat trips from the harbour, taking visitors out to see seals, dolphins, basking sharks, puffins and much more. Various trips include a 1-hour voyage to Seal Cave, a 1-hour powerboat tour of the coast and 2-hour sea safaris exploring the coastline, history and wildlife of the local area.

LEARN TO COOK
Padstow Seafood School
rickstein.com
Riverside, PL28 8BY
01841 532700 | Check website for course calendar; book in advance
Where better than Padstow to get a handle on how to cook fish, with a view of the working harbour out of the window? Half-, one- and two-day courses are available on a variety of topics, including classic seafood dishes, cooking from India, Italian seafood cookery and Spanish tapas. Advance booking is essential.

GO SEA FISHING
Emma Kate II
emmakate2.com
North Quay, PL28 8AF
01841 532762
Padstow is a working harbour and in the summer months sea fishing trips can be booked to catch mackerel and more. *Emma Kate II* is one of the regular boats offering fishing trips all year, including wreck, reef and all-day trips, 2-hour mackerel and 4-hour bass fishing trips. Enquire along the quay for other trips.

EAT AND DRINK
The Metropole 🌸🌸
the-metropole.co.uk
Station Road,
PL28 8DB | 01841 532486
This Victorian hotel has commanding views over the Padstow and Camel estuary, and where better to enjoy them but over a meal in the Harbour Restaurant, with large windows and high-backed upholstered dining chairs at clothed tables on the carpeted floor. The kitchen is driven by local supplies – fish landed in the nearby harbour, for instance – and serves them in a contemporary style.

Paul Ainsworth at No. 6 🌸🌸🌸🌸
number6inpadstow.co.uk
6 Middle Street,
PL28 8AP | 01841 532093
There's more than one celebrity chef in this town: Paul Ainsworth has wowed telly audiences on *Great British Menu* and continues to draw crowds to his Georgian townhouse restaurant, just back from the harbour. Think modern Cornish with classic integrity from Michelin-starred Ainsworth. There are two other Ainsworth establishments in Padstow: Rojanos and the Padstow Townhouse.

Rick Stein's Cafe
rickstein.com
10 Middle Street, PL28 8AP
01841 532700
The most relaxed of Rick Stein's restaurants is a casual

▲ Padstow

cafe with rooms decked out in a nautical theme. It's open all day, so call in for breakfast or an excellent cappuccino and peruse the papers, or arrive early for deliciously simple lunches and dinners – for example, fragrant cod curry from Southern India, prawns with chicken broth, feta tart or deep-fried seabass.

St Petroc's Bistro 🌀
rickstein.com
4 New Street, PL28 8EA
01841 532700

The bistro is an informal and relaxing sort of place, with simple tables and chairs on worn wooden floorboards, modern paintings on plain white walls, and professional service from attentive staff. There's a cosy bar and a pleasant lounge for pre-dinner drinks and a courtyard and garden for alfresco meals. With Rick Stein at the helm, it comes as no surprise that seafood is the main business with moules marinière and oysters among the starters, plus mains of devilled mackerel, hake and sea bream – although steaks from the grill are a feature too.

The Seafood Restaurant
@@@
rickstein.com
Riverside, PL28 8BY
01841 532700

This is where the Stein empire began – a large, always busy restaurant with a central seafood bar. Fish is the thing, of course – seafood Dieppoise, or red mullet stuffed with crabmeat and basil, and the finest of local shellfish. There are Asian, Spanish, Indonesian and Japanese influences in many of the dishes. Booking is not required at the bar.

▶ PLACES NEARBY

There are some lovely beaches near Padstow, along with a golf course by Constantine Bay and a pub run by Rick Stein in St Merryn. Rock (see page 221) is just across the water.

Constantine Bay

This long sandy beach, which is located just north of Padstow, is very popular with surfers and families alike, with a food wagon on the sands on its approach, lifeguards in peak season and dogs allowed all year. At low tide rock pools are exposed and a little pool forms in the middle of the beach, thanks to a sandbank. Parking is difficult close to the beach – parking at Treyarnon Bay and walking 10 minutes along the coast path is an option. There are toilets by the small car park and there's a little shop in Constantine village a short walk away.

The Cornish Arms
rickstein.com
Churchtown, St Merryn,
near Padstow, PL28 8ND
01841 532700

St Merryn, just outside Padstow, is home to this pub, part of the Stein portfolio. Across the road from the parish church, the pub has remained very much the village local. The pub oozes character, with slate floors, beams and roaring log fires. There are traditional pub classics like ham, egg and chips on the menu but you can still find treats such as Meen kulambu, a fragrant cod curry from Southern India, or devilled mackerel or the ever-popular moules marinière.

Harlyn Bay

This sheltered, sandy beach with dunes is considered one of Cornwall's best beaches for families. It's a safe beach for learner surfers and swimmers alike, and popular with sea kayakers too. Lifeguards patrol in the summer. There are surf schools on the beach and it's a short walk to Harlyn village. Dogs are allowed all year and there's a car park just by the beach.

Treglos Hotel @@
tregloshotel.com
Constantine Bay,
PL28 8JH | 01841 520727

An upmarket, family-run hotel overlooking Constantine Bay near Padstow, the Treglos is a late Victorian house converted into a hotel in the 1930s. The dining room is done in maroon and leafy green, with discreet artworks and ceramics here and there, and the menus offer traditional English cuisine served up with a modern approach, with specials built around a solid repertoire.

Trevose Golf Club

trevose-gc.co.uk
Constantine Bay, near Padstow,
PL28 8JB | 01841 520208
Open all year

Trevose Golf Club has its early holes close to the sea on excellent springy turf. It is a championship course and a good test, with well-positioned bunkers and a meandering stream. It can be windy. There are self-catering lodges and a restaurant.

Trevone Bay

Two miles from Padstow, Trevone Bay is another sandy beach popular with families and surfers. Dogs aren't permitted Easter to September. There are lifeguards through the summer season and the sea is safe for swimmers. Scramble over the rocks and you'll find another rocky beach here, great for rock pooling and with a natural swimming pool that appears at low tide. In the summer, the beach and the village beside it often hold events. There's a car park by the beach and it's just a short walk from the beach to the village tea shops and pub.

Treyarnon Bay

Another great sandy family beach with rock pools, Treyarnon is 11 miles north of Newquay and has a car park, a beach shop and lifeguards in summer. There can be strong undercurrents and large waves. It's a popular surfing spot for intermediate surfers. At low tide, a large rock pool great for paddling is exposed.

▶ Pendeen MAP REF 274 A4

This straggling line of small communities on the north coast of the Land's End peninsula all link to the former tin and copper mines of the area. The smaller villages of Carnyorth, Trewellard, Boscaswell and Bojewyan make up the roll call of this, the last of Cornwall's coastal mining communities. It's a startlingly dramatic place to visit, where the fractured mining landscape meets the raw beauty of the Atlantic coast.

Pendeen's Geevor Mine stopped operating in 1990 in the face of international market pressure, but was previously the mainstay of the larger area. It can be visited today, transformed into an informative heritage centre with mine workings, a museum and a fascinating underground tour.

Just south of Geevor at Levant, the power of steam is harnessed to a restored working beam engine at Levant Mine, looked after by the National Trust.

GET INDUSTRIAL
Geevor Tin Mine
See highlight panel opposite

▸ **PLACES NEARBY**

As befits the former tin mining area, there's more to see in nearby Trewellard and the moorland inland is lovely walking territory.

Levant Mine and Beam Engine
nationaltrust.org.uk
Levant Road, Trewellard,
TR19 7SX | 01736 786156
Open mid-Mar to Oct Sun–Fri
10.30–5, Nov to mid-Mar Fri
10.30–4; closed second half Dec
This unique steam-powered Cornish beam engine is the only one in the world still in steam on its original site. Perched in a stone-built engine house overlooking the cliffs, it's an evocative spot. For 110 years, Levant Mine was worked and stretched a mile out to sea at a depth of nearly 2,000 feet; a local team, known as 'the Greasy Gang', restored it after 60 years lying idle.

Morvah Schoolhouse
morvah.com
Morvah, TR20 8YT | 01736 787808
In the tiny hamlet of Morvah, with its historic church and cluster of old buildings, this cafe and gallery makes for an ideal coffee stop on the long and winding B3306 coast road.

Penwith Moors
Penwith Moors run parallel to the north coast of the Land's End peninsula through an undulating series of hills crowned with granite tors. They are noted for their ecological value and their concentration of Neolithic, Bronze Age and Iron Age remains, which include burial chambers, settlements, stone circles and standing stones. Most of the northern moors are at the heart of the Higher Level Stewardship Scheme area, within which farmers are compensated for working in sympathy with the traditional structure of the ancient landscape.

The high ground begins at Rosewall Hill just west of St Ives, and is continuous through the beautiful parishes of Zennor and Morvah. Smaller areas of moorland continue the westward-leading sequence to Chapel Carn Brea above the wide, flat coastal plateau of Land's End itself. The moorland is a splendid counterpoint to the outstanding coastline and is easily accessible from a number of points.

◂ Pendeen lighthouse

▶ **Geevor Tin Mine** MAP REF 274 A4

geevor.com
TR19 7EW | 01736 788662
Open Apr–Oct Sun–Fri 9–5, Nov–Mar Sun–Fri 9–4

This preserved tin mine and museum provides an insight into the methods and equipment used in the industry that was once so important in the area. The Geevor Tin Mine only actually stopped operation in 1990 and was closed completely a year later. Guided tours let visitors see the tin treatment plant, and a video illustrates the techniques employed. There is also a museum of hard rock mining, and the underground tour is well worth the trip.

▶ **Penzance**   MAP REF 274 B5

This grand seaside town, the capital of West Cornwall, is all
sunshine and stunning sunrises over Mount's Bay and St
Michael's Mount. The old town has beautiful Georgian and
Regency buildings, there's a 19th-century seaside promenade
and the jewel in its crown, a 1930s lido, recently refurbished.
The water may occasionally be a bit chilly, but you can warm up
afterwards in one of the town's characterful pubs, which are
welcoming and have Cornish ales and ciders on tap. Penzance
is a lively spot that saw its heyday in the 19th century as a
popular holiday spot. Gilbert and Sullivan's operetta *The Pirates
of Penzance* was a little dig at the holiday scene here, rather
than a reference to a historical smuggling past.

Today it's a great place to visit, particularly if you're into
art, as the town has long had associations with artists and the
arts. Three top quality art galleries to visit are the Exchange,
Penlee House and Newlyn Art Gallery; there are also many arts
and craft shops, especially in the attractive Chapel Street.
If you are more interested in modern and contemporary art
than that of the Newlyn School, be sure to visit Tremenheere
nearby, which has a distinctly different feel to the county's
historic garden estates, and is peppered with experiential
art and sculptures.

Penzance is not the most handsome town in Cornwall – the
modern additions to the town's architecture are bland and
characterless – but it is a living town rather than a tourist
attraction, and has a distinct character and spirit. It has a
hugely popular literary festival in early July and a colourful
summer festival called Golowan that lasts for eight days in
late June, and involves numerous cultural events and
entertainment, culminating in Mazey Day when the streets of
Penzance are closed to traffic and the main street, Market Jew
Street, is lined with stalls. Other unique-to-Penzance
experiences include Allantide, a Cornish celebration of
Hallowe'en where children are given a large red apple, and the
Montol Festival in December, where traditional Cornish
customs, including guise dancing – in which masked
participants dress up in often outlandish costumes – and a
lantern procession, take place. Both are believed to date from
pre-Christian times.

Penzance gets its name from the Cornish for 'Holy
headland', referencing a chapel called St Anthony's that is said
to have stood for more than 1,000 years on the headland where
Penzance harbour is now.

Penzance's main street, Market Jew Street, holds all kinds
of shops, including several pasty shops offering a variety of

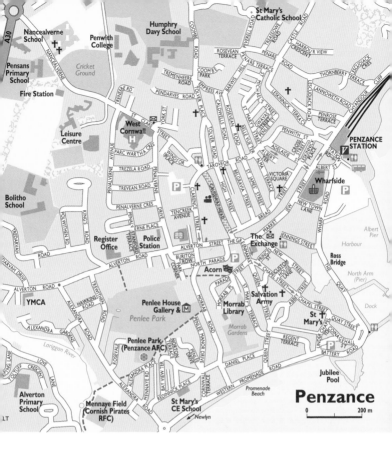

flavours. Towards the sea are Morrab Gardens and Penlee Park; the former is a lovely ornamental garden, the latter houses Penlee House Gallery and Museum.

To the west, Penzance merges with Newlyn, the major fishing port in the southwest of the county. Scores of fishing boats of all types and sizes work from here in spite of the increasing difficulties of the modern international industry. The large fish market bustles with activity in the early morning. Parking at Newlyn is difficult, and a walk along Penzance's spacious promenade and on along the seafront to Newlyn is a pleasant alternative, which can be combined with a visit to the Newlyn Art Gallery along the way. Newlyn now boasts a custom built cinema, the Newlyn Filmhouse.

Just outside Penzance is the National Trust's Trengwainton Garden, a complex of five walled gardens set amid mature woodland, at its best during the spring and early summer months. Trengwainton Garden can be reached via Heamoor, or from Tremethick Cross on the St Just road.

Another sight to visit a few miles out of town to the north is Chysauster Ancient Village, the remains of an Iron Age settlement from almost 2,000 years ago with a mysterious tunnel or 'fougou'.

A ferry goes to the Isles of Scilly from Penzance harbour, offering day trips and longer. The harbour is also the place for sea safaris and sea fishing trips, which could result in a mackerel or two for tea; they taste great on a barbecue with a little lemon squeezed over them. For walkers and cyclists, there are some lovely routes nearby, including the South West Coast Path and the First and Last Trail, linking Penzance with Land's End.

If you're looking for a beach, Long Rock Beach is a broad, sandy beach safe for swimming and good for families, leading around Mount's Bay to Marazion. Sennen, 9 miles across the peninsula, near Land's End, is your best bet for surfing (see page 256).

TAKE IN SOME HISTORY
Trereife
trereifepark.co.uk
Trereife, TR20 8TJ
01736 362750 | Open Jun–Oct Tue, Thu, Sun 11–4; house by guided tour only at 12 and 2
This Queen Anne manor house, some of which dates from the Elizabethan age, is in a stunning location near Penzance. It's open year round for bed and breakfast – unusual for an estate of this style – and is open to day visitors during the summer months only. There are modern parterre gardens, laid in 1999 and planned to suit the Queen Anne front of the house; there's also a ha-ha and parkland beyond it. In the house, a key feature are plasterwork ceilings created by Italian workers in the early 1700s.

As well as an estate to explore, the Stableyard Cafe has a menu including Cornish crab and pilchards. Check the website for events and fairs which take place at Trereife all year, including an Easter fair, a food, craft and beer festival at the end of May, the Cornwall Design Fair in August and a Christmas gift fair in November.

VISIT THE MUSEUMS AND GALLERIES
Newlyn Art Gallery and the Exchange
newlynartgallery.co.uk
New Road, Newlyn, TR18 5PZ
01736 363715 | Open summer Mon–Sat 10–5, public holidays 11–4, winter Tue–Sat 10–5
These contemporary art galleries, housed in two striking buildings (the Exchange, a former telephone exchange, is on Princes Street, Penzance; Newlyn Art Gallery is at the entrance to Newlyn) show some of the finest modern art in Cornwall. The focus is on paintings and drawing, with some events, performances and film screenings at the Exchange. Newlyn Art Gallery's Studio Cafe has a fantastic view

of the sea and both venues have great shops showcasing books, art, and the best local crafts and ceramics.

Penlee House Gallery and Museum

penleehouse.org.uk

Morrab Road, TR18 4HE

01736 363625 | Open Easter–Sep Mon–Sat 10–5, Oct–Easter Mon–Sat 10.30–4.30

This museum and gallery in a grand Victorian house specialises in the works of the Newlyn School artists, painting approximately 1880–1940, and west Cornwall's archaeology and social history. The park includes sub-tropical gardens, a sensory garden, an open-air theatre and a children's play area. Follow an enlightening gallery tour with lunch or afternoon tea in the Orangery Cafe. Cakes and pastries are freshly baked, while lunches include crab sandwiches, quiche and fish pie.

GO ROUND THE GARDENS
Morrab Gardens

TR18 4DA

Open daily 9–dusk

Penzance's Morrab Gardens is a delightful haven of green lawns, ponds and winding pathways within a network of flowerbeds and shrub borders and with plenty of benches on which to sit and take it all in. At its heart is an elegant Edwardian bandstand where musical performances are sometimes staged on summer evenings. There are many sub-tropical plants here, including a variety of Penzance's famous palm trees as well as myrtles, aloes, camellias and geraniums. There are magnolia trees that are over 100 years old.

Tremenheere Sculpture Garden

tremenheere.co.uk

Gulval, near Penzance, TR20 8YL | 01736 448089

Open Easter–Sep daily 10–5, Oct Sun–Wed 10–4, Thu–Sat 10–5, Nov–Dec, mid-Feb to Easter Fri–Sun 10–4; closed Jan to mid-Feb

So much more than a sub-tropical garden – though that's interesting and exciting enough – Tremenheere opened in 2012 as a sculpture garden with woodlands, streams and views of the coast offsetting contemporary art, experiential art and installations. There is also a covered gallery that stages exhibitions. With a monthly market, a singing group, a cafe and views of St Michael's Mount through the trees, it's a very special place. Installations are atmospheric and magical. There's an adventure map for children and well-behaved dogs are welcome.

Trewidden Garden

trewiddengarden.co.uk

Buryas Bridge, TR20 8TT

01736 363021 | Open mid-Feb–mid-Sep daily 10.30–5.30

Trewidden Garden, one of the Great Gardens of Cornwall, is a 15-acre, 19th-century garden

▲ Chysauster Ancient Village

with one of the largest tree fern dells in Europe and an impressive camellia and magnolia collection. The owners have designed a trail for children and have a cafe and plant shop on site. Head gardener Richard Morton takes free guided tours on Thursdays February to April– ring to book a place in advance. At other times, garden tours can be booked but cost extra. Dogs are welcome.

CATCH A PERFORMANCE
The Acorn
theacornpenzance.com
The Acorn, Parade Street,
TR18 4BU | 01736 363545
Box office open Thu–Fri 11–2
The Acorn is housed in an old Wesleyan chapel and has been Penzance's main performing arts venue for many years. It stages a whole range of events, including theatre, live music, poetry and drama readings, story-telling, dance, filmand lectures. The venue also hosts Penzance's annual Literary Festival (see page 50). There is a bar for refreshments. You can also buy tickets from the box office or various other venues – see the website for details.

GO BACK IN TIME
Chysauster Ancient Village
english-heritage.org.uk
Newmill, TR20 8XA
07831 757934 | Open Apr–Jun, Sep daily 10–5, Jul–Aug 10–6; Oct 10–4
Chysauster Ancient Village is what remains of an Iron Age

settlement occupied almost 2,000 years ago. The village consisted of stone-walled homes known as 'courtyard houses', found only on the Land's End peninsula and the Isles of Scilly. The houses lined a 'village street', and each had an open central courtyard surrounded by a number of thatched rooms. The site also has the remains of a fogou, an underground passage of uncertain purpose.

MEET THE SEALIFE
Marine Discovery
marinediscovery.co.uk
Shed 5, Albert Pier,
TR18 2LL | 07749 277110
Sailings Mar–Oct, weather permitting

Penzance is a great place to take safari trips to watch seals, seabirds, sharks and dolphins out on the open sea. Marine Discovery runs catamaran sailing trips along the southwest coast, from 1.5 to 4 hours long. Some voyages are suitable for children aged three and up; others only take over-sixes or over-12s. The best time to see whales – minke whales are the most common ones to be spotted – is at the end of the summer and start of autumn; basking sharks are most commonly seen around late May and June.

HIT THE BEACH
Long Rock Beach is a large swathe of golden sand and shingle stretching as far as Marazion at low tide. It's an easy beach to reach from Penzance and is very safe for swimmers, particularly children, as it takes a lot of walking through the shallow, gently deepening water to get waist deep for a swim. There are lifeguards in season.

EXPLORE BY BIKE
Cycle Centre
cornwallcyclecentre.co.uk
1 New Street, TR18 2LZ
01736 351671

There are plenty of great scenic bike rides around Penzance, including to Marazion along Mount's Bay, with a view of St Michael's Mount all the way. It's part of the First and Last Trail that runs from Land's End and links Penzance with Mousehole in the opposite direction.

Penzance Bike Hire Torwood
Alexandra Road, Penzance,
TR18 4LZ
01736 360063

SADDLE UP
The Old Vicarage
oldvicaragepenzance.co.uk
Churchtown, St Hilary,
TR20 9DQ | 01736 711508

The Old Vicarage runs a slightly unusual programme of riding activities. Along with classic beach canters and coastal and inland treks, they model themselves on the classic American ranch with Western riding, natural horsemanship, carriage driving and family bonding holidays all on offer too. Book in advance.

10 top pubs

VISIT THE SCILLIES
**Isles of Scilly
Steamship Company**
ios-travel.co.uk
Quay Street, TR18 4BZ
01736 334220 | Sailings daily in
summer, rest of year Mon, Wed, Fri,
Sat. Some sailings are affected by
tides, check online before booking
The Isles of Scilly Steamship
Company runs day trips to
St Mary's from Penzance on

Scillonian III, taking 2 hours
45 minutes. Sailings leave
Penzance at 9.15 and leave
St Mary's at 4.30. Wildlife
cruises are also on offer from
the same company, with a
chance to see seals, puffins and
dolphins. The company offers a
fly one way, sail the other
option for day trips too. For
more about the Isles of Scilly,
see page 246.

GO SEA FISHING
Bite Adventures
biteadventures.com
Penzance
07816 844674
Penzance has several angling
boats and you can join one on a
private or group sea angling trip
seeking shark, wrecks,
mackerel or pollock. The best
wreck fishing is in the spring.
Bite Adventures is a Cornish
record-breaker for its shark
fishing, having brought in the
biggest blue shark found in
southwest waters in over a
decade in 2013.

GO SWIMMING
Jubilee Swimming Pool
jubileepool.co.uk
Battery Road, Promenade,
TR18 4UU | 01736 369224
Check for opening hours
Penzance's famous art deco
pool is the largest seawater lido
in the UK and makes for an
excellent alternative to the
beach. The pool dates from
1935 and reflects the style of
the time, from its clean
geometric lines to its blue and
white decor that imparts a

touch of the Med. The pool has recently undergone major refurbishment after suffering severe storm damage. There is a large triangular pool plus a children's pool, and the whole complex is sheltered from the wind. Bring a picnic or buy lunch from the cafe.

EAT AND DRINK

Archie Browns
archiebrowns.co.uk
Old Brewery Yard, TR18 2EQ
01736 362828| Mon–Sat 9–5.30
A popular cafe serving breakfast and lunch above its attendant health-food shop, Archie Browns is tucked away off the bottom of Penzance's Causewayhead shopping street. There's no sea view but the interior is spacious and stylish. The food is varied and tasty and ranges from baked potatoes and sandwiches to Homity Pie and Goat's Cheese Stack. The emphasis is on healthy eating including vegan and gluten-free options.

The Bay@Hotel Penzance ◉◉
thebaypenzance.co.uk
The Bay, Britons Hill,
TR18 3AE | 01736 366890
A light, relaxed restaurant with all-day dining and particularly lavish Sunday roasts. The Hotel Penzance and its Bay restaurant both have permanent exhibitions by local artists on their walls. The kitchen has strong links with local suppliers and caters well for vegans, those who love

shellfish, foodies looking for a tasting menu and those who are fans of Modern Cornish cuisine.

The Dolphin Tavern
dolphintavern.co.uk
Quay Street, TR18 4BD
01736 364106
Sir Walter Raleigh is said to have smoked the first pipe of tobacco in England at this lovely 16th-century pub. These days, it serves great homemade food accompanied by a full range of St Austell beers, and has bedrooms. A typical menu might feature steak and ale pie or Newlyn crab salad.

Harris's Restaurant ◉
harrissrestaurant.co.uk
46 New Street,
TR18 2LZ | 01736 364408
The Harris family have been running their unpretentious, engaging restaurant on a cobbled side street for over

▼ Penzance harbour

30 years. The emphasis is on seafood, with nearby Newlyn providing most of it, but meat features on the menu too, along with divine desserts.

The Honeypot

thehoneypotpz.co.uk
5 Parade Street, TR18 4BU
01736 368686

Tucked away near Morrab Gardens and Chapel Street, this charming little cafe is a longstanding favourite and serves up delicious cakes, cream teas, and there a range of other delights on the menu, including seasonal favourites. They also offer lunch choices like soups, salads and jacket potatoes. Vegetarian and gluten-free options are also available. Across the way is the Acorn, Penzance's centre for live arts.

The Turk's Head

Chapel Street,
TR18 4AF | 01736 363093

This popular terraced side-street local is the oldest pub in Penzance, dating from around 1233, and was the first in the country to be given the Turk's Head name. Sadly, a Spanish raiding party destroyed much of the original building in the 16th century, but an old smugglers' tunnel leading directly to the harbour still exists. Wash down hearty pub food – steaks, burgers, fish pie – with a cracking pint of Sharp's Doom Bar, best enjoyed in the sunny, flower-filled garden.

▶ **PLACES NEARBY**

Around Penzance you'll find one of Cornwall's top ice cream parlours, a handful of classic Cornish pubs, and banana plants and rhododendrons in Trengwainton Garden.

Jelberts

New Road, Newlyn, Penzance,
TR18 5PZ | Open Easter–Sep

This far from glamorous-looking ice cream parlour is regularly hailed as one of the best in the county, and serves up just one simple, divine flavour: vanilla. Worth the drive, especially if you like to load your cone up with clotted cream on the top too. Expect queues.

Trengwainton Garden

nationaltrust.org.uk
Madron, near Penzance,
TR20 8RZ | 01736 363148
Open mid-Feb to early Nov
Sun–Thu 10.30–5

With plants from around the globe scattered throughout this 25-acre garden, there is something to inspire around every corner at Trengwainton Garden. Champion magnolias and vibrant rhododendrons make way for lush banana plants and soaring echiums. The restored walled kitchen garden was built to the dimensions of Noah's Ark and showcases contemporary varieties of fruit and vegetables. A colourfully bordered stream leads to a shady pond and a sunny terrace, with stunning views across Mount's Bay.

▲ Perran beach

▶ **Perranporth** MAP REF 275 D3

A little way south of Newquay on the north coast, Perranporth is known for its wonderful beach, backed with a mile of sand dunes. What you find in the sand dunes, known as Penhale Sands, depends on where you walk and what time of year you visit: there's a golf course, butterflies, lizards and plenty of rare plants and other insects, orienteering routes, and the odd naturist here and there. Probably not in the winter, though.

The beach itself is well worth the trip – a huge slice of sand with natural arches and rock stacks at the south end and Ligger Point exposed at low tide, 2 miles out. There's enough space for everyone and it's within walking distance of the village, making it a great family holiday spot. It's also one of Cornwall's key surf beaches.

One of the loveliest stories about Perranporth surrounds its churches. Because of drifting sands, Perranporth has had three St Piran's churches. They keep getting lost under sand: one, dating from the 7th century and apparently founded by St Piran himself, has been dug up twice in the last 100 years, but was reburied in the 1970s for its own preservation. The second church was abandoned in the 15th century and the latest was built in a village nearby when local architects had learned their lesson.

There's also a link to Winston Graham and the *Poldark* series: the novels were televised in the 1970s and are again a highly popular television series today. Graham lived near Perranporth for a time.

Other notable things about Perranporth include its surf lifesaving club, one of the oldest in the UK, which puts on an extreme triathlon in the autumn; the beach is popular with kite surfers as well as surfers, thanks to its exposed position. In the early morning, you might see dog walkers and horse-riders in the surf; in peak season the beach is closed to dogs 9–5.

HIT THE BEACH

Perranporth beach, as mentioned, is a glorious family beach with lifeguard cover in season. Watch out, though, for rip currents around Chapel Rock. Combined with Perran and Penhale Sands to the north, it's a popular surf destination, and lessons and surf hire are available. There are beach shops and food outlets close to the beach and in Perranporth itself. At low tide there's a nice walk to Ligger Point along the sands, then back through the dunes as the tide comes in.

PLAY A ROUND

Perranporth Golf Club
perranporthgolfclub.co.uk
Budnic Hill, TR6 0AB
01872 572454 | Open daily all year
There are three testing par 5 holes on the links course at Perranporth Golf Club (second, fifth, eleventh). This seaside links course has magnificent views of the north Cornwall coastline, and excellent greens. The drainage of the course, being sand-based, is also exceptional.

EAT AND DRINK

Perran Dairy
33 St Pirans Road, TR6 0BJ
01872 859389
Voted into the top rank of ice cream parlours nationally this bright and cheerful place offers a range of delicious treats made from local clotted cream and milk. Varieties include waffles and sundaes with tempting names to draw you in. Try a Big Dipper, mint sundae, white chocolate mallow dessert, or settle for a classic Cornish cream tea. It's all only a short step from the beach.

▶ Polperro MAP REF 277 D6

West of Looe on the south coast, Polperro is another of Cornwall's picturesque fishing villages, with tightly packed houses leading to a small harbour. It's an ancient place that has seen action as a fishing village for centuries, and has hosted many a smuggler since the 12th century. The pattern of narrow lanes and alleyways and steep flanking streets is enclosed by a wooded valley and the Rafiel, a boisterous stream, runs alongside it, beneath a Saxon bridge and beside the House on the Props, a historic house with rough wooden supports and a secret staircase to the sea. Polperro throngs with tourists in the summer, so you need a little imagination to see the village as it was in days gone by, when supplies were brought in by boat from Plymouth just once a week. Today only a dozen or so fishing boats are in operation from the harbour, as tourism has taken over as the main economic activity. There are lots of pretty cafes, pubs and tea gardens where you can have a freshly baked scone and homemade jam while enjoying Polperro's unique atmosphere.

Taking a walk around the harbour is recommended; there's also a great walk from here to Looe, via the shingly Talland Bay, which has a beach hut cafe and a boutique hotel serving slap-up cream teas. A bus can take you back. It's all along the Southwest Coast Path, which in the 18th century was the haunt of the King's men, looking for smugglers.

The village heritage centre can tell you more about this particular time in history, and especially about local man Zephaniah Job, a merchant known as the 'Smuggler's Banker' who helped Polperro men sent to prison and hired London lawyers for them when they were taken to court.

A word of warning: Polperro is a car-free village because the streets are very narrow. Park in the Crumplehorn car park and walk down the hill to the village. For those who find walking difficult, there's a shuttle service into the village from the car park.

VISIT THE MUSEUM
Polperro Heritage Museum of Smuggling and Fishing
polperro.org/museum.html
Harbour Studio, The Warren,
PL13 2RB | 01503 272423
Open Mar–Oct daily 10–6
This small and characterful museum in the town's former pilchard factory brings the fishing and smuggling past of Polperro back to life with memorabilia dating to the 18th century on display alongside 19th-century photographs and model ships.

ENTERTAIN THE FAMILY
Polperro Model Village
polperromodelvillage.com
Mill Hill, PL13 2RP
01503 272378 | Open Easter–Oct daily 10–6
Polperro's Model Village and Land of Legend has been going for more than 60 years, with a quaint reproduction of the village in miniature plus a show taking in seven stories of ancient Cornwall, myths, legends and smugglers' tales included. Two children are free with two paying adults.

TAKE A BOAT TRIP
The Polperro Boat Men
contact Ollie Puckey 07966 528045
Easter–Nov daily from 10am,
weather permitting
Various boat trips operate out of the harbour on a daily basis with fishing trips, half-hour coastal trips and trips to Looe or Fowey on offer. It's a great way to see the coastline and the native wildlife, and is useful if you're keen to walk the delightful coast path route to or from Looe one way.

EAT AND DRINK
The Plantation
The Coombes, PL13 2RG
01503 272223
On the banks of the River Pol, this is a traditional Victorian tea room with wooden beams, a fireplace and a cosy atmosphere. Friendly service delivers homemade cakes, excellent Cornish cream teas and hearty lunchtime meals. There's also a leafy terrace for eating outside.

▶ Polzeath   MAP REF 276 B4

World renowned as a surfing destination, Polzeath is 6 miles north of Wadebridge and has a sandy beach exposed at low tide only. There is wetsuit and board hire on the beach, but beware if you're a beginner; this may not be the place for you, as it has a few rips and can have heavy waves.

The main street of Polzeath runs along the shore and includes beach shops, ice cream parlours and cafes, largely catering for holidaymakers. There are also a lot of caravan parks and campsites nearby.

There are some lovely walks to take from Polzeath and around the beach. Start by taking the coast path west to Greenaway Beach, a family spot with rock pools, and on to Daymer Bay, a calm beach good for swimming. The route leads on to the 12th-century St Enodoc Church, which was almost buried by sand for centuries. Another lovely walk to take is from Polzeath around Brea Hill to Rock, where you can catch a ferry across the Camel Estuary to Padstow. Puffins nest in the cliffs nearby in the summer months.

Sir John Betjeman loved Polzeath and wrote many verses about it. He's buried nearby at St Enodoc Church.

SEE A LOCAL CHURCH
St Enodoc Church
Trebetherick, near Polzeath,
PL27 6LD
This church is in the sand dunes east of Daymer Bay and in the 16th century was nicknamed 'Sinking Neddy' or 'Sinkiniddy' because it looked as if it was sinking in the sand. As the wind blows on shore, sand banks up around it. At one time, it was buried almost completely in sand

and the vicar and parishioners had to enter via a hole in the roof; today it's accessible as normal through a door, but is surrounded by sand banks. Elements of the church date from the 12th century; former Poet Laureate John Betjeman wrote about the church in his poems and he is buried in the churchyard.

HIT THE BEACH
Polzeath is a busy family beach and a legend in the surfing community. Lifeguards are on hand in the summer season and there are beach facilities nearby. However, note that at high tide there's not much sand to speak of so check the tide table before you come. Dolphins have been seen offshore.

GO SURFING
Surf's Up
surfsupsurfschool.com
21 Trenant Close,
PL27 6SW | 01208 862003
This renowned surf school has turned out a few local champs in its time, and runs courses for beginners, intermediates and experienced surfers in the area, with taster lessons for those as young as seven. Weekend intensive courses involve three 2.5-hour sessions over two days and are great value for money.

▶ Port Isaac MAP REF 276 B4
Lovely Port Isaac on the north coast between Padstow and Tintagel is a popular fishing village and former pilchard-fishing port with a great fish market, characterful restaurants and pubs, and short coast path walks. Park on the outskirts of town and walk in around the headland for beautiful views and perhaps a glimpse of the occasional dolphin out at sea.

Best known in recent times for being the location of Port Wenn in the popular *Doc Martin* television series, visitors tend to walk through the town and stop for a photo at the white house that is used as the doctor's home in the show, before wandering back down to the narrow streets to cafes serving cream teas, restaurants with fresh, fish and souvenir shops.

Whitewashed cottages crowd the narrow streets and lanes, one of which is so narrow that it is known as Squeezebelly Alley. Rose Hill, a crooked lane festooned with rambling roses, steepens and dwindles to little more than a path as it nears the harbour. Fishing boats, nets and calling gulls lend atmosphere to a port from which Delabole slate, which has been quarried nearby since the early 17th century, was once shipped. Port Isaac was also a thriving fishing port up to the 19th century, when the vast shoals of pilchards made their regular appearances along the Cornish coast. Today, the pilchards are replaced by tourists, both in numbers and in economic value.

The handsome 15th-century parish church to the south at St Endellion is built in the Perpendicular style; it has a beautiful timber roof with modern bosses depicting bishops, and bench ends are carved with heraldic motifs.

A couple of miles to the east you'll find the double ramparts of Tregeare Rounds. This Celtic hill fort was excavated in 1904, and pottery from shortly before the Roman period was discovered. The fort has been identified with the Castle Terrible of Thomas Malory's 15th-century epic *Le Morte D'Arthur* – the spot where Uther Pendragon besieged the Duke of Cornwall. With Tintagel Castle just up the coast, it's a legend that seems to make sense.

EAT AND DRINK

Restaurant Nathan Outlaw
◉◉◉

nathan-outlaw.com
New Road, PL29 3SB
01208 880896

Like many a contemporary chef, Nathan Outlaw's not shy in building the Outlaw brand, but the celeb stuff doesn't get in the way of cooking fish in a masterly manner. The flagship premises sit at the top end of the village, with unsullied sea views and an understated minimal look involving neutral tones, local art and chunky wooden tables. The top-class

▼ Port Isaac

Cornish materials speak for themselves, helped along with high-flying technique and an innate sense of what works with what. Choosing what to eat is easy: there's just fish and seafood, in an eight-course tasting menu and a set lunch option, plus veggie options. The village also hosts Outlaw's Fish Kitchen (01208 88183).

The Slipway

portisaachotel.com
Harbour Front, Port Isaac,
PL29 3RH | 01208 880264
With a reputation for seriously good fresh fish and seafood, this 16th-century, one-time ship's chandlery overlooks Port Isaac's tiny harbour. Cornish Orchards cider, and real ales from Tintagel and Sharp's breweries, are available on hand pump. In the summer, the covered terrace overlooking the harbour is a good place to dine and enjoy music from local bands.

▶ PLACES NEARBY

Not far from Port Isaac in the pretty village of St Endellion there's a Victorian garden and a tea room to visit.

Long Cross Victorian Gardens

longcrosshotel.co.uk
Trelights, near Port Isaac,
PL29 3TF | 01208 880243
Open Mar–Oct daily 10–6
In the grounds of the Long Cross Hotel and Restaurant, these Victorian gardens are the only public gardens on the north coast and include windblown, lichen-clad sculptures of cherubs, a round tower, mazes, rock garden and a lake. There's a plant shop too. The 4 acres of grounds here are deeply affected by the salty sea air and apparently receive a hundredweight (8 stone) of salt per acre every year.

Port Quin

Between Port Isaac and Polzeath, Port Quin is a small hamlet and peaceful cove from where you can see sensational sunsets. The National Trust owns a couple of fishermen's cottages now turned into holiday homes in the village. Port Quin declined during the 19th century, some say because a fishing disaster took the local men, others because the mines and pilchard harvest failed.

Trevathan Farm Tea Room

trevathanfarm.com
St Endellion, near Port Isaac,
PL29 3TT | 01208 880248
This charming tea room has stunning views, serves superb teas and is also a quality farm shop, all on the edge of St Endellion village. Part of a working farm that has been farmed by the same family since 1850, it serves a famous Cornish cream tea and has a shop stocked with the farm's own fresh meat, jams and chutneys. There is also a children's play area and pets' corner.

▶ **Porthcurno** MAP REF 274 A5

The paradise beach at Porthcurno is all dazzling white seashell sand, plus towering cliffs and crystal-clear sea, making it a special place to be. But there's more to Porthcurno than that: this beautiful spot 3 miles from Land's End was at the centre of telegraph technology during World War I, at one time with undersea telegraph cables connecting it with the rest of the world. The Cable and Wireless Company ran a training college in the Porthcurno Valley, and tunnels and chambers were built in the cliffs to protect the technology from harm in 1941, during World War II. Today a visit to the Telegraph Museum tells you more, and gives access to those hidden caves.

The visitor to Porthcurno is really spoiled for choice. The main beach is marvellously persuasive for wriggling the toes; but to either side lie lovely coastal walks. Eastward is Treryn Dinas, a rocky promontory that is crowned by a vast monolith, the Logan Rock, that once rocked at the touch of a finger but is less responsive now, and westward you'll find the Minack Theatre, Porthchapel Beach and the little church of St Levan. St Levan can also be reached along the narrow road that climbs steeply from Porthcurno. There is a car park by the church. All around Porthcurno Bay are sheltered coves and exquisite tidal beaches, and the eastern side is flanked by the magnificent headland of Treryn Dinas with the beautiful Penberth Cove just to its east.

VISIT THE MUSEUM
Porthcurno Telegraph Museum
porthcurno.org.uk
Eastern House,
TR19 6JX | 01736 810966
Open summer daily 10–5, winter Sat–Mon 11–4.30
This remarkable museum is all about the history of Porthcurno Valley, which was at the centre of international cable communications from 1870–1970 and was the site of a training college until 1992. Cornish miners dug tunnels to house the entire telegraph operations during World War II and they can be visited here today. There are plenty of interactive exhibits and family activities are available through the year. The museum cafe serves snacks and treats.

CATCH A PERFORMANCE
Minack Theatre
See highlight panel opposite

HIT THE BEACH
Porthcurno Beach is beautiful, popular and safe for bathing, with a river running through it popular with paddling toddlers. There is a lifeguard presence in the summer, when dogs aren't welcome. Some of the beaches nearby are only visible at low tide and have rips, so take care.

▶ **Minack Theatre** MAP REF 274 A5

minack.com
TR19 6JU | 01736 810181
Open Apr–Sep daily 9.30–5, Oct–Mar 10–3.30 except during performances
Cornwall's famous open-air theatre, designed in the 1920s by visionary Rowena Cade and built in the 1930s, is unmissable. It is surrounded by open cliffland overlooking the beautiful Porthcurno Bay. You can clearly see why Ms Cade decided on this location for a theatre to show *The Tempest*, with raging seas as a natural backdrop. Visit in the daytime to find out more about her and her vision, and for children's shows; book well in advance for an evening show. It's a really wonderful experience.

▸ **PLACES NEARBY**

Along the coast from Porthcurno you'll find the cliffs and beach of Porthgwarra, a secluded cove safe for swimming.

Porthgwarra

Porthgwarra lies to the southwest of Porthcurno and is sheltered from the Atlantic winds by high ground leading to the magnificent granite cliff Chair Ladder at Gwennap Head. It is the most southerly extent of the Land's End Peninsula. Tunnels were carved through softer rock to allow access to the beach by donkey and trap in the days when neighbouring farmers collected seaweed to fertilise their fields, and they are the fabulous atmospheric access route to the beach today. The clifftop walks to the west are magnificent, and the area is noted for rare species of birds that often make landfall here during spring and autumn migrations.

The Logan Rock Inn
Treen, near Penzance,
TR19 6LG | 01736 810495

Named after the 80-tonne rock that balances on the cliffs nearby, this traditional pub is just as popular in the winter months for its roaring fire, as it is as a pre-theatre spot for those who are visiting the Minack Theatre in the summer months. With traditional Cornish ales, seafood dishes and a pub garden on offer, it's an inviting place. Families will enjoy the two gardens, family room and children's menu. The nearby Pedn Vounder beach is popular with naturists. If you plan to visit the Logan Rock, then you need to know that this is one of two Treens in Cornwall, the other is near Zennor.

▸ Portreath MAP REF 274 C4

This small north coast resort with a sheltered harbour lies 5 miles north of Redruth and along the coast from Porthtowan. Looking at it today, it's hard to imagine that the narrow harbour was once a key export port for the area's copper – you can barely believe that a large ship would navigate such a tight space. Today, just a few fishing boats come in and out, and the main attraction is the wide, sandy, family-friendly beach. Bodyboarders flock here when there's a big swell to ride the Vortex around the harbour wall.

Portreath is the start of the Mineral Tramways Trail, a cycling and walking route along the old tram roads used to transport ore from the mines, and there are some lovely walks along the cliffs, including a 5-mile walk to Basset's Cove along slate and sandstone cliffs topped with wildflowers and busy with seabirds.

HIT THE BEACH

Portreath has a popular north-facing beach with lifeguards in season. Like many of the beaches along the north coast, it's a surf beach and also attracts bodyboarders. There's a large car park nearby and plenty of shops, cafes, ice cream stands and surf hire shops.

CYCLE THE MINERAL TRAMWAYS TRAIL

Mineral Tramways Coast-to-Coast route
sustrans.org.uk

Elm Farm Cycle Hire
cornwallcycletrails.co.uk
Cambrose, TR16 5UF
01209 891498
This coast-to-coast route uses the old tram roads once used by miners and runs from Portreath on the Atlantic coast to Devoran on the south coast. Along the way you can see a number of important mine buildings, all linked by trails along the original tram and railway routes. It was specifically created with walkers, cyclists and horse-riders in mind and there are refreshment stops along the way. Hire bikes from Elm Farm Cycle Centre in nearby Cambrose, who have tandems, bikes for all ages, and bike seats, trailers and tagalongs for children.

▶ The Devoran to Portreath Mineral Tramway

EAT AND DRINK

The Basset Arms
bassetarms.com
Tregea Terrace, TR16 4NG
01209 842077
Built as a pub to serve harbour workers, at one time this early 19th-century Cornish stone cottage served as a mortuary for ill-fated seafarers, so there are plenty of ghost stories. Tin-mining and shipwreck paraphernalia adorn the low-beamed interior of the bar where you can wash down a meal with a pint of Skinner's real ale.

Portreath Bakery
portreathbakery.co.uk
3 The Square, TR16 4LA
01209 842612
This well-known, local bakery sells regional specialities and a huge range of pasties, both savoury and sweet.

▶ Probus MAP REF 275 E3

The village of Probus, northeast of Truro, has the tallest church tower in Cornwall. It is more than 123 feet high and is lavishly decorated. The village also has several interesting gardens: Probus Gardens has a varied display of flowers, shrubs, vegetables and fruit and, a short distance along the A390, the 18th-century Trewithen House has extensive gardens open to the public. Tregothnan tea estate (see page 267) is also nearby.

GO ROUND THE GARDENS
Trewithen Gardens
trewithengardens.co.uk
Grampound Road, Truro,
TR2 4DD | 01726 883647
Open Mar–May daily 10–4.30,
Jun–Sep Mon–Sat 10–4.30
This historic, privately owned estate has beautiful gardens renowned for their plant-hunter origins, red squirrels and a fantastic house dating from 1715 that is open for guided tours and still home to the same family, some 300 years on. The horticultural vision has stood the test of time: woodland paths are bordered by mature trees, rare blooms and incredible colours, with bird hides hidden among them. 'Trewithen' is the Cornish for 'house in the spinney'.

George Johnstone inherited the property in 1904 and devoted the rest of his life to creating and maintaining the 28-acre garden, which occupies a level site 250 feet above sea level. A great hybridist, he played an important part in the development of the popular Camellia x williamsii 'Donation', but his first love was magnolias, and the Royal Horticultural Society published his magisterial work, *Asiatic Magnolias in Cultivation*, in 1955. Many of Johnstone's plants are still to be seen today at Trewithen, and this wonderful garden is now owned by his grandson, Michael Galsworthy.

It is ironic that the Glade, perhaps the most admired part of Trewithen, came about as a result of a government order during World War I to fell 300 trees.

The lawn stretches for more than 200 yards to the south of the house, but the first part of this magnificent amphitheatre is dominated by one of the garden's great trees. Magnolia and camellia are the key species, all of which have an interesting horticultural history. Shrubs, including viburnums, azaleas, potentillas, euonymus and berberis, edge the lawn in front of the house.

The walled garden, which houses many tender plants, surrounds a pool, while a wisteria-draped pergola adds colour to this formal area. Recently planted beds of birch and sorbus, mahonia, dogwoods and roses, heathers and conifers help to make Trewithen not only a garden with an outstanding plant collection, but a place of ever-changing variety and colour.

Visitors to the house should book in advance via the website. The interior hasn't changed significantly since the 18th century, and the Great Saloon or dining room has ionic columns, views of the south lawn and rococo plasterwork. The tea shop serves traditional Cornish cream teas and there is also a plant centre.

EAT AND DRINK

The Hawkins Arms

thehawkinsprobus.co.uk

Fore Street, TR2 4JL

01726 882208

This welcoming family-friendly pub at the heart of the community offers cask beers such as Tribute, Bath Gem and a weekly guest ale, and Healeys cider. Food is traditional but with subtle touches. As well as sandwiches and tasting platters, mains include the likes of crab thermidor, braised brisket of beef and vegetarian choices, such as stilton and spinach risotto.

▶ Rame Head   MAP REF 277 F6

This headland to the east of Whitsand Bay near the Devon border on the south coast is well known to sailors leaving Plymouth as the last point of land they see on departure. It's a dramatic promontory, with the well-preserved remains of an Iron Age fort on the top of it along with heathland grazed by Dartmoor ponies.

Rame Head has been important through history: a medieval chapel and hermitage once stood here and a small 11th-century building survives, its roof mottled with moss and lichen and its walls rough with age. A warning beacon was once maintained on Rame Head as an aid to navigation, but tradition speaks of its more likely use by smugglers.

From Rame Head, the great crescent of Whitsand Bay curves to the west (see page 117); while Kingsand and Cawsand, two atmospheric villages nearby (see page 113), lie just to the north along the coast. Above Whitsand Bay, in a crook of the coast road, is Tregantle Fort, the most westerly of the line of defences that march from Fort Bovisand on the Devon shore of Plymouth Sound through a series of surviving bulwarks. They were built in the 1860s in response to fears of French invasion. Worth a visit on the narrow road to the Rame Head car park is Rame church, a beautiful example of local vernacular achitecture. Its rough slate walls and broach spire look as if they have simply grown out of the surrounding earth.

▶ Redruth   MAP REF 275 D4

Copper and tin mining created Redruth, and then abandoned it. Yet today this stalwart Cornish town is a bustling, cheerful place where Fore Street, the partly pedestrianised main street, has created a pleasant centre. Look for the delightful *Hounds of Geevor* sculptures created by Cornish artist David Kemp. In its heyday, Redruth was one of the wealthiest towns in Cornwall because of its location in the heartland of profitable mineral mining. Few such towns can boast an elegant Italianate clock tower, handsome Georgian and neo-Gothic Victorian facades, and a hinterland of fascinating industrial archaeology that has earned Redruth a place at the heart of the Cornish Mining World Heritage Site. The Redruth Town Trail leaflet, available in local bookshops, gives a glimpse of the town's intriguing and eclectic architecture.

In the early days of tin and copper mining the method of extraction was by streaming, where tinners sifted through river sand and gravel for fragments of ore. The process caused a disturbance, which released a red stain into rivers and streams, and it was this that gave the town its name, although in an odd reversal from what you would expect: 'red' coming from *rhyd* for ford, and *ruth* meaning red.

Redruth has connections with some famous modern names (see panel opposite) and a few historical ones. Leading off Fore Street is Cross Street, where there is a house with an external staircase which was once the home of William Murdock, a Scottish engineer and inventor who worked in Redruth during the late 18th century. Murdock developed a lighting system using coal gas, and his home in Redruth was the first house in the world to be lit in this way, in 1872.

East Pool Mine (see page 80) and the remains of the Wheal Coates mine (see page 227) can be seen nearby, as can Tehidy and Tuckingmill parks (see page 80 and page 81). Stithians Lake (see page 101) is a watersports and coarse fishing lake.

GO ROUND THE GARDENS
Tregullow
Scorrier, TR16 5AY
01209 820775 | Open as part of the National Garden Scheme; groups by appointment
This beautiful 15-acre private garden is best seen in the spring when bluebells create a colourful carpet under the trees. The garden was first created in the 19th century, but then lost and only redicovered in the 1970s. The current owners are replanting and clearing the estate, revealing two large walled gardens and a yew walk as they go. Cream teas are also served here.

▶ **Rock** MAP REF 276 B4

Affectionately known to some as 'Knightsbridge-on-Sea' – a nickname reinforced by the fact it is the holiday spot of choice of David Cameron – Rock is said to boast more millionaire homeowners than anywhere else in Cornwall, and is a popular holiday destination for affluent tourists.

Just across the Camel estuary from Padstow (see page 189), Rock is a small village with more than its fair share of delis and boutiques plus a watersports centre, pubs, and its own brewery. Access is best on the Black Tor Ferry from Padstow and there's also a water taxi available. Nathan Outlaw's Michelin-starred restaurant is now in Port Isaac, but you can still sample his food at the St Enodoc Hotel. Don't strain your neck looking for celebrities arriving by helicopter, though. The beach is lovely, great for swimming and very calm.

LEARN TO WATERSKI
Camel Ski School
camelskischool.com
The Pontoon, PL27 6LD
01208 862727
Waterskiing and wakeboarding lessons are on offer at this watersports school. They also have stand-up paddleboarding lessons, inflatable banana boats and kite-surfing lessons and equipment. Rock's beach is sheltered and traditional surfing isn't usually possible here as the waves aren't big enough.

PLAY A ROUND
St Enodoc Golf Club
st-enodoc.co.uk
Wadebridge, PL27 6LD
01208 863216 | Open all year
The classic links course at St Enodoc Golf Club has huge sand hills and rolling fairways. James Braid laid out the original 18 holes in 1907 and changes were made in 1922 and 1935. On the Church course, the 10th is the toughest par 4 on the course, and on the sixth is a truly enormous sand hill known as the Himalayas. The Holywell course is not as exacting. In 2017, St Enodoc was rated as 6th best in Golf World's top 100 courses.

EAT AND DRINK
Outlaw's
nathan-outlaw.co.uk
St Endonoc Hotel, Rock, Wadebridge, PL27 6LA
01208 862737
Nathan Outlaw has retained his Rock eatery in spite of expanding his Port Isaac empire (see page 212). Outlaw's set lunch menu revives old

5 born in Cornwall

▶ Mick Fleetwood – Redruth

▶ Kristen Scott Thomas – Redruth

▶ John Nettles – St Austell

▶ Rosamunde Pilcher – Lelant

▶ Rory McGrath – Redruth

favourites such as cuttlefish fritters while the seasonal menu works magic with the likes of grey mullet and offers meat and other options. There's a bar menu too, with a teasing selection from the seasonal summer menu that will bring you back for more. The setting is relaxed, and in fine weather you can eat outside on the terrace, taking in the views.

▶ Roseland Peninsula   MAP REF 275 E4

This beautiful peninsula jutting out into the sea east of Falmouth seems quietly detached from mainstream Cornwall. It can feel like another country, particularly when you're trying to drive somewhere quickly. There's much local discussion about where the Roseland begins and ends; it's certainly bordered to the west by the Fal River, with Mylor and Feock opposite, and is most famous for St Mawes, St Mawes Church and the church of St Just-in-Roseland. The very tip of the Roseland Peninsula is pierced by the twisting Percuil River that cuts deeply inland to create even smaller peninsulas.

Driving advice is necessary: instead of taking the A3078 on to the peninsula, consider taking the faster A39 south of Truro, then the B3289 past Trelissick Garden (see page 264) and cross the Fal by the King Harry Ferry. There's also a neat passenger ferry from Falmouth to St Mawes which gives you the best of the views without any parking headaches.

St Just-in-Roseland is an exquisite place. The church stands on the banks of a small creek, its mellow stonework embedded in a garden of shrubs and graceful trees that include palms as well as indigenous broad-leaved species.

On the promontory of land between Carrick Roads and the Percuil River, St Mawes (see page 243) is deservedly popular and besieged by moored yachts in summer. On Castle Point to the west stands Henry VIII's St Mawes Castle, a quiet triumph of good Tudor design over function and renowned for its symmetry and decoration. The outer arm of the Roseland Peninsula terminates at St Anthony Head, one of the properties on the peninsula cared for by the National Trust, where you'll find a lighthouse and a gun battery with an interesting history. On the east coast, further north, is Portscatho, open to the sea and with excellent sandy beaches nearby. Nare Head (see page 175) is to the east.

VISIT SOME LOCAL VILLAGES

Porthscatho

This small fishing village has a sandy and pebbly beach and a special beach restaurant on a nearby cove that runs feast nights (see right). It's better for rock pooling than swimming and there's no lifeguard cover. Parking is in the village a short walk away, where you'll also find shops, pubs and cafes. A better bet for swimming is to wait until low tide and walk across to Porthcurnick Beach.

St Just-in-Roseland

This pretty village is known for its 13th-century church overlooking an area of water known as St Just Pool and is surrounded by semi-tropical shrubs and plants. The path from the road to the church is carved with verses from the Bible. Next to the church is Pascoe's Boatyard, which has been in operation since the 18th century.

GET OUTDOORS

St Anthony Head

nationaltrust.org.uk

At the southernmost tip of the Roseland Peninsula, this promontory guards the entrance to the Fal estuary with a white 19th-century lighthouse guiding the passage of ocean liners and fishing boats. It's a lovely area for walking, with wildflowers and seabirds, and the peninsula ends with two sandy beaches, Great Molunan and Little Molunan, and grey seals on the rocks. There's a car park by St Anthony Battery, where the former officers' quarters are now holiday homes, and the gun battery, which was in operation from the early 19th century to the late 1950s, is underground. It's open one day a year; consult the National Trust website for details.

EAT AND DRINK

Driftwood ⊛⊛⊛

driftwoodhotel.co.uk

Rosevine, near Portscatho, TR2 5EW | 01872 580644

This elegant boutique bolt-hole perches on the clifftop above the rugged coastline around Gerrans Bay, in 7 acres of grounds with a wooded path leading down to its own beach. The restaurant, with its huge windows giving quintessentially Cornish views, is a supremely relaxing spot, done out with an understated beachcomber-chic look. The menu features the best ingredients Cornwall can offer, brought together in intelligently designed compositions. There's real flair in selecting ingredients for their striking originality and how they work together on the palate.

Roseland Inn

roselandinn.co.uk

Philleigh, TR2 5NB
01872 580254

A lovely, peaceful setting near the village church, a rose-clad frontage and an unspoiled bar with a homely atmosphere combine with good cooking to make this 17th-century pub a real find. Dine on local farm meats and fish landed at St Mawes in the low-ceilinged bar, with its slate floors, cushioned settles and winter log fires. The stable door leads to a suntrap terrace.

▶ St Agnes MAP REF 275 D3

This large village on the surf coast west of Newquay has beaches, independent shops and a legend about a carnivorous giant. The town and area around it have been mined since prehistoric times – Stone Age remains near New Downs and Polberro date from 4000 BC – but today it's known as a great surf spot and family holiday destination. The ruined mining buildings along the cliff tops add a sense of drama; but let's get back to the giant.

Legend has it that a giant called Bolster lived in the cliffs near St Agnes and feasted on children and adults according to his whim. It was said that he was so large he could stand with one foot on St Agnes Beacon and the other on Carn Brea, 6 miles away. He fell in love with a young girl called Agnes and, to spare her, knights and locals gathered on Chapel Porth Beach, challenging him to a fight to the death. Young Agnes herself outwitted the giant by setting him a challenge to fill a hole on Chapel Porth Beach with his blood as proof of his love. This hole, Agnes knew, had a crack in it and could never be filled. The giant bled to death on the beach in front of her.

This story is retold with giant puppets and music on May Day in Chapel Porth each year for the Bolster Festival. It's one of a few festivals that take place here and demonstrate St Agnes' unique community spirit and sense of fun. It's a great place to visit. In September, the World Bellyboard Championships celebrate a simpler age of surfing, where no wetsuits, leashes or fins are allowed and contestants turn up with plain wooden boards and swimming costumes, and retro bathing caps for fun too. It's an enjoyable event, very inclusive, and pokes fun at the more serious surf industry up the coast at Newquay.

In the village itself, there's a small local museum with MP3-guided walks around the village and independent shops, pubs and cafes.

St Agnes has four beaches: Trevaunance Cove, Trevellas Porth, Chapel Porth and Porthtowan, which is known in particular for its surf. With significant mining heritage dotted around the cliffs nearby, cliff walks are particularly interesting. Between St Agnes Head and Porthtowan you'll find one of Cornwall's last surviving ancient heathlands, with heather and spiders that somehow survived despite the soil contamination caused by the mines. Keeping things pollution free is still a big concern here; the environmental charity Surfers Against Sewage was formed in 1990 to improve the water quality of the beach here, along with that of Chapel Porth and Trevaunance

Beaches, at a time when surfers were falling ill because of sewage in the water. Today the water quality is good and is monitored closely.

To the west lies St Agnes Beacon, reached by following Beacon Drive to a National Trust parking area on its north side. A good path leads easily to the summit and to spectacular views along the coast to north and south. The heathland around here is significant, says the National Trust, and represents some of the last remaining ancient heathland in Cornwall, with rare plants and butterflies.

Just to the north of Chapel Porth, reached along the coast path, are the impressive remains of the Towanroath Engine House, restored by the National Trust. Dating from 1872, it housed the massive steam engine used to pump water from the nearby Wheal Coates mine. Some of the industrial buildings around St Agnes have been converted into residential units.

VISIT THE MUSEUM

St Agnes Museum

stagnesmuseum.org.uk
Penwinnick Road,
TR5 0PA | 01872 553228
Open Easter–Oct daily 10.30–5

This award-winning local history museum covers all aspects of life in St Agnes, from the mines to the sea, with exhibitions on 19th-century mining and the painter John Opie, and a large, mounted leatherback turtle. There is a treasure hunt for children and a shop selling local crafts. The museum also offers an MP3 audio guide pre-programmed with a commentary taking you around St Agnes.

HIT THE BEACH

St Agnes has four beaches: Porthtowan, which is a fine family and surf beach; Chapel Porth, where revellers gather for the Bolster Festival in May; Trevaunance Cove, for surf and rock pools; and Trevellas Porth, a small pebbly cove.

Chapel Porth

This cove near St Agnes, with a dramatic entry point, has a long stretch of sand, reduced greatly at high tide, and is looked after by the National Trust. It has a welcoming cafe and is popular with surfers. Lifeguards are on the beach mid-May to September, and dogs are banned Easter–September. The National Trust car park is on the beach; beware the incoming tide, which can be swift.

Porthtowan Beach

Porthtowan Beach is large, busy and beloved of surfers. There's a bar across the road from the beach, and wetsuit and board hire available; lifeguards watch over the beach in high season. There's a car park nearby and at low tide it's possible to walk to Chapel Porth beach, otherwise accessible by the coast path. It's a Blue Flag beach.

Trevaunance Cove

Chapel Porth is not the only beach in St Agnes to hold events – this beach holds an Easter dog race (St Agnes is that kind of place) and an RNLI day in August. It's a decent surf beach, with limited sand and mostly pebbles, and is also good for rock pooling. There's lifeguard cover and dogs are allowed all year; have a beer at Driftwood Spars (see below) when the sun is going down to experience it like the locals.

Trevellas Porth

This quieter pebbly cove is popular with snorkellers and fishermen. It's the only one of St Agnes' beaches to have no lifeguard, and it has rock pools to explore at low tide. There are no facilities at the beach. When the tide is out, you can walk to Trevaunance Cove.

▲ Trevellas Porth

EAT AND DRINK

Driftwood Spars

driftwoodspars.co.uk
Trevaunance Cove,
TR5 0RT | 01872 552428
Named after the wooden beams, salvaged from wrecks, used in its construction, this family-run pub occupies a building that was, in sequence, a 300-year-old tin miners' store, chandlery and sail loft. It stands next to the South West Coast Path in the stunning

Trevaunance Cove and comprises a pub with bedrooms, a dining room, two beer gardens, three bars, a microbrewery and a shop. The Sunday roast comes highly recommended.

The Miners Arms

Mithian, TR5 0QF
01872 552375
The curiously light interior of this historic 16th-century pub adds yet another layer of mystery to the legends of its past. Over the centuries it has served as a courthouse, a venue

for inquests, a smugglers' lair and even a house of ill repute. Relax beneath the low-beamed ceilings while admiring the wall paintings of Elizabeth I and choose from classic dishes cooked from local produce.

Rose-in-Vale
Country House Hotel ⊛⊛
roseinvalehotel.co.uk
Mithian, TR5 0QD
01872 552202
This creeper-clad, stone-built Georgian country house hides in its own little valley, amid highly attractive gardens. The Valley, its chandeliered dining room, showcases contemporary country-house cooking. Attention to detail extends to canapés and amuse-bouches, and Sundays see a carvery operation spring into action.

▶ **PLACES NEARBY**
Wheal Coates mine
nationaltrust.org.uk
Chapel Porth
North of Chapel Porth in the heart of old mining country, standing on a lonely stretch of coastline, is the engine house of the Wheal Coates mine. It is one of many such distinctive buildings, which are a feature of the Cornish countryside, and once housed

the engine that provided the essential services of winding, pumping and ventilation for the mine. Wheal Coates is an important relic of the county's industrial past, and has been restored by the National Trust, which cares for much of this historic coast. The coast path to the south from Chapel Porth leads to Porthtowan.

Cornish Cyder Farm
thecornishcyderfarm.co.uk
Penhallow, Truro, TR4 9LW
01872 573356

Healey's has been making cider for more than 25 years and offers free tours of its farm. This includes a look around the press house, bottlery and jam kitchen and a little tasting. Children are entertained with a quiz as they look round, and orchard walks can be accompanied with a member of the team for an insider's take on how the cider is made. You can also take a tractor ride around the orchards or visit the friendly farm animals in their enclosure.

▶ **St Agnes (island)**
see **Isles of Scilly**, page 248

▼ Towanroath Engine House, Wheal Coates mine

▲ St Austell clay works

▶ **St Austell** MAP REF 276 B6

The St Austell Bay area, which includes Fowey, Mevagissey and the Eden Project, is an area worth exploring. St Austell town has overcome the disadvantage of its raw industrial hinterland of the clay country and today is a busy shopping venue, its largely modernised centre enhanced by some fine traditional buildings. It is also famed for its beer. The town's brewery produces some of the county's most distinctive drinks, from Tribute to Smugglers, Admiral's Ale and Proper Job.

The white peaks of Cornwall's clay country dominate the landscape around St Austell: great spoil heaps from the area's successful china clay quarrying industry. Even when it was a mere village, St Austell was the centre of good farming country, open-cast tin extraction and stone quarrying. To the north is Cornwall's most startling industrial landscape, from which clay has been extracted on a massive scale. The clay was once used for making porcelain but is now used mainly in paper-making. About 3 million tons are produced in the St Austell area annually. Much waste is generated and the great, snowy tips have created a strangely compelling landscape that now hosts the Eden Project and its biomes. The Wheal Martyn Museum and Country Park in Carthew to the north of St Austell on the B3274 includes a museum all about china clay, with examples of how it's used in our daily lives today.

Modernisation of the centre of St Austell has been achieved with some sympathy. Fore Street and the area around Holy Trinity church have been conserved and the Town Hall is in bold Renaissance style, a granite palazzo incorporating a splendid market hall with its interior still intact. Holy Trinity has sculpted figures set within niches in the tower, which itself is faced with Pentewan stone from the coastal quarries to the south. The pearly-grey stone has a warmer tinge when wet.

Further north is the village of Roche, with its adjacent Roche Rock. This remarkable outcrop of quartz schorl, an altered form of granite, is unique in Cornwall and a startling feature in the midst of the industrial landscape. The largest outcrop is crowned by the ruins of the chapel of St Michael, built in 1409.

GET INDUSTRIAL

Clay country circuit

The best way to appreciate the clay country is to drive through it – explore the area north and west of St Austell between the B3279 and the B3274, which takes in Nanpean, Roche, the Roche Rock, and Wheal Martyn Museum and Country Park at Carthew (see right). The vast spoil tips of the St Austell clay country are composed of feldspar and quartz. The raw clay is stripped from the faces of the pits by high-pressure hoses creating flooded pits, their translucent green and blue waters adding to the odd surrealism of this 'lunar' landscape.

Wheal Martyn Museum and Country Park

wheal-martyn.com
Carthew, PL26 8XG
01726 850362 | Open mid-Jan to Mar Sun–Fri 10–4, Apr–Oct 10–5, Nov–Dec 10–4

Set within 26 acres of woodland, Wheal Martyn provides a fascinating day out. The site includes the UK's only china clay museum, set within a complete 19th-century clay works, telling the story of Cornwall's second-most important present-day industry. Key features are Cornwall's largest working waterwheel, spectacular views of a wooden working clay pit with machines at work, nature trails, a children's challenge trail,

5 top local brews

Ask for these local ales and ciders to show you're in the know:

▶ Betty Stogs (Skinner's)

▶ Cornish Rattler (Healey's)

▶ Black & Gold Pear (Cornish Orchard)

▶ Tribute (St Austell)

▶ Doom Bar (Sharp's)

a play area, indoor interactive displays, as well as a cafe and a gift shop.

GET OUTSIDE

Footsteps of Discovery

footstepsofdiscovery.co.uk

07899 928131

Survival courses in St Austell.

TOUR THE BREWERY

St Austell Brewery

staustellbrewery.co.uk

63 Trevarthian Road, PL25 4BY

0345 2411122 | Visitor centre open all year Mon–Fri 10–5.30, Sat 10–4; tours Mon–Sat 11–3 by arrangement

If local ales interest you, St Austell Brewery's visitor centre offers hour-long tours of the brewery, including free samples and two half pints of beer at the end. The brewery itself dates from Victorian times and includes a museum. Children over eight only (soft drinks are available), and book in advance as the tours take limited numbers of people.

EXPLORE BY BIKE

Pentewan Valley Cycle Hire

pentewanvalleycyclehire.co.uk

1 West End, Pentewan,

PL26 6BX | 01726 844242

There are lots of routes in the nearby area that are suited to two wheels. The Pentewan Valley is one place to explore, around St Austell, and you can also reach Heligan, Mevagissey and Charlestown easily. One thing to note: if you cycle to the Lost Gardens of Heligan or the Eden Project, you'll get a reduction on your entry fee. Pentewan Valley Cycle Hire in the nearby village of Pentewan hires bikes, trailers, tagalongs and more by the half day, day or week.

PLAY A ROUND

St Austell Golf Club

staustellgolf.co.uk

Tregongeeves Lane,

PL26 7DS | 01726 74756

Open daily all year

St Austell's challenging inland parkland course was designed by James Braid and offers glorious views of the surrounding countryside. It is undulating, well covered with tree plantations and well bunkered. Notable holes are the eighth (par 4) and 16th (par 3).

EAT AND DRINK

Boscundle Manor ◉◉

boscundlemanor.co.uk

Boscundle, PL25 3RL

01726 813557

The hotel stands in 5 acres of grounds, within easy distance of the Eden Project. Its restaurant is very much a draw in its own right, done out in a traditional and decidedly romantic manner, with candlelight, mellow pinky-red colour tones, and tables dressed up in white linen. The chef sources much of the produce locally, and everything is made in-house, from bread to ice cream. The à la carte menu is a satisfying blend of classical technique and contemporary touches, with flavour combinations working in harmony.

The Cornwall Hotel, Spa & Estate 🏅
thecornwall.com
Pentewan Road, Tregorrick,
PL26 7AB | 01726 874050
This luxurious Victorian country house with a spa and woodland holiday homes in 43 acres of tranquil grounds has a smart restaurant, Arboretum, and a more informal brasserie, Acorns. The Elephant Bar & Brasserie's menu treads an uncomplicated modern path, keeping step with the seasons and making good use of regional ingredients. There are fine views over the Pentewan Valley make it a fine spot for a pre-dinner cocktail.

▶ St Columb Major   MAP REF 275 E2

St Columb Major is set on high ground 5 miles east of Newquay; the 'Major' is to distinguish it from the smaller village of St Columb Minor on the coast. There are a few interesting places to visit nearby. In the village itself there are some unusual architectural touches, including an Italianate Gothic building of red and yellow bricks that now houses a bank. Opposite is the attractive Red Lion Inn, and much of the main square dates from the Regency period. Off the A39 east of the village, there's the Devil's Quoit, the remaining capstone of an ancient burial chamber; the supporting stones were removed in 1870, but it's still an impressive slab.

Families and those who particularly like owls and birds of prey may enjoy the two largest attractions nearby, the Screech Owl Sanctuary and the Cornish Birds of Prey Centre.

MEET THE BIRDLIFE
Cornish Birds of Prey Centre
cornishbirdsofprey.co.uk
Winnards Perch, St Columb,
TR9 6DH | 01637 880544
Open Apr–Oct daily 10–5
This family-run centre cares for injured, rescued and neglected birds of prey and has a play area, ponies and a waterfowl lake. There are more than 50 birds housed here – ranging from kookaburras to hawks, vultures and owls – and with regular flying sessions, visitors have a chance to see why they're so special. Falconry experiences are on offer too, and there are also three fishing lakes and a play area.

Screech Owl Sanctuary
screechowlsanctuary.co.uk
Goss Moor, St Columb,
TR9 6HP | 01726 860182
Open mid-Mar to Oct daily 10–5; check the website for other opening times
This sanctuary does not only look after screech owls: expect to see meerkats, emus, ponies and pygmy goats too. It's a fun mini-zoo/farm for families, with a hand-tame area and falconry displays, a children's play area and a tea room.

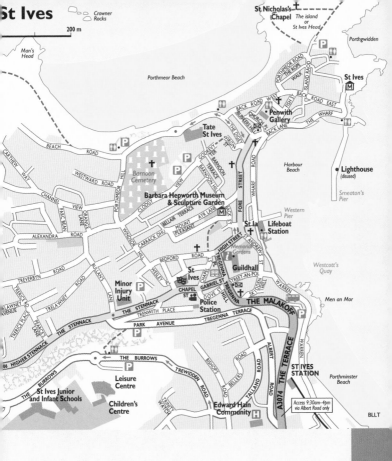

▶ St Ives MAP REF 274 B4

The English nursery rhyme 'As I was going to St Ives, I met a man with seven wives...' has featured in Hollywood movies, magazines and books. St Ives in Cambridgeshire lays claim to the song, also, but Cornish St Ives claims to have more cats. In Cornish St Ives, you too will not be alone: the town has half a million day visitors in high summer. St Ives is a wonderful seaside town with a rare quality of air and light that has drawn painters and artists – the sea in the harbour is a pellucid turquoise – and it has a unique character. The only negative thing is the parking – do your best to arrive by train on the St Ives line, or park out of town to make your visit a happy one.

St Ives' unique character springs from its fishing traditions, its artistic inheritance and its tourism industry. They might clash at times, but the combination of the three makes it an ever-lively place to visit. As well as being an archetypal Cornish fishing port, it also has magnificent sandy beaches, top-rated beach cafes, fab boutiques, ice cream parlours and restaurants, and two of the best art galleries in the county, if not the country.

Tate St Ives is perhaps its most famous landmark. The gallery stands above Porthmeor Beach in a former gasworks building; its curves and crests are as white as the waves below. The Barbara Hepworth Museum and Sculpture Garden is an equally important artistic attraction here, celebrating the work of the much-lauded English sculptor.

St Ives is a delight overall whether you like art or not because of its narrow, canyon-like streets, ubiquitous granite cobbles and clear, sea-mirrored light. The parish church of St Ia is one of the finest in Cornwall. St Ives' harbour area, known locally as Downalong, is a maze of exquisite granite buildings where you catch satisfying glimpses of shady courtyards and passageways.

And there are always those beaches to escape to: Porthminster, to the south, is sheltered and calm; Porthmeor,

▼ St Ives viewed from Godrevy Point

to the north, is a bit more lively and popular with the surfing crowd. There are several smaller beaches at the harbour and in the lee of the Island, the breezy, green promontory that juts out to sea from a low-lying neck of land.

The price of all this is potential overcrowding at the busiest holiday periods. Avoid dawdling through St Ives by car and be prepared for a lot of pedestrian traffic in the narrow Fore Street and along the busy harbour front. There is a park-and-ride scheme at Trenwith above the town and another at Lelant Station, southeast of the town, which uses a little branch line.

Whatever you're doing in St Ives, it will be a pleasure: eating cake in Tate St Ives' cafe with views of slate rooftops, seagulls and the sea; paddling on the beach, slurping cornets of local ice cream; or walking along the coast to either side of town. St Ives also has excellent places to eat – the beach cafe on Porthminster Beach is regularly judged as one of the best in the UK.

VISIT THE MUSEUMS AND GALLERIES

Barbara Hepworth Museum and Sculpture Garden

tate.org.uk/stives
Barnoon Hill, TR26 1AD | 01736 796226 | Open Mar–Oct daily 10–5.20, Nov–Feb Tue–Sun 10–4.20

Visiting the museum and garden is a unique experience offering a remarkable insight into the work and outlook of one of Britain's most important 20th-century artists, Dame Barbara Hepworth. This is where she worked, in Trewyn Studio, which, along with her beautiful gardens and home, form the museum.

Hepworth, her husband, Modernist-Abstract painter Ben Nicholson, and their young children, moved to St Ives in 1939 at the outbreak of the war. Some of her bronze, stone and wood sculptures are on display in the garden which she used for viewings. Inside are paintings, drawings and her archive. A combined Tate St Ives/Barbara Hepworth Museum ticket saves 20 per cent; there are also discounts for those visiting by public transport.

Ben Nicholson walking tours

Tate St Ives and the Barbara Hepworth Museum also offer a Ben Nicholson walking tour, showing the town through the eyes of the artists' colony he and his wife established. St Ives had a huge influence on his work. The multimedia walking tour is available on an iPod Touch for those who have already paid entry to either museum, and there's a small extra fee. Ask at the desk. The walking tour is downloadable for free from the website for those who already have an iPod, smart phone or similar device.

Penwith Gallery

penwithgallery.com
Back Road West, TR26 1NL
01736 795579 | Open Mon–Sat 10–5.30, free admission

The Penwith Society of Arts was founded by 19 local artists in 1949, and still continues today. This small gallery, also founded in 1949, regularly exhibits its members' work and shows the works of leading contemporary artists with paintings, sculpture and ceramics.

St Ives Museum

Wheal Dream, TR26 1PR
01736 796005 | Open Easter–Oct Mon–Fri 10–5, Sat 10–4

In St Ives' old harbour area of Downalong, this museum traces the history of the town in a building that used to house its pilchard-curing cellar and the famous Troika pottery. It's an independent museum maintained by volunteers and including items of mining and fishing history, with tiny models of cats and kittens in the display cases for children to seek out, in a nod to the nursery rhyme.

Tate St Ives
See highlight panel opposite

▶ Tate St Ives MAP REF 274 B4

tate.org.uk/stives
Porthmeor Beach, TR26 1TG | 01736 796226
Open Mar–Sep daily 10–5.20; Oct–Feb 10–4.20 (visitor centre only).
Check website for confirmation of opening hours

This world-class contemporary art gallery is on the edge of the town in a beautiful building, with swirling white curves and a view out to sea. A new extension was opened in 2017, adding almost 600 square metres of new gallery space and studios, all hidden from view from outside but spectacular inside. As the home of post-war British Modernism, it is the natural place for a gallery of this calibre. Exhibitions embrace the best of modern and contemporary art. Along with paintings by leading artists of the St Ives School including Patrick Heron – who designed a stained-glass window for the entry hall – Peter Lanyon and Terry Frost, you might find works by Turner, Juergen Teller, Barbara Hepworth and more. There are regular changing exhibitions and twice-daily free tours of the collection.

There's also a Tate shop, stocking the very best art books and a selection of top Cornish crafts and goodies, plus a cafe with a view and a great line in cakes and light bites, worth the visit in itself.

GET OUTDOORS
Godrevy Head
The National Trust property of Godrevy Head is at the eastern end of St Ives Bay and is the first of a sequence of high, rugged cliffs of dark slate that run uninterruptedly to the northeast. Offshore from the headland stands Godrevy Island and its crowning lighthouse. There is ample parking at Godrevy Head on grassy downs that are reached along a winding road. Paths lead across and around the headland; the offshore waters attract grey seals. To the south lies Gwithian Beach (see page 109), and inland is the village of Gwithian where there is a handsome church and an attractive pub.

HIT THE BEACH
St Ives has four beaches, Porthminster, Porthmeor, Porthgwidden and Harbour

▼ St Ives harbour

beaches, while the gorgeous white-sand Carbis Bay beach is just a mile to the east.

Carbis Bay
A mile to the east of St Ives, and linked to the town of Lelant (see page 125), Carbis Bay beach is one of the finest in Cornwall. Owned by the Carbis Bay Hotel, it has sub-tropical surroundings and no surf to speak of, making it a prime and popular family spot. It's a gorgeous white-sand beach with views to the lighthouse. Nearby Porthkidney Sands is an RSPB bird sanctuary for its seabirds. Walks on the coast path from here take you to St Ives.

Harbour Beach
St Ives' Harbour beach is backed by shops, cafes and fast food outlets right in the centre of the town and is a great place to eat an ice cream or fish and chips, overlooking the harbour. The water is clean and fine for swimming. Watch out for the robber gulls. There's no parking nearby and no lifeguards on duty.

Porthgwidden Beach
By St Ives Island, a short walk from town, Porthgwidden is a family-friendly stretch of sand with safe swimming and plenty of sun. You can walk to and around St Ives Island to Porthmeor beach, and there are a cafe and beach huts here too. The car park nearby gets very busy in season. There are no lifeguards.

Porthmeor Beach

St Ives' largest and most popular beach, Porthmeor is the beach under Tate St Ives. Safe for families, it's also popular with surfers and there is a summer surf school on the beach. Lifeguards patrol from May to September. It's also a Blue Flag beach, and has a beach cafe and shops nearby. The parking situation is tricky – if you can, park out of town and use park-and-ride as there is rarely a space on the narrow streets nearby.

Porthminster Beach

The second-largest St Ives beach, Porthminster is sandy, north facing and sheltered and has great facilities. It's a Blue Flag beach and has views of the town and Godrevy lighthouse. Along with a famous beach cafe (see page 240) it also has beach huts and mini-golf, and lifeguards patrol May to September.

TAKE A BOAT TRIP
St Ives Fast Rib Rides
07824 633447
stivesfastribrides.co.uk

St Ives Boats
stivesboats.co.uk
outside the Lifeboat Station, Wharf Road, TR26 1LF
07773 008000
Sea cruises, seal-watching trips and fast rib rides are all available from St Ives harbour. Dolphins and basking sharks are often sighted. St Ives Boats runs hour-long trips 3 miles

west to Seal Island where there is a colony of grey seals.

GO SEA FISHING
St Ives Boats
stivesboats.co.uk
outside the Lifeboat Station, Wharf Road, TR26 1LF
07773 008000 | Fishing trips depart daily, weather permitting
St Ives Bay sees plenty of mackerel between May and September and local fishing charters can take you out to catch them with 1.5- and 2-hour trips teaching you the basics of hand-line fishing. Wreck and reef fishing for other fish species, including cod, haddock and pollock, is also available, as are 4-hour fishing trips.

GO SURFING
St Ives Surf School
stivessurfschool.co.uk
Porthmeor Beach | 01736 793938
Porthmeor is the place to head for surf lessons, where the St Ives Surf School also hires out boards and wetsuits. With group and private lessons available, they also offer stand-up paddleboard hire, lessons for calm days and sea kayak guided tours.

EAT AND DRINK
Carbis Bay Hotel @@
carbisbayhotel.co.uk
Carbis Bay, TR26 2NP
01736 795311
The family-run Carbis Bay Hotel and spa has stunning views over the eponymous bay from its lofty position, and the sandy beach is only a minute away.

Sands Restaurant serves a contemporary menu, with plenty of seafood as well as meaty options.

The Garrack ◉
garrack.com
Burthallan Lane, Higher Ayr, TR26 3AA
01736 796199

Both the restaurant and conservatory at this hotel offer uninterrupted sea views over St Ives. The room itself has been given a stylish contemporary look, with high-backed leather seats and lamps on the tables. The kitchen reaches out to global cuisines to add variety to the modern British menu. All of the bread is baked in-house and the pastries on offer taste consistently good.

Moomaid of Zennor
moomaidofzennor.com
Wharf Road, TR26 1LG
01736 799285

5 ice cream parlours

There are many ice cream parlours in St Ives but it's worth walking past them to find this little gem, serving luxury Cornish ices in traditional flavours such as clotted cream and fudge, right through to orange and mascarpone, and almond and amarena cherry. There's a small seating area inside but the best thing is to take a cornet to the beach. Watch out for seagulls – they love the ice cream almost as much as we do.

Porthgwidden Cafe
porthgwiddencafe.co.uk
Porthgwidden Beach, TR26 1PL
01736 796791

This relaxed and intimate cafe, with a notably Moroccan feel, is on the quietest beach in St Ives. Call in for smoked salmon and scrambled egg, freshly baked muffins or croissants from 8am. Pick a sunny day and head straight for the terrace for cracking views. Afternoon teas on the terrace are an experience to savour.

Porthminster Beach Cafe ◉◉
porthminstercafe.co.uk
Porthminster Beach, TR26 2EB
01736 795352

In a region with no shortage of places to eat with an accompanying sea view, the landmark white building surveying Porthminster beach stands head and shoulders above much of the competition. This multi-award-winning cafe, with its decked terrace overlooking Porthminster's shining sand, makes sure that the spanking fresh local fish and seafood is subjected to a globetrotting array of fusion influences.

Porthminster Kitchen ◉

porthminster.kitchen
Wharf Road, TR26 1LG
01736 799874

A companion venue to the Porthminster Beach Cafe just along the bay, the Kitchen also enjoys a bracing seaside location. Slick, stylish decor resists the indignity of seashells, and the menus deal in populist global cuisine with a Cornish accent.

The Queens ◉

queenshotelstives.com
2 High Street, TR26 1RR
01736 796468

This local, welcoming pub is just a short stroll from the harbour in a granite-fronted Georgian building, with a pleasing ambience of unclothed tables, sofas and bare floorboards inside. The menu might be short and the dishes on offer may sound a little straightforward, but there's flair on display in the cooking: it's relaxed and friendly but with real skill too.

The Rum and Crab Shack

rumandcrabshack.com
Wharf Road, TR26 1LG
01736 796353

Just as the name suggests, this quirky little place serves

5 smuggler's pubs

rum and crab, as well as lobster, mackerel pâté, crab soup and tempura squid, all with a view of the sea. It's a rustic-chic, trendy spot with lovely staff and it's good for children too. A great, unusual spot for lunch or tea in St Ives.

The Sloop Inn

sloop-inn.co.uk
The Wharf, TR26 1LP
01736 796584

A trip to St Ives wouldn't be complete without visiting this 700-year-old pub, which is perched right on the harbourside. Slate floors, beamed ceilings and nautical artefacts decorate the interiors, while the cobbled forecourt is an unbeatable spot for people- and harbour-watching, preferably with a pint of local Doom Bar. Be aware that The Sloop can get very busy at times.

▶ **St Just** MAP REF 274 A5

St-Just-in-Penwith – not to be confused with St-Just-in-Roseland – is a sturdy Cornish town 8 miles west of Penzance, and the closest town to Land's End. Originally the centre of the tin-mining industry in this area, here you'll find weathered granite buildings, a 15th-century parish church and a market square with pubs, cafes and shops. It is the ideal base from which to explore the mining coast of the Land's End Peninsula.

The elegant headland of Cape Cornwall lies to the west, rugged, shapely and crowned with the chimneystack of a long-defunct mine. On the southern edge of the cape, small fishing boats work from Priest's Cove. From the cove, a stony track leads up to the rocky headland of Carn Gloose. The impressive burial chamber of Ballowall lies about 150 yards inland. The cape, and the coastline to either side, is in the care of the National Trust.

To the north lies the remarkable mining area of Kenidjack and the Nancherrow Valley, a historic mining landscape that is being preserved by the Trust. A mile north of the town along the B3306 is the village of Botallack, and the nearby coastal area is particularly rich in old mine buildings.

SEE A LOCAL CHURCH
St Just Church
High Street, TR19 7EZ
Built of large blocks of worked granite, St Just Church is entered through a handsome battlemented porch. It dates from the 14th to the 16th century. There are many exciting features to be found in the church. The oldest is a memorial stone dating from the 5th or 6th century inscribed 'Silus lies here'. Then there is a Saxon cross shaft reused as a lintel. The church was restored in 1866, when six wall paintings were discovered. Two remain: one of St George and the Dragon, the other a 'Warning to Sabbath Breakers'. There are two medieval crosses in the churchyard, one depicting a crucifixion.

PLAY A ROUND
Cape Cornwall Golf and Leisure Resort
capecornwallgolfclub.co.uk
Cape Cornwall, TR19 7NL
01736 788611 | Open daily all year
The walls are an integral part of this, Britain's first and last 18-hole course overlooking the only cape in England, with views of the north Cornwall coast and old fishing coves. The course features a flat front nine and challenging back nine, and has scenic, wild coastal views.

EAT AND DRINK
The Cook Book
thecookbookstjust.co.uk
4 Cape Cornwall Street, TR19 7JZ
01736 787266
A much-loved institution, this delightful cafe and bookshop offers breakfasts, homemade

cakes and scones and tasty lunches. Feed mind and soul into the bargain by browsing – and buying – some of the 5,000 books displayed in the three upstairs rooms.

▶ **PLACES NEARBY**

Close to St Just are the famous Corwons Mine, Botallack, the historic church of St Credan, in Sancreed, and Carn Euny, the remains of an Iron Age village.

Crowns Mine

nationaltrust.org.uk
Botallack, TR19 7QQ

Just to the north of St Just is the Botallack mining area, now part of a World Heritage Site. The focus of the area is the dramatic cliff-edge Crowns Mine. The surrounding area is rich in mining remains and served as a key background to the BBC's *Poldark* series. The area is in the care of the National Trust, which has a small museum and a gallery/performance space in the nearby Count House, once the assaying centre for the mines.

Carn Euny Ancient Village

english-heritage.org.uk
Near Brane, 2 miles from St Just
0370 333 1181 | Open at any reasonable time

Carn Euny is the remains of an Iron Age settlement that was occupied until late Roman times. Surviving features include the foundations of stone huts and an intriguing curved underground passage or 'fogou'.

St Credan's Church

Opposite Glebe Farm,
Sancreed, TR20 8QS

The pretty granite church dates from the 15th century, and still has the base of its rood screen with original paint and pictures of a spotted goat, a jester, a triple-headed king – perhaps representing the Trinity – birds and other beasts. The 15th-century font has shield-bearing angels at the corners. In the churchyard here are two very early full-length crosses, possibly from the 10th century, both with crucifixions carved into them.

▶ **St Martin's**
see **Isles of Scilly**, page 249

▶ **St Mary's**
see **Isles of Scilly**, page 250

▶ **St Mawes** MAP REF 275 E5

This pretty seaside town on the Roseland Peninsula has a harbour full of yachts in the summer months, thanks in part to Hotel Tresanton, its upscale boutique hotel, which draws a select and wealthy crowd. The town itself is a pleasant place to visit, with a shoreline road, two shingle and sand beaches and St Mawes Castle, built by Henry VIII, at its western end. It's one of the best-preserved military fortresses that Henry built and is lavishly decorated. There are plenty of beaches nearby to visit if you want sands or secret coves (see Roseland Peninsula, page 222), and there is a ferry from the town across the Fal River to Falmouth. There is a lovely walk from the castle to St Just-in-Roseland, where there is a pretty church, St-Just-In-Roseland, surrounded by sub-tropical gardens; see page 223.

TAKE IN SOME HISTORY
St Mawes Castle
english-heritage.org.uk
Castle Drive, TR2 3AA 01326 270526 | Open Apr–Jun, Sep Sun–Fri 10–5, Jul–Aug Sun–Fri 10–6, Oct daily 10–4, Nov–Mar Sat–Sun 10–4

This castle was Henry VIII's most picturesque fort, one of a defensive chain built between 1539 and 1545 to counter an invasion threat from Catholic France and Spain. Although it was designed to mount heavy guns, great care was taken with its design, including carved Latin inscriptions in praise of Henry VIII and his son, Edward VI. It fell to Parliamentarian forces in 1646 with only a single shot being fired, which is one reason why it remains in such good condition.

HIT THE BEACH
The two family beaches in St Mawes, Tavern and Summers, are good for swimming and are on either side of St Mawes harbour. Summers has rock pools to explore at low tide.

GO KAYAKING
St Mawes Kayaks
stmaweskayaks.co.uk
The Quay, TR2 5DG
07971 846786

St Mawes Kayaks rents out one- and two- to three-person kayaks as a great way to see the Roseland Peninsula from the water. From St Mawes you can explore St Anthony's Head, pass below the lighthouse and spot seals, with a route taking you to Great and Little Molunan beaches on the way back; there's also an option to explore the Upper Fal with a kayak drop-off point at Turnaware Bar.

▼ St Mawes Castle

▲ St Mawes harbour

TRY SAILING

St Mawes Sailing Club
stmawessailing.co.uk
1 The Quay, TR2 5DG
01326 270686
The St Mawes Sailing Club runs events and offers classes in a variety of craft, from dinghies to yachts and cruisers. Children must be aged 8 and above to take part in classes.

EAT AND DRINK

Hotel Tresanton ⊚⊚⊚
tresanton.com
27 Lower Castle Road,
TR2 5DR | 01326 270055
St Mawes' uber-chic boutique hotel is one of Cornwall's A-list weekend retreats. Its restaurant is decked out in nautical style and has a modern Mediterranean-influenced menu, using local goodies. On the menu: Porthilly oysters, hand-dived scallops, monkfish, halibut, Cornish lamb and pork all with delicious trimmings.

The Victory Inn
victory-inn.co.uk
Victory Hill, TR2 5DQ
01326 270324
Named after Nelson's flagship, this friendly fishermen's local near the harbour adopts a modern approach to its daily lunch and dinner menus. Eat downstairs in the traditional bar, or in the modern and stylish first-floor Seaview Restaurant with a terrace that looks across the town's rooftops to the harbour and the Fal River. Booking is advisable in the summer.

▶ St Michael's Mount
see **Marazion**, page 159

▶ Isles of Scilly   MAP REF 274 b2

Palm trees, clean and clear water, fine white sands and an
even more temperate climate make the Isles of Scilly feel much
further than 28 miles away from the UK mainland. They are a
soothing holiday spot, reached by ferry from Penzance or plane
from Exeter, Newquay or Land's End, with sea views, coastal
walks, ancient sights, and superb bird- and wildlife-watching
on both land and sea.

Also known as the Fortunate Islands or the Sunshine
Islands, a hundred or so islands and islets make up the
archipelago. Only five islands are inhabited – St Agnes,
Bryher, St Mary's, St Martin's and Tresco, total population
2,200 – and together they offer a rare combination of
seascapes, golden beaches and crystal-clear sea, with quiet,
green corners inland.

Scillonians are outstanding seagoers, and the tradition of
small-boat handling is maintained by the fishermen and by the
boatmen who run pleasure trips. These boat trips are an
essential part of getting the best from any visit to the Isles of
Scilly, whether you're seal watching, puffin spotting or just
keen for a pleasure cruise.

▲ St Martin's

The inter-island launches connect daily to and from
St Mary's and also make trips between the islands so you
can tour them at your leisure. Some of the finest trips are
those to the outlying uninhabited islands and to the marine
wildernesses of the Western Rocks, the Norrard Rocks and the
Eastern Isles, where seabirds can be seen at close quarters
and seals lie at their ease on sea-sucked ledges.

Entertainment on the Isles of Scilly is of a richly traditional
nature. There are numerous slide shows and delightful talks in
the local community hall of each of the islands. Island boatmen
especially are noted for their salty wit. Cricket is a popular
sport and every year local festivals take place, from the Walk
Scilly walking festival in March to folk festivals, the World Pilot
Gig Championships and the Tresco and Bryher Food Festival in
September, a feast of local goodies including Bryher crab and
lobster, St Martin's wine and wild-food foraging walks.

The best time to visit is late spring or early summer,
when the wild flowers are in bloom but the peak holiday
season has not yet started, for the best chance of a deserted
beach to yourself.

▶ Bryher MAP REF 274 a1

Bryher is the smallest of the five inhabited islands, less than a mile across at its widest point and about 1.5 miles from top to bottom. A little to the west of Tresco, which looks like a bustling metropolis by comparison, it consists of a gentle undulation of granite hills leading down to sweeping sandy beaches crunchy with seashells. Hell Bay may sound like something out of the Wild West, but the west of Bryher is entirely peaceable, and makes a supremely relaxing location for the Atlantic-facing boutique hotel in its little cove.

Bryher faces Tresco across the narrow channel of New Grimsby Sound, and island life is focused on the beaches that fringe the Sound. Here boats draw up at a granite quay, or at the jetty, built as one of Anneka Rice's famous 1980s television challenges to extend landing times on Bryher and now known fondly as 'Annequay'.

HIT THE BEACH

Bryher's Great Par is an inspirational place. It's featured in several Michael Morpurgo books (ask the children), including *Why the Whales Came*. We'd bet they came for the sands, sun and sea just like the rest of us – it's also a good beach for snorkelling and swimming. Another famous beach spot is Hell Bay, an Atlantic-facing cove that received many a shipwreck in the 18th and 19th centuries. Along the coast, if you can find it, is High Rock Cave, a 30ft-high cave that is one of the island's largest caves, and was once used by smugglers.

EAT AND DRINK

Hell Bay ⊕⊕⊕
hellbay.co.uk
TR23 0PR | 01720 422947
Large windows in the restaurant look over tussocks of windswept grasses to the sea. It's a simply decorated, light-filled room, hung with Cornish artworks. Local materials are as good as it gets – seafood is caught off the island itself, and local farmland supplies much of the fresh produce, while mainland Cornwall contributes meats and artisan cheeses. Daily changing menus are carefully balanced between European tradition and modernity.

▶ St Agnes MAP REF 274 a2

Just over a mile wide, St Agnes has a special atmosphere of serenity. It is the most southerly of the group and is separated from St Mary's by the deep water channel of St Mary's Sound. The Turk's Head Inn and the Post Office are at the hub of the community, which goes to show how small it is. To the east the main island is linked by a narrow sandbar to the smaller tidal 'island' of Gugh, and off its western shore is the protected bird island of Annet. Beyond Annet lie the dramatic Western Rocks – reefs that end at the Bishop Rock Lighthouse.

EAT AND DRINK
Covean Cottage
coveancottage.com
01720 422620
In this quiet tea shop you can enjoy clotted cream fresh from the Isles of Scilly's only dairy with delicious local homemade jam on freshly baked scones, served on delicate vintage plates. With the English roses in vases on the table, afternoon tea here is a quintessential Isles of Scilly experience.

▶ St Martin's   MAP REF 274 b1

The most northerly island in the group, St Martin's is 2 miles in length and just over half a mile wide. Landing on St Martin's can be adventurous at certain stages of the tide, when walking the plank to reach the sandy shore from launches is necessary. Just wandering here is exhilarating, though the lure of magnificent beaches such as Great Bay on St Martin's northern shore tends to distract.

HIT THE BEACH
As if you needed the encouragement, Great Bay in St Martin's is a gorgeous, dramatic swathe of sand and sea on the north side of the island, with rock pools at low tide and gently shelving waters. It's a great swimming spot.

GO WINE-TASTING
St Martin's Vineyard
stmartinsvineyard.co.uk
Higher Town, TR25 0QL
01720 423418 | Tours during the summer Tue–Thu 11–4
The UK's most southwesterly vineyard produces white wines that go well with seafood, as luck would have it, as well as red and rosé wines. Tours can be either self-guided or guided and include tastings. There's also an apple orchard.

GO DIVING
St Martin's Dive School
scillydiving.com
Higher Town, TR25 0QL
01720 422848
Who wouldn't want to see what's going on in these clear seas? St Martin's Dive School offers lessons, dive charter, single dives and snorkelling alongside seals. That's an offer you won't find anywhere else. There are shallow reefs, wrecks and beautiful fish to see in the waters all around the islands.

EAT AND DRINK
Adam's Fish and Chips
adamsfishandchips.co.uk
Highertown, TR25 0QN
01720 423082
Locally caught fish and chips made from potatoes from the owner's family farm

feature on the menu of this simple cafe, which has indoor seating and a larger outdoor garden under a canopy. It's really all about the fish here, with pollock as the star and lobster making an appearance in the salads. If you want a pasty, you have to pre-order.

▶ St Mary's MAP REF 274 b2

St Mary's is the largest of the Isles of Scilly. Its main settlement of Hugh Town is the marine metropolis of the islands, and it is from Hugh Town Quay that the passenger launches leave for the exciting sea trips that are an essential part of holidaying on Scilly. There are beaches on the north and south sides of Hugh Town, the southern bay of Porthcressa being particularly delightful. A footpath follows the coastline for a 9-mile circuit, passing several well preserved prehistoric sites on the way. Early flower growing developed in Scilly from the late 1860s and daffodils and narcissi are still exported from the islands, though the trade has declined in recent years.

TAKE IN SOME HISTORY

Buzza Tower

Buzza Hill

This squat tower and well-known Grade II listed landmark was originally a windmill built in the early 1800s, and was renamed King Edward's Tower in honour of a visit by Edward VII in 1902. It stands on land that is thought to contain the remains of a Bronze Age cairn and there's a great view over Porthcressa Beach. Buzza Hill is an important wildlife area with Hottentot fig among other species growing around the quarry at the base of the hill, a popular picnic area.

The Garrison

english-heritage.org.uk

An unmissable walk on St Mary's is the round of The Garrison, the hilly cape-like peninsula that lies east of Hugh Town. The Garrison was a fortified site from Tudor times, when its walls were laid out in the shape of an eight-pointed star. The walk takes about an hour and starts at the harbour end of Hugh Town's main street and finishes at Porthcressa Beach.

VISIT THE MUSEUM

Isles of Scilly Museum

iosmuseum.org

Church Street, Hugh Town, TR21 0JT | 01720 422337

Open Easter–Sep Mon–Fri 10–4.30, Sat 10–12, Oct–Easter Mon–Sat 10–12

The mission of this museum is to preserve the traditions and spirit of the islands and help visitors to understand local traditions and their place in history. Items include Romano-Britain finds thrown up during a storm in the 1960s, a summer wildflower display, local art and stuffed birds.

GO BACK IN TIME
Bant's Carn Burial Chamber and Halandy Down Ancient Village
english-heritage.org.uk
North of St Hugh

On a cliff top a mile north of Hugh Town with views of the sea, this Bronze Age burial mound has an entrance passage and inner chamber and makes for a good walk on a breezy day. On the slopes below it are the remains of an Iron Age settlement that was used for around 500 years until the end of the Roman period. The burial mound was excavated in the 1900s but was found to be almost empty; it's thought that it was originally over 13 feet high. The English Heritage website has a short audio tour available for downloading to MP3 players, iPods and iPhones to accompany a walk around these ancient monuments.

HIT THE BEACH
Bar Point is one of St Mary's most scenic beaches, a sandy stretch backed by dunes between McFarland's Down and the Innisidgen Bronze Age tombs with views to St Martin's and Tresco. It's actually the location of a long-eroded causeway between the islands. Porthlaw is another beautiful scenic spot, a white-sand beach with views of Buzza Hill and the tower on the top of it.

EXPLORE BY BIKE
St Mary's Bike Hire
24 Porthmellon Business Park, TR21 0JYT | 07552 994709

St Mary's is a lovely place to cycle, with few cars, of course, and with views of the sea all around. St Mary's Bicycle Hire rents out bikes, tagalongs, child carriers and tandems by cash or cheque (by prior arrangement) by the half day, day or week.

TAKE A BOAT TRIP
Island Sea Safaris
islandseasafaris.co.uk
Old Town, TR21 0NH
01720 422732

Boat cruises are the thing to do to explore around these beautiful islands. Try Crusader from St Mary's Harbour for daily direct trips to the other islands, scenic cruising and wildlife spotting. Sea Quest also runs from St Mary's with a glass-bottomed boat showing the underwater world on an ocean cruise; and Island Sea Safaris runs 1- and 2-hour-long boat trips to see seals and local wildlife around the islands, from the Hugh Town quay.

St Mary's Boatmen's Association
scillyboating.co.uk
The Strand, TR21 0PT
01720 423999

A collective of 10 excursion boats offering a whole range of trips around the islands, from gig boat races to birdwatching tours.

▲ Bant's carn

TAKE A RETRO COACH TOUR
Island Rover
islandrover.co.uk
Holgate's Green, TR21 0JT
01720 422131
Island Rover offers guided
coach tours of the island,
running at 10.15 and 1.30 with
full commentary on a stylish
retro turquoise bus. Note that
dogs and children are not
allowed. The bus times the
tour to allow visitors to catch
the midday boat to Tresco,
so it's timed well for any
day trippers.

SADDLE UP
St Mary's Riding Centre
scillyonline.co.uk
Maypole, TR21 0NU
01720 423855
Why not saddle up and see St
Mary's by horse, riding along
the beach, or along the cliffs
and on the heathland? St Mary's
Riding Centre is the only riding
establishment in the Scilly Isles
and caters for beginners and
experienced riders alike.
Children must be four or older.

EAT AND DRINK
**The Tanglewood Kitchen
Company**
tanglewoodkitchen.co.uk
Hugh Street, TR21 0LR
01720 422454 | Mon–Fri
8.15–4.30, Sat 8.15–1
This award-winning takeaway
and eatery, with limited seating,
specialises in a range of dishes
from crab and asparagus
quiche to lamb hotpot.

▶ Tresco MAP REF 274 a1

Tresco lies at the sheltered heart of the islands. It is more of a show place than the rest of Scilly, a private domain where there is an atmosphere of carefully regulated life and gentle pace. The exquisite sub-tropical gardens surrounding Tresco Abbey House are the main focus of the island. A priory to St Nicholas was established by Benedictine monks during the 12th century; the scant ruins that remain are now incorporated into the Abbey Gardens, where Burmese honeysuckle, Australian scarlet bottlebrush, aloes, dracaenas, mimosa, gigantic ice plants and a host of other exotics line the terraced pathways. Dogs must be kept on leads on Tresco.

VISIT THE GALLERY
Gallery Tresco
tresco.co.uk
New Grimsby Harbour,
TR24 0QE | 01720 424925
Open early Feb–Nov
This fine art gallery shows paintings inspired by Cornwall and the Isles of Scilly in an airy converted boatshed. It's a great place to find a classy souvenir, and holds several exhibitions a year showcasing the work of new and established artists. The gallery also stocks local craft items and jewellery.

GO ROUND THE GARDENS
**Abbey Garden
and Valhalla Museum**
See highlight panel overleaf

▶ Abbey Garden and Valhalla Museum MAP REF 274 a1

tresco.co.uk

Tresco Abbey, TR24 0QQ | 01720 424108 | Open daily 10–4

These 14-acre gardens, dating from 1834, are home to many exotic plants, including the South African proteus, tender geraniums from Madeira, tall date palms from the Canary Islands and the striking Chilean myrtle, which has orange bark. There are also acacias, eucalyptus and the New Zealand *Metrosideros tomentosa*, which is 80 feet tall and produces crimson flowers in summer.

Around St Nicholas's Priory, honeysuckles, the blue-flowering *Convolvulus mauritanicus* and pretty Mexican daisies spill out of cracks in the ancient walls and arches, and there is a magnificent rock garden excavated into a 40-foot cliff below. The Middle Terrace has an area known as Mexico, and is covered with the turquoise flowers of *Puya alpestris* from Chile. Further along, a stone summerhouse is overgrown with Burmese honeysuckle.

One of the best sights here is Valhalla, a building open on one side, which contains some of the figureheads of ships that have tragically foundered on the treacherous rocks around the Isles of Scilly in the course of the last three centuries. Abbey Garden also has a cafe serving light snacks and cakes.

HIT THE BEST BEACH IN BRITAIN
Pentle Bay

Pentle Bay on Tresco was rated as one of Britain's top 20 beaches by the *Daily Telegraph*, a beautifully situated white-sand bay with an emerald sea lapping at its shore and islands leading your eye out to the horizon. Best of all, the beach does not get as busy as you might expect as it's on the opposite side of the bay from where the boats land. Go see what all the fuss is about.

GO WINDSURFING
Isles of Scilly Sailing Centre

sailingscilly.com
Old Grimsby, TR21 0NE
01720 422060 (St Mary's),
01720 424919 (Tresco)
Open Jul–Aug only

Sailing, windsurfing and powerboating are all on offer at the Isles of Scilly Sailing Centre, along with kayak and boat hire by the day. The Scillies are a watersports paradise and this watersports centre has suitable options whether you're a beginner or an experienced old hand.

EAT AND DRINK
New Inn ◉

tresco.co.uk
New Grimsby, TR24 0QQ
01720 422849

Just a few steps away from this characterful old inn is the quay at New Grimsby and the first of a string of white-sand beaches that garland this sub-tropical island. The bar is partly created

10 Cornish sayings

- **Teazy asn adder** – moody
- **Rough as rats** – of poor or uncouth upbringing
- **Drekly** – later, if at all
- **Got feet like half-crown shovels** – got big feet
- **Face like a whitewashed wall** – pale
- **So daft as a carrot half scraped** – not very clever
- **Black as pit** – very dark
- **Mazed** – a bit daft
- **Thick as a hedge** – a thick mist
- **A brave step** – a long walk

from salvage from local wrecks giving a rustic maritime feel. Scilly-brewed beers populate some of the handpulls on the bar, whilst Scillonian provender forms the backbone of the well-balanced menu, including locally caught shellfish and island beef. Three beer and cider festivals are held over the summer.

Ruin Beach Cafe

tresco.co.uk
Ravens Porth, Old Grimsby,
TR24 0QQ | 01720 424849

This beach cafe is open all day and serves breakfast, lunch, afternoon tea and dinner along with fantastic sea views. It has a wood-burning oven – handy for its pizzas – and also has a good children's menu. Views are towards St Martin's and the Eastern Isles.

▲ Sennen Cove

▶ Sennen   MAP REF 274 A5

Holiday snaps of Sennen Cove can be deceptive, its white sand and clear turquoise water looking more like the Caribbean than Cornwall. It's the most westerly surf spot in the country, renowned for its waves, and is close to the small harbour and fishing village of Sennen. With little fishing boats pulled up to the quay and a 150-year-old lifeboat station to visit in summer, it's a photogenic place. It also has its own legend – the Hooper of Sennen Cove was said to send a dense mist to prevent fishermen sailing out into incoming storms.

The village proper is on the higher ground alongside the A30, while Sennen Cove has the main attractions of the beaches and fine granite cliffs to the south. A car park at the far end gives access to the cliff path and to Land's End on foot – it's roughly a half-hour walk (1.5 miles) along the cliffs from the beach. This southern end of the cove spills into the ocean and has a laid-back atmosphere. The nearby wood and granite Round House contained the capstan that was used for hauling boats out of the water. It is now a craft shop and gallery.

There are two beaches: as well as Sennen Cove, Gwenver Beach to the north is a serious surfing and bodyboarding beach and a suntrap on a good day. It's harder to reach and the smaller of the two. Lifeguards are on hand in the summer months, but do take care as tidal currents can be fierce.

HIT THE BEACH
Gwenver Beach

Gwenver is known for having some of the county's best surf. Access is via a long flight of broad steps down grass slopes that test the lungs on the way back. It's a dog-friendly beach all year and has a car park at the top of the approach steps. There are lifeguards on duty in peak season, and their advice should be strictly followed.

Sennen Cove

This is one of the most beautiful beaches in Cornwall, a curve of white sand with water so clear you can see through it from the cliff tops. The steep cliffs on Pedn-men-du headland at the western end of Sennen are popular with rock climbers, and there's plenty to do at the beach beyond swimming, sunbathing and surfing, with a variety of cafes, food outlets and beach restaurants plus a small art gallery. There is also a surf school and surf hire on the beach. Lifeguards patrol in season.

GO SURFING
Smart Surf School

sennensurfschool.com

The Blue Lagoon, TR19 7DF

01736 871817

Sennen Surfing Centre

sennensurfingcentre.com

Churchtown House, TR19 7AD

01736 871227 | Open Apr–end Oct

In the UK's most westerly surf spot, what else? There are two surf schools on the beach offering wetsuit and board hire and lessons, plus surf'n'stay options with the nearby Whitesands Hotel and nearby campsites and cottages, and 1–5 day courses for those bitten by the bug. Instructors here are accomplished and have travelled the world surfing and teaching.

EAT AND DRINK
Little Bo Cafe

thelittlebocafe.weebly.com

Sennen Cove, TR19 7DF

01736 871900

A cheerful cafe on the Sennen Cove seafront with outside seating and glorious views alongside the seaward railing. It's a great place to stop for coffee or cream teas but breakfast and light lunches are also served plus evening sharing platters and other treats. On offer is a fine selection of tasty, well-sourced food, from mackerel pate to homity pie, delicious crab cakes, salad bowls and a range of sandwiches.

▶ Tintagel MAP REF 276 C3

Tintagel, on Cornwall's north coast between Bude and Padstow, can feel like a bit of an Arthurian theme park at times, which is both good and bad. Good because who wouldn't want to visit Tintagel Castle dreaming of King Arthur and the Knights of the Round Table – it's one of England's most enduring stories – but bad because, seriously, King Arthur-themed fudgeries and fish and chip shops are just pushing it over the edge. Get past the rampant commercial exploitation of the legends and you'll find the incredible ruined castle moulded to the blunt summit of 'the Island' of Tintagel Head a real joy to visit. There's more here than a whiff of ancient legend: the castle is 13th century, but historians suggest it was the site of an Iron Age enclosure, a Celtic monastery and a Roman signal station. The prominence of the Island suggests that it was used as a defensive site from the earliest times; it's now watched over by English Heritage.

Barras Nose to the north and Glebe Cliff to the south are in the care of the National Trust. It's tempting to say that the hinterland is in the care of the King Arthur industry, but Tintagel village offers a little more than that. The antiquated Old Post Office (National Trust) at the heart of the village is a delightful building: a small 14th-century manor house with a central hall rising the full height of the building which became a post office in Victorian times. King Arthur's Great Halls in Fore Street is another remarkable token of dedication to a theme, packed with Arthurian memorabilia and with a light and sound show.

TAKE IN SOME HISTORY
Tintagel Castle
See highlight panel overleaf

VISIT THE MUSEUMS
King Arthur's Great Halls
Fore Street, PL34 0DA
01840 770526
Get inspired for a visit to Tintagel by first stopping at this 1930s building on Fore Street. It contains 72 stained-glass windows illustrating the Arthurian tales by Veronica Whall, a pupil of William Morris, a round table, granite thrones, and a light and music show telling more about the legends.

Tintagel Old Post Office
nationaltrust.org.uk
Fore Street, PL34 0DB
01840 770024
Open early Apr–Sep daily 10.30–5.30, Mar, Oct 11–4
A rare survival of Cornish domestic medieval architecture, this 14th-century yeoman's farmhouse is well furnished with local oak pieces and has a distinctive undulating slate roof. One room was used during the Victorian period as the letter-receiving office for the district. Inside today are relics from the Victorian era; there's also a peaceful cottage garden.

EAT AND DRINK
Granny Wobbly's Fudge Pantry
grannywobblys.co.uk
Fore Street, PL34 0DB
01840 770595

This jolly shop sells handmade fudge in five flavours – vanilla, rum and raisin, chocolate, butterscotch and maple and walnut – plus a different mystery flavour each week. It has an ice cream parlour next door and a sister shop in Wadebridge. A great place to buy boxes of fudge to take home as gifts or souvenirs.

▶ **PLACES NEARBY**

It's not all myths and legends; just over 2 miles south of Tintagel the coastal settlement of Trebarwith Strand has a beach and more.

The Mill House Inn
themillhouseinn.co.uk
Trebarwith, PL34 0HD
01840 770200

This converted 18th-century mill house is halfway up the wooded valley from the surfing beach at Trebarwith. The bar is big, with flagged floors and a wood-burning stove, and has Sharp's ales on tap. Enjoy drinks and barbecues out on the terraces, or a more intimate dinner in the contemporary Millstream Restaurant.

The Port William
theportwilliam.com
Trebarwith Strand,
PL34 0HB | 01840 770230

In one of the best locations in Cornwall, this former harbourmaster's house lies

---

5 top castles

▶ **Tintagel Castle**
page 261

▶ **St Michael's Mount**
page 159

▶ **St Mawes Castle**
page 244

▶ **Restormel Castle**
page 156

▶ **Pendennis Castle**
page 95

---

directly on the coastal path, 50 yards from the sea. There is an entrance to a smugglers' tunnel at the rear of the ladies' loo. The daily-changing specials include gourmet burgers, chicken, leek and apple pie, fish pie, local mussels and even venison sausages.

Trebarwith Strand
This sandy and rocky beach is accessible via the South West Coast Path as well as from the car park 5 minutes' walk away, and is a good surf and family beach. The beach is completely covered at high tide and incoming tides can be swift, so check before you turn up; there are local lifeguards on hand in season. The added bonuses are that dogs are allowed all year, and there is a beach shop and a cafe in the village but no surf hire.

▶ **Tresco**
see **Isles of Scilly**, page 253

▶ **Tintagel Castle** MAP REF 276 C3

english-heritage.org.uk
Castle Road, PL34 0HE | 01840 770328
Open Apr–Sep daily 10–6, Oct 10–5, Nov–Mar Sat–Sun 10–4;
check website for variations

Overlooking the wild Cornish coast, Tintagel is one of the most spectacular spots in the country. Where to start? Well, as it's the birthplace of King Arthur, according to popular myth, don't head straight to the ruins but watch the video in the visitor centre about searching for the legend before you start. It's a long walk down to the ruins on the cliff top, and it's well worth it. For those less mobile, a Land Rover does return trips. The castle is closed on exceptionally windy days.

Recent excavations have revealed Dark Age connections between Spain and Cornwall, alongside the discovery of the 'Arthnou' stone suggesting that this was a royal place for the Dark Age rulers of Cornwall, so who knows – perhaps the legends have roots in history.

The 13th-century ruined castle is a magical place to visit, with wooden doors studded with metal, overgrown cottage gardens and stone walls crumbling down the cliff. In the summer, history is brought to life with storytelling sessions, an archaeology week and a family trail. After visiting the castle, wander down to the beach and find Merlin's Cave and a shorter tunnel that opens up in the meadow above the cliffs.

▲ Truro Cathedral

▶ **Truro** MAP REF 275 E4

At the heart of Cornwall, Truro is one of the county's great towns, with cobbled streets, independent shops selling artisanal cheese, homemade bread and surf clothing, and a great cathedral right in the middle. Holidaymakers tend to head to seaside towns and villages but missing Truro would be missing a treat: there's always something going on here, thanks to its year-round programme of events, from fashion shows to hip hop.

It's impossible to miss Truro's great cathedral, which catches the eye from all quarters. It rises from the heart of the city, all honey-coloured stone and lancet windows reflecting the sun, with its great Gothic towers piercing the sky. Long before it was built here in the late 1800s – the first cathedral to be built on a new site since Salisbury in 1220 – the site held a Norman castle, while a Dominican friary stood near the river. The cathedral makes up for their loss and is known for its Victorian stained-glass windows, said to be among the best in the UK.

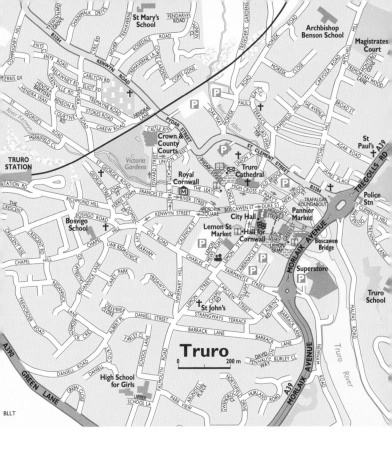

The history of the town of course centres on mining. In the late 18th century, it was the political and cultural centre of Georgian Cornwall, hence the beautifully proportioned buildings here, and in the last years of the century the striking buildings on Boscawen Street and Lemon Street were built. Today Boscawen Street is a broad, cobbled space, entered at both ends from narrow thoroughfares. The granite facade of the City Hall is on this street, and Lemon Street survives as one of the finest examples of a late Georgian street in Britain, its houses perfectly aligned to either side of a broad avenue.

There are hidden glories in Truro amid the modern developments which reflect the town's importance today. From the Moorfield car park, a lane leads to Victoria Square, but parallel and to its right is the elegant Georgian crescent of Walsingham Place. Throughout the heart of Truro, the lanes connecting the main streets are lined with attractive shops, cafes and restaurants. From the west end of Boscawen Street, King Street leads up to the pedestrianised area of High Cross in front of the cathedral. The stylish Assembly Rooms, with a facade of Bath stone, stand nearby.

Seen from its forecourt, the cathedral seems crowded in by buildings instead of being the dominating presence that commands the view from outside the city, but the west front with its soaring towers is exhilarating. The foundation stones of the cathedral were laid in 1880 and the western towers were finally dedicated in 1920. Truro's cathedral is a Victorian building, early English Gothic in design but with strong French influences that are seen in the great spires. The interior is glorious, vaulted throughout with pillars and arches in elegant proportion. There are beautiful individual features such as the exquisite baptistery.

Pydar Street runs north from the cathedral as a pleasant pedestrian concourse. A short distance away is the stylish Crown Court, and below here are the Victoria Gardens. Boscawen Park, by the River Truro, is reached along the road to Malpas.

The Royal Cornwall Museum in River Street is worth visiting for a sight of a real Egyptian mummy and a Cornish giant, among its many treasures. The art gallery has works by John Opie, the 18th-century portrait painter, who was born near St Agnes. Truro is an excellent shopping centre with numerous independent and specialist shops in its narrow, characterful streets. The Hall for Cornwall hosts shows, events and touring acts of the calibre you'd expect for the capital of the county: anything from Peppa Pig for the under-sevens to breakdancers, touring West End shows and comedians such as Billy Connolly.

Near to Truro you'll find Trelissick Garden, another of Cornwall's key garden estates, and Trewithen Gardens, in the village of Probus (see page 218).

VISIT THE MUSEUM
Royal Cornwall Museum
royalcornwallmuseum.org.uk
River Street, TR1 2SJ
01872 272205 | Open Tue–Sun 10–4.45; library closed 1–2pm, all day Thu and Sat pm
Cornwall's oldest museum is famed for its internationally important collections. Visitors can see large collections of minerals, a real Egyptian mummy and the Cornish Giant. The art gallery has a fine collection of paintings from the Newlyn and St Ives Schools, and regular temporary exhibitions. The museum runs a range of family activities throughout the year along with a regular programme of lectures. You can contact the museum for details of events and activities.

GO ROUND THE GARDENS
Trelissick Garden
nationaltrust.org.uk
Feock, TR3 6QL
01872 862090 | Open mid-Feb to Oct daily 10.30–5.30, Jan to mid-Feb, Nov–Dec 11–4

Set amidst more than 500 acres of park and farmland, with panoramic views down Carrick Roads to Falmouth and the sea, Trelissick Garden is well known for its large collection of hydrangeas, camellias, rhododendrons and tender plants. In the garden's sheltered position many unusual and exotic plants also thrive, including sub-tropical species from South America and Tasmania. The large walled garden has fig trees and climbing plants, and there is a shrub garden. The Cornish apple orchard contains the definitive collection of Cornish apple varieties and is particularly lovely in the spring, when the trees are covered in blossom. Two galleries on the property display Cornish arts and crafts. Check the website for musical and theatrical events.

The grounds were laid out with carriage drives and planted with trees during the 1820s to take full advantage of the picturesque views. The parkland is criss-crossed with pathways, which provide some delightful walks. The beautiful gardens and deciduous woods, which run down to the Fal River, make a particularly pleasant place to work up a healthy appetite for, or to walk off the indulgence of, one of the excellent afternoon teas served here. The traditional spread of sandwiches, cakes and scones might include the the Trelissick fruit slice – a speciality – and

▲ Fisherman on the pier at Truro

there are 20 varieties of tea to choose from. Light lunches are also available. Booking is advisable for Sunday lunch and for anyone with any special requirements. One of the best ways to visit is by river on a boat trip from Truro (see Enterprise Boats below).

TAKE A BOAT TRIP
Enterprise Boats
falriver.co.uk
01326 741194
Enterprise's red and turquoise boats sail regularly from Truro to Falmouth and St Mawes along the banks of the Fal River. It's a pleasant way to travel and explore. The regular trips stop at the National Trust's Trelissick Garden and Malpas. En route, expect to see plenty of other boats, and historic and Tudor houses. Boats run from the town quay.

WATCH A PLAY
Kneehigh
kneehigh.co.uk
01872 267910
Cornwall's most dazzling theatre company knocks the socks off any other creative company in the UK. Its home in the summer months is the Asylum, a purpose-built tent amid the beautiful country just outside Truro (check the website for the precise location, as it changes). Magic is in the air as traditional stories – often children's or folk tales – are reworked with drama, song, circus skills and theatricality. Much is talked about seeing shows at the Minack – the Asylum is just as good, if not more inventive, surprising and memorable.

PLAY A ROUND
Truro Golf Club
trurogolfclub.co.uk
Treliske, TR1 3LG | 01872 278684
Open daily all year
This is a picturesque and gently undulating parkland course with lovely views of Truro and the surrounding countryside. The course offers a great challenge to golfers of all standards and ages. The many trees and shrubs offer open invitations for wayward balls, and with many fairways boasting out of bounds markers, play needs to be safe and sensible. Fairways are tight and the greens small and full of character, making it difficult to play to your handicap.

EAT AND DRINK
Charlotte's Tea House
Coinage Hall, 1 Boscawen Street, TR1 2QU | 01872 263706
This tea house on the first floor of the old Coinage Hall presents a sanctuary of Victorian tranquillity just a few steps from the busy main street below. As well as teas from the Tregothnan Estate, they serve an extensive range of homemade cakes plus scones, quiches, soups and light lunches.

Fig Cafe
figcafe.co.uk
Lemon Street Market, TR1 2QD
01872 271733
Fig Cafe is located on the bright and airy upper mezzanine of the Lemon Street Market, itself worth a visit for its colourful array of stylish shops and cafes and for the Atrium Gallery. Fig Cafe is open for breakfast, light lunches, and afternoon tea and coffee. Downstairs is Fig2Go, the takeaway arm of Fig Cafe.

Hooked Restaurant & Bar ⊚
hookedcornwall.com
Tabernacle Street, TR1 2EJ
01872 274700
On a quiet city-centre street, Hooked is a buzzy restaurant with wooden floors and tables, fashionably exposed brickwork, high ceilings, banquettes and brown and cream leather-look seats, and some 'fish shoal' lampshades reflecting the seafood credentials of the place. Tapas dishes are available daytime and evening.

The Old Ale House

old-ale-house.co.uk
7 Quay Street, TR1 2HD
01872 271122

Close to the old riverside quays, this bare-boarded, heavily beamed pub is Skinner's Brewery tap, so a reliable pint is certain; Truro-made Apple Slayer and Lyonesse real ciders are first-rate too. A collaboration between Skinner's and Devon's River Cottage-trained chefs lies behind the upstairs restaurant, which showcases Cornwall's best produce. The pub holds a beer and cider festival every spring.

Tabb's Restaurant ◉◉

tabbs.co.uk
85 Kenwyn Street, TR1 3BZ
01872 262110

Tabb's occupies a white corner building that looks like a private house. Inside is a soothing colour scheme of lilac and lemon, with comfortable chairs and a friendly atmosphere. The cuisine is modern European, and everything that's served is produced on the premises, from the complimentary soup to petits fours.

The Wig and Pen

wigandpentruro.co.uk
Frances Street, TR1 3DP
01872 273028

This city-centre pub includes Quills Restaurant in the basement, serving modern pub classics and specials on the menu to go with the HSD and Tribute beers. Everything is made in house, including the crisps and pork scratchings. Watch the world go by from the sun terraces. The cellars are apparently haunted by the ghost of a woman run over by a stagecoach in Victorian times.

▶ PLACES NEARBY

Truro is surrounded by lots of foodie attractions, including a cider farm (see page 228) and a tea estate. There's also a golf course for working it all off.

Boscawen Park

visittruro.org.uk
Malpas Road, TR1 1UE

This is where Truro's children come to play with their families. A lovely riverside venue with bedding displays and a play area with climbing games, slides and swings. There are also tennis courts (to book them, call 01872 274776) and there is free parking.

Killiow Golf Club

killiowgolf.co.uk
Kea, TR3 6AG | 01872 270246
Open daily all year

This picturesque and testing parkland course in the grounds of Killiow Estate has mature trees, water hazards, small greens and tight fairways, making this a challenge for all golfers. Five holes are played across or around water. There is a floodlit, all-weather driving range and practice facilities.

Tregothnan

tregothnan.co.uk
The Woodyard, Tresillian,
TR2 4AJ | 01872 520000

Known for having the UK's most successful tea plantation, Tregothnan is a private family garden and has been home to the Boscawen family since the early 14th century. Garden visits are by group tour and prior arrangement only (see the website); among the things to see are the Diamond Woodland, planted to celebrate the Queen's Diamond Jubilee, 100 acres of impressive exotics and a tea plantation whose climate mimics that of the Himalayan foothills. There are also regular special events, such as tea tastings and masterclasses.

If you want to stay over at Trego, the inviting Wild Escape accommodation selection includes old school cottages in ancient plum orchards as well as secluded stone-built creekside houses to rent.

▶ Wadebridge   MAP REF 276 B4

Wadebridge is known as the start of the Camel Trail, a route along the old railway that has been cleared and reworked for walking, cycling and horse-riding. The town itself is charming, with pedestrianised streets, independent shops, cafes and boutiques and a decent deli. Back in the early part of the 20th century, it was a busy town, and today it supports more than just the tourist industry so you'll find more than buckets and spades in the shops.

The old bridge dates from the mid-15th century and it is said that it was built on foundations of woolpacks, the area being noted for its wool production. To the west, modern technology has spanned the wider estuary with a lofty road bridge that has eased much of the town's traffic problem.

Close to the town of Padstow and the village of Rock, there are beaches to explore nearby, along with a family theme park and St Enodoc Church, part-covered by sand, where Sir John Betjeman is buried. If you want to know more about the former Poet Laureate, the Wadebridge Concern for the Aged centre has memorabilia on display.

VISIT THE MUSEUM
John Betjeman Centre
concernwadebridge.org.uk
Wadebridge Concern for the Aged, Southern Way, PL27 7BX
01208 812392 | Open Mon–Fri 9–4.30
This Concern for the Aged centre is in the main building of the old Wadebridge railway station. Inside, along with meeting rooms, there is a memorabilia room dedicated to Sir John Betjeman with furniture and personal items that belonged to the poet. Betjeman died in 1984 and he is buried at St Enodoc Church in Trebetherick (see page 210).

ENTERTAIN THE FAMILY
Callestick Farm Cornish Ice Cream
callestickfarm.co.uk
Callestick, TR4 9LL
01872 573126 | Open Easter–Sep
Mon–Sat 10-5.30, Sun 10–4.30,
Oct Mon–Sun 10–4
Callestick Farm nestles in a quiet valley setting and is famous for its ice cream manufactory using milk from the 300 cows that graze on the farm. Visitors are welcome at the farm and invited to watch the ice cream-making process. The variety of ice cream that is on offer is mouth-watering. There is also a popular tearoom there and a play area for youngsters.

HIT THE BEACH
Daymer Bay
Daymer Bay is a sandy beach backed by dunes and sand hills. It's a little off the beaten track, safe for swimming and has no lifeguard presence or facilities to speak of. Braey Hill to the south of the beach can be climbed, and St Enodoc Church is nearby. Parking and toilets are nearby and dogs are allowed all year.

CYCLE THE CAMEL TRAIL
Bridge Bike Hire
bridgebikehire.co.uk
The Camel Trail, PL27 7AL
01208 813050

Camel Trail Cycle Hire
cameltrailcyclehire.co.uk
Eddystone Road, PL27 7AL
01208 814104

The route of the old Atlantic Coast Express, from Wadebridge to Padstow, is now the main part of the 18-mile Camel Trail, a recreational walking, riding and cycling route that passes through varied countryside alongside the River Camel. This traffic-free trail is ideal for all the family as the surface is mainly smooth and virtually level, with one gentle climb from Wadebridge to Poley's Bridge. It is ideal for wheelchair users, prams and buggies, and those who have difficulty walking on uneven surfaces. There are plenty of benches and picnic tables along the way where you can stop and enjoy the views.

The Camel Trail can be joined at several points: Padstow, Wadebridge and Boscarne Junction to the west of Bodmin, where it swings north to continue through Hellandbridge to terminate at Poley's Bridge.

PLAY A ROUND
St Kew Golf Course
stkewgc.com
St Kew Highway, PL30 3EF
01208 841500 | Open all year
St Kew Golf Course is an interesting, well laid out parkland course with six holes with water and 15 bunkers. It's in a picturesque setting with 10 par 4s and eight par 3s. Nine extra tees have now been provided on the course, allowing a different teeing area for the back nine.

EAT AND DRINK

The Quarryman Inn

thequarryman.co.uk
Edmonton, PL27 7JA
01208 816444

Close to the famous Camel Trail, this friendly 18th-century free house has evolved from cottages that housed slate workers from the nearby quarry. Several bow windows add character to this unusual inn. The Quarryman's menus change frequently, but look out for the regular house speciality hake, monkfish, king prawns and mussels in Portuguese sauce.

Relish Food & Drink

relishfoodanddrink.co.uk
Foundry Court PL27 7QN
01208 814214

Located in a delightful cobbled area just off busy Molesworth Street, this colourful licensed cafe has cornered the quality coffee title with a fine selection on offer served with a great barista flourish. The home-baked cakes and biscuits are delicious, and you can buy some of the goodies at the adjoining deli.

The Tea Shop

6 Polmorla Road, PL27 7ND
01208 813331

Fresh local produce takes pride of place on the menu at this bright and cosy tea shop, and everything on the menu is homemade. The choice of 40 teas and around 30 cakes, including boiled fruit cake, strawberry pavlova and apple and almond cake, make it really special. Ice creams and light lunches are also on offer.

Trehellas House Hotel & Restaurant ⊛

trehellashouse.co.uk
Washaway, PL30 3AD
01208 72700

Trehellas House has an interesting past: initially an inn that also served as the local courthouse in the 18th century, then a farm, and a pub again in the 1970s. It's now a country-house hotel with an appealing restaurant serving punchy modern cooking with Cornish produce at its heart.

▶ PLACES NEARBY

Four miles southwest of Wadebridge, St Breock Downs' great standing stone is set amid a nature reserve on Rosenannon Downs run by the Cornwall Wildlife Trust.

St Breock Downs Monolith

english-heritage.org.uk
Rosenannon | Open any reasonable time

This, Cornwall's largest and heaviest standing stone, is located on the summit of St Breock Downs with fabulous views to the sea. It was originally 16 feet tall, weighs nearly 18 tons and dates from the Late Neolithic to mid-Bronze Age, around 2500–1500 BC. There are many other Bronze Age relics and monuments in the nearby area. Dogs on leads are welcome.

Watergate Bay
see **Newquay**, page 183

Whitsand Bay
see **Kingsand & Cawsand**, page 117

Zennor MAP REF P274 B4

Storm-tumbled cliffs and wheeling gulls guard Penwith's wild, Atlantic shoreline and it's easy to imagine how and why the local legend of the mermaid of Zennor came to mind. The mermaid is said to have seduced a local chorister into the dark waters below Zennor Head, with promises of a life under the sea together. In the local church of St Senara, you can see a bench-end with a relief of a mermaid carved into it. On quiet evenings, the smooth heads of seals pop up in the bay and perpetuate the legend.

The village itself, along the coast from St Ives, is wild and impossibly romantic, with rough, tawny hills sloping down towards the echoing sea cliffs. Between hills and sea lies a narrow coastal plateau of small, irregular fields whose Cornish 'hedges' of rough granite date from the Iron Age. Because of these historic treats, this long-farmed landscape has earned Zennor protected status for ecological and archaeological reasons. There are outstanding coastal and inland walks radiating from the village.

Access to Zennor Head and to the coast path is on foot down a narrow lane that starts behind the Tinners Arms. Zennor Head has a flat top, but its western flank is spectacular. Towering cliffs fall darkly into a narrow gulf, where the sea crashes white against the shoreline far below. If you can tear yourself away from thoughts of mermaids, it is an invigorating 6-mile walk east to St Ives along some of the most remote coastline in Cornwall.

GO BACK IN TIME
Zennor Quoit

This megalithic burial chamber is about a mile east of Zennor and dates from 2500–1500 BC. One of the eight remaining quoits on West Penwith Moor, it's in good condition. Archaeologists have found Neolithic pottery and cremated bones here and suggest that it was used for burial and/or cremation rituals; originally, it was probably covered by a mound. It can be found by driving along the B3306 between Zennor and St Ives. Sperris Quoit, 330 yards away, is a more tumbledown example of the same.

EAT AND DRINK

The Tinners Arms

tinnersarms.com

TR26 3BY | 01736 796927

There is timelessness about this famous Cornish pub with its stone floors, low ceilings, cushioned settles, winter open fires and craft beers such as the eponymous Tinners and Mermaid. Other local treats are Cornish gin and Polgoon wine. Food is based on the best fish and meat from local suppliers. Outside there is a peaceful garden and large terrace with sea views. The Tinners is noted for its music and storytelling evenings.

▶ PLACES NEARBY

A short drive from Zennor takes you to the Gurnard's Head, a promontory with evidence of ancient residents, and a gastro pub named after it.

Gurnard's Head

Just over a mile to the west of Zennor Head outside St Ives lies Gurnard's Head, a long, elegant promontory that rises to a great, gnarled headland ringed with sheer black cliffs. There are remains of embankments across the neck of this Iron Age site and on the flanking slopes are the rough remains of Iron Age houses. Promontories such as Gurnard's Head may have been 'cliff castles', or perhaps simply ceremonial gathering places and even trading sites.

Gurnard's Head may be reached from the B3306, but parking is limited. The coast path between Zennor Head and Gurnard's Head makes for a pleasantly rough walk of about 1.5 miles. Both headlands are in the care of the National Trust.

The Gurnard's Head

gurnardshead.co.uk

Near Zennor TR26 3DE

01736 796928

The Gurnard's Head collects awards like picking blackberries around the adjoining fields and cliffs. High-end dining from a sensibly manageable menu includes delicious fish dishes, the fish sourced locally and well-prepared. There are good alternatives for meat eaters also, all served up in the bar area or the main dining room with its nod to the area's artistic legacy on every wall. Outside there's a spacious garden area, which can be airy at times, but it's good Cornish sea air.

Rosemergy Farmhouse Cream Teas

rosemergy.com

Morvah, TR20 8YX | 01736 796557

Open Apr–Oct Thu–Tue 1.30–5.30, Jul–Aug daily. Phone to confirm Oct openings

Cornish cream teas at their very best in a spectacular location is what Rosemergy Farmhouse is justly famous for. They are all served in a spacious dining room or, alternatively, in the lovely garden.

0   10 miles
0   10   20 kilometres

Lundy

Ilfracombe

Bideford

Isles of Scilly

Bude

DEVON

Launceston

276–7

Wadebridge

CORNWALL

Bodmin

Liskeard

Newquay

Lostwithiel

Torpoint

274–5

Truro

St Austell

Redruth

St Ives

Camborne

Penzance

Falmouth

Helston

Land's End

Lizard Point

ATLAS

★ A-Z places listed

• Places Nearby

A   **B**   **C**

1

White Island

St Martin's

New Grimsby   Old Grimsby

Bryher   Tresco

Higher Town

Abbey Garden & Valhalla Museum

Samson

Eastern Isles

Bant's Carn & Halandy Down   A3110

2

Hugh Town   A3111

The Garrison   St Mary's

Old Town

Middle Town   Gugh

Annet

St Agnes

Isles of Scilly

Western Rocks

3

Portreath

Godrevy-Portreath Heritage Coast

St Ives Bay

Godrevy Head   Tehidy Country Park   East Pool Mine

Gwithian   Tuckingmill Valley Park

St Ives

4

Carbis Bay   Camborne

Gurnard's Head

Penwith Heritage Coast

Zennor   Lelant   Gwinear

Trencrom Hill   Hayle

Morvah   Schoolhouse

Chysauster Ancient Village

Levant Mine & Beam Engine

Pendeen   Penwith Moors

Crowns Mine

Geevor Tin Mine   Gulval   Godolphin House

Trengwainton Garden   Penzance   Marazion   St Hilary

St Just

Carn Euny Ancient Village   Sancreed   Trereife   St Michael's Mount

Perranuthnoe   A394

Helston

Trewidden Garden   Newlyn

Praa Sands

5

Whitesand Bay

A30   St Buryan

Flambards

Sennen   The Merry Maidens   Mousehole   Mount's Bay   Porthleven

Land's End   Trevescan   Lamorna

Loe Pool

Porthcurno   Treen   Minack Nature Reserve   Gunwalloe

Porthgwarra   Minack Theatre

Mullion

Chocolate Factory and Craft Centre

Mullion Cove

6

The Lizard Heritage Coast

A   **B**   **C**

A   **B**   **C**

1

2

Crackington
Haven

*Pantire Point - Widemouth
Heritage Coast*

Boscastle ★

3   Tintagel ★   Lesnewth ●
       Bossiney

Trebarwith ●
Strand   Arthurian
          Centre ●

Delabole ★   Camelford ★

Port Isaac   Lanteglos ●
Bay   Pencarrow ●

Port   Rough
Port   Isaac   Tor ●
Quin ●

Padstow Bay   Long Cross
Polzeath ★   Victorian Gardens ●

Hayle Bay   Trebetherick ●   St Endellion ●

Trevose Head
Heritage Coast   Trevone ●
Bay   Prideaux   St Tudy ●

Harlyn ●   Place ★
Bay   ★ Rock

4 Constantine Bay ●
                Blisland ●

Treyarnon Bay ●   **Padstow**
       St Merryn ●

○ Porthcothan

          Wadebridge

Bedruthan Steps ★   Washaway ●

275   Camel Valley
      Vineyard ●   **Bodmin**
   The Japanese   St Breock   Cardinham
    Garden ★   Downs Monolith ★   Woods

Mawgan ★   Pinsla
Porth   St Mawgan ○   Cornish Birds   Garden ●
          of Prey Centre ★   Lanivet ●

Watergate Bay ★   Lanhydrock ●

5 Tolcarne ★   ★ St Columb
Beach   Major   Restormel
Beach ★   Castle ●

Crantock ★   **Newquay**   Screech Owl
          Sanctuary ●   Roche ○   **Lostwithiel**

rt   Trerice ●   DairyLand   Bugle ○
         Farm World ●

Lappa Valley   Summercourt ○   Wheal Martyn   The Eden
anporth   Steam Railway   Museum & ●   Project ★
         Country Park   ○ St Blazey   Golant ●

            St   Par ○
6 ennallow   St Stephen ○   Austell ★   Boscundle ●   **Fowey**
lestick ● Marazanvose   Carlyon   Polruan ○
         Charlestown ★   Bay
rose   Ladock ○   *St Austell*   Gribbin
ater   Grampound ○   *Bay*   Head
      Probus ★   Trewithen ●   **Lost Gardens**

A Tresillian   **B**   **C**

Index, themed

Page numbers in **bold** refer to main entries

Index, places

Page numbers in **bold** refer to main entries; page numbers in *italics* refer to town plans

The Automobile Association wishes to thank the following photographers and organisations for their assistance in the preparation of this book.

Abbreviations for the picture credits are as follows – (t) top; (m) middle; (b) bottom; (l) left; (r) right; (c) centre; (AA) AA World Travel Library.

4tl AA/A Burton; 4tr AA/A Burton; 4bl AA/A Burton; 5r AA/A Burton; 5bl AA/J Wood; 8–9 AA/J Wood; 11 AA/J Wood; 12t AA/C Jones; 12b AA/R Tenison; 13t AA/A Burton; 13m AA/C Jones; 13b AA/R Moss; 14t Arcaid Images / Alamy; 14m AA/C Jones; 14b AA/J Wood; 15 AA/R Moss; 16 AA/R Tenison; 18 AA/A Weller; 19 AA/R Tenison; 20 AA/A Burton; 21 Courtesy of The Eden Project; 22 AA/J Wood; 23 AA/J Wood; 24 digitalunderwater.com/Alamy; 25 AA/J Wood; 26 AA/S&O Mathews; 30–1 AA/A Burton; 32 Jack Sullivan/ Alamy; 33 AA/J Love; 34 AA/C Jones; 35 AA/A Mockford & N Bonetti; 36–7 AA/J Love; 38 Chris Lawrence/Alamy; 40 David Pearson/Alamy; 41 AA; 42 AA/A Burton; 43 AA/J Tims; 44 Andrew Ray/Alamy; 45 AA/ R Tenison; 46 AA/J Wood; 49 AA/A Burton; 50 AA/J Wood; 52 AA/A Burton; 54–5 AA/A Burton; 56 AA/C Jones; 60 AA/R Moss; 62 AA/J Wood; 63 AA/R Moss; 64 AA/R Moss; 72 Derek Stone/Alamy; 77 Loop Images Ltd/Alamy; 80 mauritius images GmbH/Alamy; 86 AA/J Wood; 89 Courtesy of The Eden Project; 91 Michael Willis/Alamy; 92 Matt Jessop/Courtesy of The Eden Project; 94 AA/C Jones; 96 Courtesy of National Maritime Museum/Bob Berry; 102–3 Kevin Britland/Alamy; 105 AA/N Ray; 108 AA/N Ray; 111 AA/R Moss; 114 AA/J Wood; 118 AA/R Moss; 120 AA/A Burton; 121 AA/C Jones; 122 AA/R Moss; 129 AA/J Wood; 130 AA/J Wood; 131 AA/J Wood; 132 AA/R Moss; 136–7 Peter Barritt/Alamy; 142 AA/R Moss; 145 David Chapman/Alamy; 148 AA/J Wood; 150 AA/J Wood; 151 AA/N Ray; 157 AA/R Moss; 158 AA/R Moss; 160–1 Anne-Marie Palmer/Alamy; 162 AA/C Jones; 167 AA/R Tenison; 168–9 AA/C Jones; 170 AA/J Wood; 172 AA/A Burton; 176–7 Andrew Ray/Alamy; 178t AA/R Tenison; 178b AA/J Wood; 181 AA/J Wood; 184–5 Kevin Britland/ Alamy; 192–3 AA/R Moss; 196 AA/A Burton; 197 AA/C Jones; 202 AA/A Lawson; 205 AA/A Lawson; 207 AA/A Burton; 212 AA/T Teegan; 215 AA/R Moss; 217 AA/J Wood; 226–7 AA/A Burton; 228 AA/A Burton; 229 AA/R Tenison; 234–5 AA/J Wood; 237 AA/J Wood; 238 AA/A Burton; 244 AA/A Lawson; 245 AA/J Wood; 246–7 Peter Barritt/Alamy; 252–3 AA/R Moss; 254 Peter Barritt/Alamy; 256 AA/A Burton; 260 AA/R Moss; 261 AA/C Jones; 262 AA/R Moss; 265 AA/M Lynch

Every effort has been made to trace the copyright holders, and we apologise in advance for any unintentional omissions or errors. We would be pleased to apply any corrections in any following edition of this publication.

Series editor: Rebecca Needes   Proofreader: Sandy Draper
Author: Laura Dixon   Designer: Tom Whitlock
Updater: Des Hannigan   Digital imaging & repro: Ian Little
Project editor: Creative-Plus   Art director: James Tims

Additional writing by other AA contributors. *Lore of the Land* feature by Ruth Binney. Some content may appear in other AA books and publications.

Has something changed? Email us at travelguides@theaa.com.

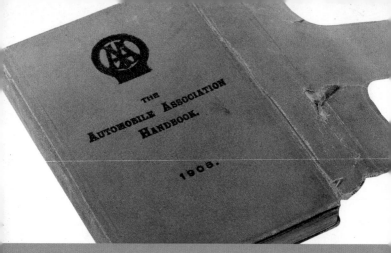

YOUR TRUSTED GUIDE

The AA was founded in 1905 as a body initially intended to help motorists avoid police speed traps. As motoring became more popular, so did we, and our activities have continued to expand into a great variety of areas.

The first edition of the AA Members' Handbook appeared in 1908. Due to the difficulty many motorists were having finding reasonable meals and accommodation while on the road, the AA introduced a new scheme to include listings for 'about one thousand of the leading hotels' in the second edition in 1909. As a result the AA has been recommending and assessing establishments for over a century, and each year our professional inspectors anonymously visit and rate thousands of hotels, restaurants, guest accommodations and campsites. We are relied upon for our trustworthy and objective Star, Rosette and Pennant ratings systems, which you will see used in this guide to denote AA-inspected restaurants and campsites.

In 1912 we published our first handwritten routes and our atlas of town plans, and in 1925 our classic touring guide, *The AA Road Book of England and Wales,* appeared. Together, our accurate mapping and in-depth knowledge of places to visit were to set the benchmark for British travel publishing.

Since the 1990s we have dramatically expanded our publishing activities, producing high quality atlases, maps, walking and travel guides for the UK and the rest of the world. In this new series of regional travel guides we are drawing on more than a hundred years of experience to bring you the very best of Britain.